CHANGING IDENTITIES
ANCIENT ROOTS

CHANGING IDENTITIES
ANCIENT ROOTS

the history of west dunbartonshire from earliest times

edited by IAN BROWN

EDINBURGH UNIVERSITY PRESS

Edinburgh University Press Ltd
22 George Square, Edinburgh

Typeset in 11/13 Minion
by Servis Filmsetting Ltd, Manchester, and
printed and bound in Great Britain by
Cromwell Press, Trowbridge, Wilts

A CIP record for this book is available from the British Library

ISBN 978 0 7486 2560 4 (hardback)
ISBN 978 0 7486 2561 1 (paperback)

Contents

Figures

Plates

Foreword

It is an honour to introduce this History of West Dunbartonshire. The concept in commissioning the book was to draw together the history of the disparate parts of West Dunbartonshire in one major publication in order to place the many different aspects of this geographic area in perspective, in terms of social, economic and historic importance and the diversity of its cultures. There have been many books and pamphlets about the various communities that were drawn together ten years ago when the reorganisation of Scottish local government took place and West Dunbartonshire Council was formed from disaggregation of Strathclyde Regional Council and the merging of two District Councils. Corporately, this book engages with this area's rich legacy and marks the prospects for cross-cultural and economic regeneration.

Professor Ian Brown and the distinguished group of historians who have written the book have done a remarkable job. They have not only compiled a well-researched document with facts and figures; they have looked at this area as a place where people settled, worked and created world-class industries and art. Their research, reaching even before the Christian age, places West Dunbartonshire at the heart of Scottish history as a significant strategic area bordered by the River Clyde, Loch Lomond and the Kilpatrick Hills. This comes across in each of the chapters in terms of military and political importance and industrial and creative development throughout the ages.

This publication rightly places West Dunbartonshire at the heart of Scotland's collective identity. It could not have come into being without the support of elected colleagues and officers of the Council, who immediately recognised the importance of drawing all our communities together in one publication. It connects our past with the present and points us towards the future. It makes a clear statement, not just about geographic location, but about the identity of all the communities that define West Dunbartonshire in a socio-political context.

Cllr Denis Agnew
Convener of Cultural Services
March 2006

Gerry McInerney
Director of Corporate Services
March 2006

CHAPTER 1

The Continuing Stream

Ian Brown

The essence of this history may be found in the conception that identity is no one thing. West Dunbartonshire was founded ten years before the year of publication of this book. Yet, as will be clear, the change of name enshrined by law and implemented in 1996 simply offered a new identity to a region, or perhaps sub-region, that has time and again changed its identity and no doubt will again. Much has been written of the detail of the local history of the region and, particularly, the towns it includes. Many of these titles can be found in the bibliography, and their authors' approach places a premium rightly, given their books' function, on the minutiae of location and events. Other histories have specialised in other ways: particularly, of course, Ian Johnston's remarkable and detailed studies of the history of Clydebank shipbuilding firms[1] and Patricia Dennison's study with Russel Coleman of historic Dumbarton as part of the Scottish burgh survey.[2] This history adopts a different approach and value system. While it is concerned with the area now called West Dunbartonshire, it seeks to set that concern in the larger context of Scottish and indeed international historical developments. It sees West Dunbartonshire not simply in terms, important as they are, of local significance, but as embodying, as any region must, the larger history of the greater communities of which West Dunbartonshire forms part. As communities and values – whether political, economic, industrial, cultural or demographic – change in both the region and the larger polity, so the interactions of such change sustain the identities of West Dunbartonshire. In response, West Dunbartonshire reflects and influences changes in identity and meaning at national and international levels. In one sense, then, West Dunbartonshire has an identity as a new local governmental creation. Simultaneously, however, and certainly more importantly, it is an identifiable region with deep roots. These have nourished and shaped the region's modern range of identities and, as this book shows, had a – perhaps surprisingly – powerful impact, through its cultural expression, its industries and its people, on the shaping not just of Scotland, but the larger world.

Part of the methodology that allows this book to open up these larger perspectives has been that of engaging distinguished historians and scholars of culture to bring their wide-ranging perspectives to the topics addressed in this book's chapters. Each of the contributors has an international reputation for research and scholarship. The scholarly craft of each demonstrates the difference between history as a modern version of the local annals of the Middle Ages and the interpretative insight expected of a contemporary historian or cultural critic. This means that, while proper attention is paid to the individual detail of events that took place in West Dunbartonshire, each chapter deals with the ways in which larger questions found expression in West Dunbartonshire and how West Dunbartonshire often helped change or redefine those larger questions. At times, the focus of these chapters moves away from the region itself in order to open up such larger questions before returning focus to the region to illuminate the interplay between the local and national. Larger questions of practice in, for example, the professionalising sporting culture of the late nineteenth century and their immediate impact on the football teams of the area, most prominently Dumbarton, Renton and Vale of Leven, are explored illuminatingly by Bob Crampsey in this way. Equally, the foundation of Clydebank as an industrial nineteenth-century company town is seen as part of the larger process of change in nineteenth-century Scotland as the impact of industrialisation and related demographic change unfolded. The importance of a major literary figure such as Tobias Smollett is understood in the larger context of the development of literacy and the writing of novels in Britain in the eighteenth century. The opening up of such a fruitful understanding of the interaction between the local, the national and international is supported, as we have observed, by the involvement in the writing of this history of historians and cultural scholars who each bring deep understanding of larger historical and cultural themes to their examination of West Dunbartonshire's history.

One way of summarising this process is to say that West Dunbartonshire becomes a microcosm for national events. This is, however, probably, to do less than justice to what this book seeks to achieve. Certainly, West Dunbartonshire can be seen, like many other regions of Scotland, as a microcosm of the larger community. Yet this history seeks to go further than such a simple – if valuable – insight. It seeks to recognise the very specificity of West Dunbartonshire, while showing that it is not simply a microcosm of the whole: a somewhat passive conception. Rather, it shows it as an active partner with the larger community in shaping its own identities and those of Scotland, and the wider world.

In order to facilitate this, after the current introductory chapter and before the conclusion, the chapters in this book fall into two broad categories. The next three chapters, by Simon Taylor, Ted Cowan and Richard Finlay set out the historical developments in the area of West Dunbartonshire from the earliest times until the present. In doing this, they provide both a sequential history of the area and a cross-referencing of that history to the major developments in Scotland's governance, political settlements, economics and industry throughout that long period. The following four chapters, by Alan Riach, Paul Maloney, Bob Crampsey and Paul Maloney again, address a variety of aspects of social and cultural expression from the Middle Ages on, with an increasing emphasis on the modern period. In this way, the book sets out to offer two complementary perspectives. One is focused on West Dunbartonshire's place in the developing history of Scotland. The other focuses on the ways in which the emotional and intellectual life of the communities of West Dunbartonshire are particularly embodied in, reflect and exemplify cultural activities and pastimes found throughout Scotland. In this way, the texture of life in the societies of West Dunbartonshire may be seen and felt both in terms of the longer historic perspective and through the immediate details of specific cultural expressions of community.

Within this framework, Simon Taylor's chapter reminds us of the early importance of the area. A large number of factors, of course, mark the area as having crucial potential importance for geographic, trading and military reasons. These include such natural features as what is now called Dumbarton Rock, the navigability of the Clyde and the Vale of Leven's offering a way into and out of the Loch Lomond valley and, hence, to the north of Scotland. The area was important as the location for the western terminus of the Antonine Wall and, so, as a site of Roman occupation for the brief period the Romans sought to settle so far north in Scotland. Later, Dumbarton was capital for a substantial period of the kingdom, Al Clud, that has come to be called Strathclyde. Taylor reminds us of the strong tradition that Saint Mungo was born in the area. By the nature of such things, of course, it is impossible to verify any such claim, but the fact the claim is made at all signifies the importance attached to the area as a site of cultural and even cultic interest. Its importance and the dynamic changes in its standing during the first millennium are reflected indirectly by its linguistic history, to which Taylor pays particular attention. Having been the capital region of the British kingdom of Al Clud, it was an obvious target for the expansionism of more recent and aggressive neighbours, such as the Scots and the Vikings. West Dunbartonshire was a fulcrum of interpenetration, conflict and exchange between the separate Pictish, Gaelic and British kingdoms with intermittent impact by the Vikings. Taylor shows, using specific place-name evidence, the overlaying of the earlier history of the area by the incursion of the Gaelic culture. This was to be dominant in the area for centuries, even, for a time, after the Scots and Scots English languages had developed in status and implicit power. West Dunbartonshire's early history, then, embodies the linguistic complexity that underlies the continuing three-language status of Scotland. It is only, as Taylor notes, relatively late in the day that Scots names come to be developed in the area.

Local place-names perhaps crystallise for us the complexity of language, cultural and even industrial developments that underlie, and provide evidence of, political pressure and conflict. Dumbarton, *the fort of the Britons*, is a Gaelic name that both appropriates and yet continues to identify the site as a historic pre-Gaelic, British centre. Balloch, derived from *bealach*, the Gaelic word for a pass, marks the geographic and trading importance of the town so named. The importance of that town in the later medieval period is also marked by its role as seat of the earls of Lennox. Lennox, which extended further west, north and east of the present West Dunbartonshire, was the regional earldom that replaced earlier kingdoms as a local unit of government within a united polity of Scotland. The complex interactions and changes Taylor so clearly brings out highlight the great antiquity of a number of the settlements in the area. Their antiquity and the Gaelic derivation of their names remind us by implication of the relatively recent foundation of one of the major towns being studied in this history: Clydebank. Clydebank's name is, of course, derived from the Clyde Bank Engineering and Shipbuilding Co., owned by J. & G. Thomson Ltd. Having founded the Clyde Bank Iron Shipyard at Govan in 1851, the firm soon found the site there too cramped. In 1871, it established new works at Dalmuir, a process which led to the entire firm moving in 1874 to a greenfield site between Dalmuir and Yoker on farmland that included the tiny village of Barns O' Clyde, opposite the mouth of the River Cart. As Ian Johnston notes:

> With no amenities whatsoever, the new yard had enormous hurdles to overcome before an adequate infrastructure, including homes for working people, could be provided. Over the course of the 1870s and 1880s, the town of Clydebank, which took its name from the shipyard, was established, recording in the process the highest growth rate for any town in Scotland at that time.[3]

While the firm was to be taken over in 1899 by John Brown's, the town's foundation marked that of a new industrial company town. Yet, its Scots name contains the Scotticised version, *Clyde*, of the older pre-Gaelic British name, *Clud*, of the river on which it lies and whose existence was of such importance in the history of West Dunbartonshire. Linguistic complexity marks underlying cultural, political and industrial complexity as part of the great richness of the area's history.

This linguistic, cultural and political complexity provides a theme running throughout Ted Cowan's chapter on the history of the area from the thirteenth to the eighteenth centuries. He draws attention to the central importance of water, both the waterways of the Clyde and Leven and the great expanse of Loch Lomond, in the history and significance of West Dunbartonshire in national life. He reminds us that historically the area shows many Highland and Gaelic cultural features, though with a very significant 'Lowland' fringe along the Clyde coast. For an area so relatively small, it has, to an extraordinary extent, encompassed the developing changes in Scottish government and governance of the period with which Professor Cowan's chapter deals. During that period, West Dunbartonshire sees, and for long resists, the process of Normanisation, with its impact on the ways in which the government and the nation are organised. It sees the establishment of Dumbarton as a burgh in 1222, quite explicitly as a bulwark of a certain version of 'civilisation' in contradistinction to the native traditions that had prevailed in the area until that time. It is often hard now to see West Dunbartonshire as a frontier area, but Cowan makes it very clear just how much it was effectively such an area throughout the five centuries he discusses.

Professor Cowan traces, too, the ways in which changes and conflicts in West Dunbartonshire reflect and, indeed, express larger developments affecting the Scottish nation as a whole. He describes with lively clarity the changes in designation and perception of the region of Lennox, of which modern West Dunbartonshire is a central area: from the status of Celtic kingdom through to a feudal earldom with significant, and not always happy, links to the blood-royal. He explores the ways in which the medieval history of the area, at least until the Reformation changed religious institutions so radically, embodies the conflict between local landowners and the Church Militant. In this, he makes the striking point that the absence of abbey foundation in the area is surely a mark of the ways in which, even after the changes in governance following the development of feudalisation, local, older, means of expressing religious devotion and piety survived. He discusses the importance of the castle at Dumbarton, in particular through the period of English aggression that culminated in King Robert the Bruce's victory at Bannockburn. He reminds us of the great affection the Bruce clearly must have felt for the area, building himself a manor at Cardross to provide, in effect, a country retreat for himself, where, in time, he died. But, after the Bruce, the area still retained its critical role in Scottish power politics, holding out for a time for Queen Mary in the struggles after her flight to England and retaining its political significance even up until the time of the Act of Union. As Cowan observes in his chapter, 'In terms of the treaty of 1707, Dumbarton was listed as one of four Scottish castles that were always to be maintained and kept in repair'.

Such significance for the area marks its borderline nature between Highland and Lowland, between Gael and non-Gael. The area of modern West Dunbartonshire has always had a critical and dynamic relationship with its hinterland around Loch Lomond and been a central player in the history of the larger area of the West of Scotland as a whole. Professor Cowan draws attention yet again to the ways in which it is not only developments in the specific area of modern West Dunbartonshire that this book reflects, but the area's wider context and impact. He offers us a fascinating and detailed case study of the impact of the borderline nature that for a long time marked out the region in the later part of his chapter. There, he addresses the treatment of the MacGregors and their relationship with, on the one hand, the royal court and, on the other, the Campbell earls of Argyll. His exposition of that conflict – the values that underlay it, the changing power relationships and the centralising governmental pressures that were bearing down on an older way of life – is illuminating. Cowan concludes his chapter with a telling and somehow moving incident when, in response to MacGregor involvement in the 1715 Rising, a raiding party from Lowland areas including Dumbarton, Kilpatrick, Paisley, Rosneath and Rhu marched round Loch Lomond to put down the MacGregors and ended up removing such of the MacGregor boats as were still fit to be used and destroying those that were damaged. In this somewhat desultory and even petty expedition may be seen the embodiment of the great changes explored in Cowan's chapter. He concludes with the image of the shock waves from the 1755 Lisbon earthquake disturbing even the waters of Loch Lomond. So, a great natural catastrophe marks the seismic agricultural and industrial changes then about to erupt.

Just as in earlier times, West Dunbartonshire was the scene of significant national – and indeed international – events and cultural, political and religious change, so, from the 1750s onwards, it continued to act as a crucible and test-bed of developments in modern Scottish history and as a force for economic change. As Richard Finlay very clearly shows, West Dunbartonshire was one of the centres for the development of the Industrial Revolution in Scotland. Of course, there had been industries, often of an agricultural kind, in the area before. Since at least 1460, for example, the monks of Paisley Abbey operated a corn mill at Duntocher, and later Duntocher Burn provided power for waulkmills, an ironworks and a spade forge.[4] It was in the middle of the eighteenth century, however, that new industries developed with greater dynamism in the context of the Industrial Revolution. Glassmaking, for example, was first established in Dumbarton in 1777, while, in the Vale of Leven, the textiles industry was then thriving. Glassmaking, however, by the middle of the nineteenth century faded in significance, while the textile industry increased its role in the local and national economy and shipbuilding, with its multifarious related industries and trades, found in West Dunbartonshire a major centre. In that, it epitomises the identity of Scottish communities and their industries in much of the west of the Scottish central belt during the nineteenth and twentieth centuries.

Given the symbiosis between community and industry, it is inevitable that the ebb and flow of industrial and economic change, recession and boom, should have a powerful impact on the citizens of West Dunbartonshire. Professor Finlay provides throughout his chapter vivid illustrations of just how difficult at times the people of West Dunbartonshire found both their living conditions and their very survival. The energy and power of the local industries was derived mainly from shipbuilding and textiles, but included a key industrial crossover between textiles and engineering in the manufacture for a time of most of the world's sewing machines. This took place in the gigantic Clydebank Singer factory, completed in 1884–5. At its best, such energy marked West Dunbartonshire as a centre of innovation, invention and pioneering of new working methods and technical problem-solving. The working people of West Dunbartonshire included some of the very best engineers in the world and the productivity of the area was prodigious. At the same time, as Finlay also reminds us, some of the most dangerous work in the textile mills was undertaken by workers who were little more than children. Their small size allowed them to work with moving looms and under heavy machinery in a way no fully-grown person could and, in so doing, to face dangers to health and safety that modern legislation renders unimaginable in Western Europe.

It is a paradox that twice, when industry was facing the risk or the reality of severe downturn, war helped out the local economy. It even, for example, helped revive the fortunes of the Argyll works, which, initially set up to manufacture cars, very quickly became in the First World War a munitions factory. An area bound up with creativity and invention found itself a central cog in the United Kingdom's war machine. And, in 1941, as Finlay vividly describes, the war came to Clydebank with a ferocity and impact not exceeded, because of the nature of the area's housing stock, anywhere in Britain. In the First World War, Beardmore had had a fledgling aircraft-manufacturing wing; in the Second, the Luftwaffe destroyed or damaged all but a very few of the houses in Clydebank. Not only has West

Dunbartonshire reflected the development and recession of modern industry, it is also representative, even iconic, in the way it suffered the impact of industrialised war. It is also iconic in the way its citizens dealt with the terror they had suffered.

In politics, too, the citizens of West Dunbartonshire reflect and represent wider national movements. The gradual acquisition of the franchise by all citizens led to the changes in political power and control Finlay discusses. Similarly, the changes in social and health care, particularly since the Welfare State reforms following the 1944 Beveridge Report, have had a steady impact on the area. In many ways, the famous work-in at Upper Clyde Shipbuilders in Clydebank in 1971 reflects the positive dynamic of a workforce that takes pride in its communities and its crafts. It also reflects one of the last stages of an industrial tradition that had come, in the statism associated with the Welfare State, to be dependent on government support and old-fashioned working methods. As Finlay points out, the very location and topography of the surviving yards meant that they were too small and too far from deep water to keep up with modern shipbuilding methods. Arguably, they survived as long as they did because, firstly, their support formed part of a parallel strategy to that which saw post-war reforms in state support for healthcare and, secondly, because the necessity in a modern democracy of providing – somehow – employment protected them from the direct impact of brutal market forces. The experience of West Dunbartonshire in coping with these complex political, economic and social changes embodies that of many declining industrial areas not only of Scotland and the United Kingdom, but Western Europe at large. As Finlay points out clearly, one of the solutions, still often supported by government subvention, was the bringing in of industries whose headquarters lay elsewhere. For a time, this branch economy approach sustained employment, but by its nature it had shallow roots. When a cheaper source of labour or an economic crisis in another part of the world emerged, the economy of West Dunbartonshire suffered as the opening and closure in the post-war era of the Timex factory, to take just one example, exemplifies.

Despite these contretemps, West Dunbartonshire has sought again and again to refocus and relaunch itself and its industrial identity. One metaphor for this may be seen in the way that the old Beardmore shipyard is now the base for both a major hotel complex and a hospital building, the latter originally designed and developed as part of a public-private enterprise and now having a national role in the public health service. Such a development is far from being without controversy both in its conception and implementation. Nonetheless, what it certainly represents is an active desire both nationally and locally to ensure that the economy and people of the area respond dynamically to changes in the world economy and to the changing balance in modern Scotland between what are, broadly speaking, service and manufacturing industries. The underlying theme of the three directly historical chapters of this book, by Simon Taylor, Ted Cowan and Richard Finlay, is clear. West Dunbartonshire has had – and retains – a central importance in the development of the nature of Scotland and its political, linguistic, industrial and economic identities. As the title of this book suggests, West Dunbartonshire has had many identities over the centuries. It has also, in discovering and expressing those identities, drawn on and given expression to ancient roots.

The various means of expressing and celebrating identity, individual, local, regional and national, form an overarching theme of the four chapters contributed to this book by Alan Riach, Paul Maloney and Bob Crampsey. Alan Riach traces the development of literary and visual expressions of the culture of West Dunbartonshire from the time of the Celtic kingdom through to the work of artists working at the present moment. He reminds us of the enormous impact of some of the leading artists both from West Dunbartonshire, as it now is, and of those who have a close association with the area. His chapter, given the nature of its topic, considers literary influences derived not only from the specific area of West Dunbartonshire, but includes reference to such towns no longer in the county as Helensburgh. It examines the wider contextual impact of sister areas, including the areas surrounding Loch Lomond, with its critically important formative and expressive role in the development of the Romantic Movement in Europe. Paul Maloney's first chapter, meantime, explores the forms and dynamics of popular culture and entertainment from the thirteenth century, when, in 1222, Dumbarton was founded as a burgh, to the most recent period. This chapter forcefully reminds us of the range of manifestations, many very ancient, which underlie expressions of popular culture and entertainment even into modern times. An underlying theme of his chapter, one to be reflected later in the context of sport by Bob Crampsey, is that of the constant tension between the outflowing of the human spirit and the need perceived by the authorities to control and manage that outflowing. Whether talking of the attempts to censor and ban plays in the post-Reformation period or the ways in which licensing hours were enforced in the early twentieth century, Maloney draws us into a deep appreciation of the range and depth of popular culture and its manifestation in West Dunbartonshire.

This chapter flows naturally into the next two, Bob Crampsey's on sport and Paul Maloney's on theatre, music hall and cinema. Both of these chapters begin in the second half of the nineteenth century. Each draws attention to the processes by which both sport and theatrical performance became professionalised and industrialised. Both draw attention to the detailed history of their topics. A theme of Bob Crampsey's lively chapter is that of the ways in which the early national, and even international, domination of sport, particularly football, by the teams of the area declined after the first, at least professedly, amateur period of organised sport. This happened as sports became more professional when, given the quasi-industrial growth of larger teams with larger fan-bases in the larger towns and cities, the power and impact of teams from smaller communities fell away. Crampsey identifies developments in sport in the area, but he particularly reminds us about what was called 'King Football', enlivening his exposition with illuminating anecdotes and examples. He draws attention, for example, to the extraordinary extent of the achievement of nineteenth-century West Dunbartonshire football teams in the pre-professional era. His reminder astonishes still:

> West Dunbartonshire teams, even after all this time, have won more Scottish Cup victories, with six, than those of any other non-metropolitan area of Scotland and more even than those of the city of Dundee with their total of two.

Crampsey also examines and pricks the inflated bubble of reputation that lies behind the claim of Renton in 1888 to be the first World Champions of football, revealing the simple device they employed to ensure they remained undefeated in that title to this day. Nonetheless, as he shows, the very effrontery of the claim marks the high achievement of sportsmen in West Dunbartonshire in the latter part of the nineteenth century. And he draws attention to the singular achievement of individual sportsmen from West Dunbartonshire since then. This includes what is surely one of the greatest series of achievements of any sportsman anywhere: those represented in the career in modern times of Jackie Stewart.

Maloney, meantime, draws together, for the very first time, a remarkable range of material concerning the development of professional theatre and music hall in West Dunbartonshire. He provides vivid and entertaining detail of the variable quality, especially in the early part of his period, of the buildings in which performances took place. He also reminds us that, as the towns of the Vale, Dumbarton and Clydebank grew more and more populated, so the need grew commensurately for entertainment. Maloney does not, of course, suggest that the popular forms he discusses in his earlier chapter disappeared, although they inevitably evolved, but he does show how they came to be complemented by recognisably modern forms of theatre and professional production.

This book, then, sets out to balance the particular and the typical. It sets the history of West Dunbartonshire and its preceding governance manifestations in the wider context. In this context, West Dunbartonshire is both a specific example of larger movements and an important player in and shaper of these movements. It recognises the impact of individual talent and skill as well as the impact of larger political and economic forces. This chapter's title, 'The Continuing Stream', is capable of many interpretations. This history as a whole explores a wide variety of possible interpretations of this metaphor, while reminding us constantly that the history of the area is profoundly engaged with the flow, in a literal sense, of those great 'streams', the rivers Leven and Clyde.

NOTES

1 For example, Johnston, Ian (1993), *Beardmore Built: the Rise and Fall of a Clydeside Shipyard* (Clydebank: Clydebank Libraries and Museums Department) and Johnston, Ian (2000), *Ships for a Nation: John Brown & Company Clydebank* (Dumbarton: West Dunbartonshire Libraries and Museums).

2 Dennison, E. Patricia and Coleman, Russel (1999), *Historic Dumbarton* ([Edinburgh]: Historic Scotland in association with Tuckwell Press).

3 Johnston, Ian (2000), *Ships for a Nation: John Brown & Company Clydebank* (Dumbarton: West Dunbartonshire Libraries and Museums), pp. 12–13.

4 Hood, John (2004), *Old Bowling, Duntocher, Hardgate, Milton and Old Kilpatrick* (Catrine: Stenlake Publishing), p. 40.

CHAPTER 2

The Early History and Languages of West Dunbartonshire

Simon Taylor

This chapter will attempt to tell the story of West Dunbartonshire from Roman times until the twelfth century, with a very brief backward glance into the prehistoric period. While the main period covered here cannot be termed 'prehistoric', to call it 'historic' is slightly optimistic. It will soon become clear that during much of this time the sources are few and far between, and are difficult to interpret. Perhaps 'proto-historic' is the better term. The approach considered the most useful in telling the story of this 'proto-historic' period is to present the different types of evidence as fully as possible, so that the reader herself or himself can judge the solidity or otherwise of the conclusions drawn. The evidence has been divided into various categories: archeological, hagiographical (that is, the writing of saints' lives, in this case the life of St Patrick), historiographical (that is, the writing of annals and other brief historic texts) and toponymic (that is, derived from the analysis of place-names).

DEFINING THE MARCHES

West Dunbartonshire Unitary Authority Council area (hereafter West Dunbartonshire) began operation in 1996. It was created in 1995 by the merging of Dumbarton and Clydebank District Councils and areas which had been part of the pre-1975 county of Dunbartonshire. Historically this county, earlier a sheriffdom, formed part of the earldom of Lennox, which also included western Stirlingshire.

The earldom of Lennox is best defined in terms of medieval parishes, the basic units of church administration, themselves based on earlier territorial divisions. These parishes can therefore be seen as the building blocks of medieval Scotland. Thus, the most accurate definition of medieval Lennox is provided by the deanery of Lennox within the diocese of Glasgow.

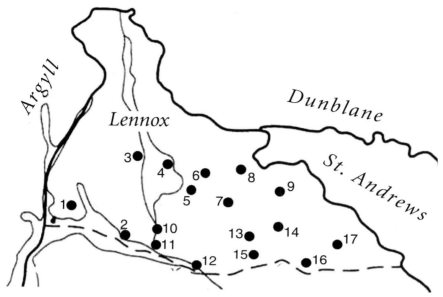

Figure I The Lennox Deanery of Glasgow Diocese c. 1300, with its parishes, the best indicator of the extent of the northern part of the early medieval kingdom of Al Clud or Dumbarton. Adapted from *Atlas of Scottish History to 1707* ed. P. G. B. McNeill and H. L. MacQueen (Edinburgh, 1996), pp. 350–1, by kind permission.

1. Neveth (now Rosneath); 2. Cardross; 3. Luss; 4. Inchcailloch (now Inchcailloch or Buchanan); 5. Kilmaronock; 6. Drymen; 7. Killearn; 8. Balfron; 9. Fintry; 10. Bonhill; 11. Dumbarton; 12. Kilpatrick; 13. Strathblane; 14. Campsie; 15. Baldernock; 16. Kirkintilloch; 17. Monyabroch (now Kilsyth)

It stretched from Loch Long in the west to Kirkintilloch (including Cumbernauld) in the east, with a boundary running through the eastern end of the Campsie Fells north to beyond the northern end of Loch Lomond. See Figure 1. This makes the Campsie Fells an important east–west barrier, rather than a north–south one. To the north of these hills, the eastern boundary of the Lennox is formed by the enormous marshy area known as Flanders Moss, through which the Forth meanders eastwards. In fact the River Forth in its upper reaches forms part of the boundary of the Lennox, making it the only Scottish earldom bounded by the two great rivers of central Scotland, the Forth and the Clyde.

The earldom of Lennox is the successor of the early medieval kingdom known variously as the kingdom of Al Clud or Dumbarton. It is likely that the western, northern and eastern boundaries of this kingdom did indeed survive fairly intact, even if there were major political, cultural and linguistic changes within these boundaries in the centuries between the fall of Dumbarton in 871 and the emergence of the earldom of Lennox in the second half of the twelfth century.

West Dunbartonshire occupies only a small proportion of the earldom of Lennox, but a central part, not geographically, but politically, since it contains the old capital of the kingdom of Al Clud (British 'rock of Clyde'), later known as Dumbarton Rock (Dumbarton being Gaelic 'fort of Britons'). West Dunbartonshire also includes the chief residence of the earls of Lennox at Balloch. In terms of pre-1975 parishes, it includes all of Dumbarton and Old Kilpatrick, most of Bonhill and Kilmaronock, and a small part of Cardross. The part of Kilmaronock excluded from modern West Dunbartonshire consists mainly of the lands of Catter, which also played an important part in the medieval earldom as a place where the earl's justice was dispensed. This included the earl's gallows, mentioned in a charter of 1371 ('at our gallows of the Catter').[1] These gallows probably stood on the large mound beside Catter House, visible from the important route-ways that passed nearby, in order to reinforce their grim message to as many people as possible.

PREHISTORIC TIMES

Visible remains of prehistoric human activity have survived chiefly in those areas where later settlement was sparse, such as the uplands of the Kilpatrick Hills. Some of these have given rise to names in both Gaelic and Scots. In West Dunbartonshire there is a high concentration of the enigmatic cup-and-ring markings, dating from the Neolithic period (c. 4000–c. 2500 BC). Some of the best preserved are from Greenland, north-west of Bowling,[2] and Auchnacraig and Whitehill by Faifley, on the south-east edge of the lands of Cochno. The name Cochno, containing Gaelic *cuach* 'bowl, cup' (whence Scots *quaich*), appears to be a direct reference to these cup-like markings.[3] A document of 1609 mentions 'the auld monument of stane callit the *Commoune-kist*', that is 'cist of the common', which marks one of the boundaries of Dumbarton common grazing.[4] This refers to the remains of a stone cist or coffin on Auchenreoch Muir, where the parishes of Bonhill, Kilmaronock and Dumbarton meet (NS432803), and is named *Common Kist* on the Ordnance Survey 6-inch 1st edition map (1864). It probably also gave rise to the nearby hill-name 'Hill of Standing Stanes'.[5] The cist was part of a Bronze Age (c. 2500–c. 750 BC) burial cairn, still a conspicuous enough feature millennia later to function as an important boundary marker. On the lands of Shanacles farm in Kilmaronock there is a large Bronze Age cemetery (NS409838). Shanacles derives from Gaelic *seann eaglais* 'old church'. There is no record of there ever having been a church here, and 'old church' probably refers to this burial site: a good example of a prehistoric feature being 'christianised'. The settlement Old Kirk, which lies immediately south-west of this same cemetery, rather than being a translated name from Gaelic into Scots, is more likely to be a similar response to this feature by Scots-speakers.

During the Iron Age (from c. 750 BC) Celtic language and culture were introduced into Britain. This was also the age of hill-forts, the best local examples of which are Carman fort[6] south-west of Alexandria, Sheep Hill by Auchentorlie, and Dumbowie[7] on the lands of Colquhoun (north of Dumbuck). Dumbarton Rock probably also had an Iron Age fort, but its traces have been all but obliterated by later building work. The extensive crannog or artificial island-dwelling offshore at Dumbuck can be fairly precisely dated to the end of the first century BC.[8] This, along with the above-mentioned hill-forts, would probably still have been occupied when the Romans appeared in southern Scotland in the later first century AD. Around this time our area emerges from prehistory into history, when Roman sources record a Celtic people called the *Dumnonii* occupying much of west central Scotland, including West Dunbartonshire. The name, also found in south-west England, contains a Celtic word meaning 'world' or 'deep'.[9]

ROMAN TIMES

For a short time, the most northerly boundary of the mighty Roman Empire ran through central Scotland, from Bo'ness on the Forth to Old Kilpatrick on the Clyde. This is now known as the Antonine Wall, named after Emperor Antoninus Pius, who 'defeated the Britons through the actions of the governor, Lollius Urbicus, and driving off the barbarians, built another wall of turf',[10] the other wall being Hadrian's Wall, which was already in existence. Begun in or shortly after AD 142, the Wall was 59 kilometres long, and was built on a stone foundation. It was around 4.5 metres wide, and rose to at least 3 metres. Between 6 and 9 metres to the north ran a ditch, and north of that the so-called outer mound, made out of the spoil from the ditch.[11] Along its southern side there were eighteen or so forts and fortlets, which housed the soldiers who garrisoned it. Four of these forts, of very varying size, are in West Dunbartonshire: Old Kilpatrick, a large fort at the very end of the Wall, and the much smaller Carleith, Duntocher and Cleddans.[12] There was also a Roman road, the so-called Military Way, which ran roughly parallel with the Wall about 46 metres to the south.[13]

Although the Wall was highly defensible, this does not appear to be its primary purpose. Rather it should be seen as a means of border

Figure 2 Distance slab from the Antonine Wall, Ferrydyke, Old Kilpatrick, recording in abbreviated form the completion of 4411 (IIII CDXI) feet of the Wall by the 20th Legion *Valeria Victrix* ('XX VV'), and the dedication to Emperor Antoninus Pius, giving him his full name and title 'Emperor Caesar Titus Aelius Hadrian Antoninus Augustus Pius father of the Country'. The wild boar was the emblem of the 20th Legion. © Hunterian Museum and Art Gallery, University of Glasgow.

control, a way of monitoring and controlling movement into and out of the Roman-occupied zone. It was, however, fully functional for only about twenty years: Emperor Antoninus died in AD 161; and the final order to retreat to Hadrian's Wall was given around AD 164. Despite its very short active life, the Wall made a lasting impact on the physical and cultural environment of West Dunbartonshire. For example, it may have played a role in situating the birth of St Patrick at Old Kilpatrick, while local place-names Carleith, Cleddans, Duntocher, and Hardgate all refer to it: **Carleith** (*Carlyth* 1654 Blaeu map), either British or Gaelic 'grey fort'; **Cleddans**, Gaelic *cladhan* 'little ditch', with a Scots plural: the diminutive might be intended to be ironic, as the ditches involved are hardly small! Whatever its

connotations, *cladhan* (or perhaps an otherwise unrecorded Scots word
*cledden or **cladden* – the symbol * is used in this context to mark a hypo-
thetical reconstruction of a word based on existing linguistic data – borrowed from Gaelic) was a standard word to refer to impressive early
earthworks in central Scotland. There are two other places with the same
derivation on the Wall itself: Cleddans east of Kirkintilloch, and The
Cleedins near Falkirk, as well as two others in Lanarkshire.[14] **Duntocher**
(*Drumthocher* 1226 x 1228 – the symbol x is used in this context to mark a
range of dates within which the usage can be dated)[15] contains Gaelic *druim*
'ridge' and *tochar* 'causeway', probably referring to the stone base of the Wall
itself. Finally, **Hardgate**, which lies a few hundred metres north of the Wall
and north-east of Duntocher, is a Scots name meaning 'hard road', and
probably refers to the same feature as *tochar* in Duntocher.

ST PATRICK

The belief that St Patrick was born and brought up in Dunbartonshire goes
back a thousand years or more, and did much to shape the later social and
ecclesiastical history of medieval Dunbartonshire. However, this does not
mean that the belief is true. Patrick lived some time in the fifth century and,
in the centuries following his death, he became the most important saint of
Ireland. There was plenty of time for stories and legends to grow up around
him. His own writing (the so-called *Confessio*) states that he came from
within the bounds of Roman Britain, more specifically from near a place
called variously *Bannauem Taberniae*, *Bannauenta Berniae*, *Bannauem
Taburnia*, etc. (the different forms coming from different readings of
different manuscripts). The Irishman Muirchú, who wrote a Latin Life of
Patrick in the second half of the seventh century, adds that it was not far
from the Irish Sea (which Muirchú calls 'our sea'), and that it is now *Uentre*.
Unfortunately, it is not known where this was, either!

The first text that links Patrick's birth place with Al Clud (Dumbarton) is the
so-called Tripartite Life of Patrick, written in Ireland in Irish. There are problems with the dating of this text, but it probably started life in the tenth century
and attained its final form in the twelfth.[16] It reads (translated from Irish):

> As to Patrick, then, of the Britons of Al Clud (*Ail Cluaide*) was his origin
> [. . .] In *Nemthur*, moreover, this holy Patrick was born; and the flag-
> stone (*lec*) whereon he was born, when anyone commits perjury under
> it, pours forth water as if it were bewailing the false testimony. But if the
> oath be true the stone (*in cloch*) remains in its proper nature.[17]

Secondly, a little later this same text tells of a miracle that Patrick, as a boy, performed 'in the palace of Al Clud (*Ail Chluaide*)'. Thirdly, in the episode concerning Patrick's capture, he and his family are described as being 'Britons of Strath Clyde' (*Bretnaib Sratha Clúathe*).

However, this is not the first time that Nemthur is mentioned as Patrick's birth place: an Old Irish poem about Patrick known as Fiacc's Hymn, which was probably composed in the eighth century, opens with the words:

Génair Pat*raic* inNemthur, iss*ed* adfét hiscelaib . . .[18]
(Patrick was born in Nemthur, this is told in stories . . .)

But there is nothing here to say where Nemthur was. The commentary (also in Irish) on this line states: ' "In Nemthur" that is a city which is in North Britain, namely Al Clud (*Ail Cluade*)',[19] but this was not written until the eleventh century, by which time the Patrick-Dumbarton link was firmly established.

There are two separate issues here: firstly, where or what is Nemthur, and where did the information come from that Patrick was born there? Secondly, how did the place where Patrick was born and raised become associated with Dumbarton?

Let us start with the first issue: where or what is Nemthur? The great Scottish place-name scholar William J. Watson, working back from stage two, and accepting the identification of Nemthur with the Dumbarton area, pointed out that the first element was the Celtic word *nemeton* 'sacred place' (Old Irish *nemed*, which in the early Christian period could also mean 'church, sanctuary'). He also, quite rightly, pointed out that a name containing this element occurs in the south-western corner of the Lennox, surviving today in the name Rosneath 'headland of Neath', where Neath is older *Neuet* (1182 x 1199 *Pais. Reg.* 157). The area known as Neath was almost certainly more extensive than the Rosneath peninsula, and in fact the parish of Rosneath had outlying parts which reached as far as the western bank of the River Leven. Watson concludes that Nemthur is an older or alternative name for Dumbarton Rock (deriving from Celtic **Nemetodúron* 'stronghold of the *nemeton*': this is also the derivation of Nanterre in France).[20] Attractive as this theory is, it must be rejected as being founded on a ghost form: *Nemthur* developed from a scribal misreading of the name which occurs in Muirchú's Life of Patrick as *Uentre*, and which he confidently gives as an alternative name for Patrick's birth place (see above). Alternatively, *Uentre* may be a misreading of an original *Nemthur*. Whatever form Muirchú intended, it was originally no more linked to Dumbarton than was *Bannauem Taberniae*. This link was only forged through the later tradition that Patrick was born on the

Clyde, and it is this tradition that will now be examined. Any such examination must begin with Patrick's contemporary, the British ruler Coroticus.

COROTICUS

Two pieces of writing by Patrick have survived, together covering about thirteen pages of modern printed text. The longer one is the *Confessio*, already mentioned in connection with the place of his birth. The shorter one is known variously as 'Letter to Coroticus' or, more accurately, 'A Tract on the Crimes of Coroticus'.[21] Coroticus is a ruler whose soldiers attacked a settlement in Ireland where Patrick had very recently baptised a group of Irish men and women. In this raid, some of the newly baptised had been killed, others had been carried off into slavery, and booty had been taken. Patrick immediately wrote to these soldiers, asking for the return of some of the booty as well as of the baptised prisoners. This simply caused uproarious laughter. The letter has not survived. Patrick then wrote a longer tract, which addresses various audiences, including Coroticus himself and the Christian community in Britain. In this, in his capacity as bishop, Patrick excommunicates Coroticus and his men until they have given back what they have taken. It is this text that has survived. It is generally accepted that Coroticus was a ruler of a British kingdom, and was at least nominally Christian. It is also accepted that his kingdom was in the north, since three times the Picts are mentioned (in extremely unflattering terms) as Coroticus's allies and customers for slaves.

The name Coroticus has developed in Welsh as Ceredig. In a genealogy of the kings of Al Clud that dates from around 900, an early ancestor of these kings is one *Ceritic guletic*, that is Ceredig *gwledig* 'Ceredig the wealthy', or 'Ceredig the ruler'.[22] It cannot be known for certain whether this is the Coroticus whose behaviour so outraged Patrick, but this is the assumption generally made by scholars.[23] It also seems to have been the assumption made by the compiler of the Book of Armagh in about the year 800. In a heading or description of one of the chapters in Muirchú's Life of Patrick, Coroticus (who appears in the Irish form of his name, *Coirthech*) is described as king of Ail (*regem Aloo*).[24] This is thought to represent Ail Cluaithe, the Gaelic form of Al Clud. In Muirchú's story itself, which dates from the late seventh century (as opposed to the heading, which is over 100 years later), Coroticus (*Coirtic*) is simply called 'a certain British king'. As a punishment for his unrepentant attitude to his crimes, Patrick prays to God 'to expel this godless man from this world and the next', whereupon he is changed into a fox in front of his whole court, runs away and is never seen again![25] The Coroticus-Al Clud link will have strongly helped to foster the later belief that Patrick himself originated there.

ST PATRICK AGAIN

Besides this Coroticus-Patrick-Al Clud link, there is another more general point to be made about locating Patrick's birth and childhood on the Clyde. By the time that records begin in earnest in the late twelfth century, it is clear that the church of (Old) Kilpatrick is the centre of the Patrick cult in the Lennox: its name means in Gaelic 'church (*cill*) of Patrick' (first appearing as 'the church (*ecclesia*) of *Kilpatrik*' 1182 x 1199),[26] and two fine pieces of tenth-century Christian sculpture have come from the site.[27] The position of this church is very significant, lying as it does at the western end of, and just within, the Antonine Wall. For the Gaelic-speaking settlers who were moving into this area after the fall of Dumbarton in 871 (if not before), the Wall would have been a visible symbol of the limit of the Roman Empire. In fact Old Kilpatrick must have been one of the first parts of Britain within the Wall to be settled by Gaelic-speakers. It was well known that Patrick was a citizen of that Empire, and, coupled with the Coroticus-Al Clud link discussed above, this was enough for people to put two and two together and make six.

While, as is clear from the above, there is no certainty as to the dating of these Patrick traditions, the slim and fragmented evidence, both textual and circumstantial, points to the tenth century as the period when Patrick became associated with the Dumbarton area. Certainly a 'dossier' or collection of stories relating to Patrick's birth and childhood in Al Clud existed early enough to be incorporated into the Tripartite Life of Patrick, and it makes most sense to see this 'dossier' as having been put together in Al Clud itself. By this time, it was standard practice in any written saint's life to have a section on childhood miracles, and so the Al Clud material was meeting a real hagiographical demand. It provided thirteen miracles, from his birth to the time of his captivity and enslavement in Ireland. It is by far the earliest piece of literature directly relating to, and almost certainly composed in, Dunbartonshire, and deserves to be better known. These stories are to be found in the *Tripartite Life*, pp. 9–17 (original Irish on even pages, English translation on odd). They include the story of the stone on which he was born (told above); the triple miracle at his baptism, of the well, of the curing of the priest, Gornias, blind and flat-faced, and of Gornias's sudden ability to read (which was at the time of composition obviously not considered to be a prerequisite of a priest). This baptism episode ends with the words 'and there stands the well by the altar, and it has the form of a cross, as the wise declare' (*Tripartite Life*, p. 9).

Figure 3 Early medieval cross-shaft associated with Old Kilpatrick. It was later used as a footbridge at Sandford nearby, was set up in the garden of Mountblow House, also nearby, then was removed to Kelvingrove Museum in 1884, where it remains today. For more details see Batey 1994, pp. 63–5. Photo: Glasgow Museums © Glasgow City Council (Museums).

An integral part of these stories of the young Patrick is the fact that he was fostered, as in all but one of the post-baptism miracles foster-parents (chiefly a rather grumpy foster-mother) play a part. They paint a vivid picture of a rural economy dependent on dairy production from both sheep and cattle, and of lands liable to flooding and owing tribute both in kind (of curd and butter) and in labour duties to the local ruler in the 'palace' of Al Clud. Dairy production continued to play an important role in the Lennox economy and system of tribute: a mid-thirteenth-century charter stipulates as part of the rent for the lands of Luss the provision, in lieu of common army service, 'two cheeses from each house in which cheese is made'.[28] One of the miracles (the bringing back to life of his foster-father) even takes place at an 'assembly of the Britains' (the Irish word used is *dáil*, today the name for the Irish Parliament). For a summary of all these miracles, see the Appendix to this chapter.[29]

THE KINGDOM OF AL CLUD

The earliest undisputed reference to this kingdom is made by Adomnán, abbot of Iona, who died 704. He is best known as the author of the Latin *Life of St Columba*, the founder of the monastery of Iona, who died 597. In Book I, chapter 15 of this Life, Rhydderch (Roderc) son of Tudwal (Tothal)[30] is described as ruling *in petra Cloithe*, that is 'in the rock of Clyde'. Latin *petra* 'rock' translates the British (and Gaelic) *al/ail* 'rock', standing for Old Gaelic *Ail Cloithe*, that is Dumbarton Rock. In the *Life of St Columba* Rhydderch is presented as a man beset by enemies, and worried about meeting a violent end. He therefore sends to Columba, described as his friend, to find out his fate. Columba replies that he will die in his own bed, in his own house, which, Adomnán informs us, is what indeed happened.[31] It was a rare enough occurrence for a king of a small kingdom in post-Roman Britain to die peacefully in his bed, and Rhydderch's worries will have been shared by most rulers of that time. Later Welsh literature hints at enmity between Rhydderch and Columba's main political supporter, Aedán mac Gabráin, king of the Scots of Dál Riata (Argyll), Rhydderch's western neighbour, which, if true, would make Adomnán's story especially ironic.[32] However, the evidence for this enmity is late and open to different interpretations. It is also recorded that Rhydderch was part of an alliance of British kings fighting against the Northumbrian English, who were expanding into what is now northern England and southern Scotland from their power base around Lindisfarne and Bamburgh.[33]

While a continuous historical narrative cannot be told of Al Clud, the few records that do exist from the centuries following the bed-death of

Rhydderch around 600 paint a picture of a kingdom frequently at odds with, less frequently in alliance with, its neighbours, the Scots to the west, the English to the south, and the Picts to the north and north-east. In 642, under their king, Ywain (Owen), they defeated the Scots of Dál Riata at the battle of Strathcarron on Al Clud's eastern borders (now in Stirlingshire), killing the Scottish king Domnal Brecc, grandson of Aedán mac Gabráin. This same Ywain was a brother or half-brother of the famous Pictish king Bruide (Brude), both sons of Beli, king of Al Clud till c. 640. Bruide son of Beli is best known as the victor at the battle of *Dunechtan* against the Northumbrian English in 685, a battle traditionally sited at Dunnichen near Forfar, Angus, although recently a site on the west shore of Loch Insch in Badenoch, at Dunnachton, Inverness-shire, has been proposed.[34] The close family ties between the rulers of Al Clud and Pictland at this time must point also to close political alliance, one that would have been facilitated by the closeness of language: British and Pictish were very similar and mutually intelligible.

This close Pictish alliance in the seventh century stands in stark contrast to the hostilities between the Britons of Al Clud and the Scots of Dál Riata that are recorded in annals in the late seventh and early eighth century, in the form of four battles, starting in the year 678. An annal for that year records 'the slaughter of the kindred of Lorn in Tiriu, between Ferchar Fota and the Britons, who were the victors'.[35] Ferchar Fota son of Feradach was the head of the Cenél Loairn (kindred of Lorn, whence Lorne in Argyll, one of the divisions of Dál Riata) and overking of Dál Riata at this time. Tiriu remains unidentified, but was presumably somewhere near the border between Al Clud and Dál Riata. This hostility continued into the opening decades of the eighth century, with another three battles between the two peoples recorded within a period of thirteen years. The British victory in 704, described as the slaughter of the men of Dál Riata (Scots) in the valley or by the loch of Lomond (*in Ualle Limnae*,[36] or *ic linn limniae*) is first of these.[37] The Scottish victory in 711 is next, described as the defeat of the Britons by the Scots at the unidentified place called *Loirgg Ecclet* (mentioned in the *Annals of Ulster*). The name suggests the battle took place on a route-way (*lorg*) connecting the two kingdoms, perhaps at the north end of Loch Long, or in Glen Falach at the north end of Loch Lomond. And, six years later in 717, the Scottish victory is described as taking place at a stone called Minuirc, again unidentified, but probably also on or near the Dál Riata-Al Clud border. The name appears to be British, the first element being British **main* (Welsh *maen*) 'stone', and it is possible, though not provable, that it is the stone which later became known (in Gaelic) as *Clach nam Breatann* 'the Stone of the Britons'. This still stands in Glen Falach marking the ancient boundary of Al Clud (later Lennox) and Pictland, and near the boundary with Dál Riata.

The story lying behind these 'headlines' may well be more complicated than one of Scots versus Britons. Recently, James Fraser in 'Strangers on the Clyde' has made a good argument for a 'special relationship' between the British of Al Clud and the Cenél Comgaill, a division of Dál Riata that has left its name in Cowal, the district of Argyll immediately west of Al Clud. This relationship, which expressed itself in close co-operation on both secular and ecclesiastical fronts, grew up in the seventh century and continued into the eighth, that is, over the period of recorded hostility between the British and (the rest of) Dál Riata. He argues that it was this alliance which helps explain how this relatively small British kingdom managed to survive for so long against all the odds. His careful reconstruction of this alliance out of a diverse range of difficult and disparate evidence is a stark reminder of just how fragmented our sources are for this period. It is also a salutary warning against oversimplification of what must have been a highly complex and nuanced network of shifting political, cultural and ecclesiastical alliances.

The last three of the above-mentioned battles between the Scots and the Britons took place during the reign of Beli son of Elfin, who reigned for twenty-eight years, a reasonably long reign for a king in this period. He died in 722, to be succeeded by his son Tewdwr (Teudebur) – the name which became English Tudor – who reigned for at least as long as his father, dying some time between 750 and 752. Towards the end of his reign, the sparse historic notices point to a deterioration of relations between Britons and Picts, with a battle between them perhaps in 744 and certainly in 750, when the brother of the Pictish king Unuist I was killed. This latter battle was at a place called variously *Catohic* (*Annals of Ulster*), *Moce-tauc* and *Mygedawc* (both from Welsh sources[38]), which can probably be identified with Mugdock, Strathblane parish, Stirlingshire. In the same year, the annals record 'the ebbing of the power of Unuist, king of the Picts', who had dominated northern politics for the past twenty years, and this may well have been as a result of the British victory at Mugdock and its aftereffects. In the same year as the battle of Mugdock (750), however, an English source (the Continuation of Bede's *Historia Ecclesiastica*)[39] records that Eadberht, king of Northumbria (737–58) 'added the plain of Kyle (*campum Cyil*) along with other lands (*cum aliis regionibus*) to his kingdom'. Kyle, now a district within Ayrshire, had probably formed part of the kingdom of Al Clud up until this time, and shows that the kingdom was under attack from both the north-east (by the Picts) and the south (by the Northumbrians), with the enemies probably acting in alliance. This alliance was still active six years later, when the Picts and Northumbrians together, under their kings Unuist and Eadberht respectively, attacked the town of Al Clud (Dumbarton) and forced the Britons to surrender. This was on 1 August 756. Nine days later, however, on 10 August, the same source (Simeon of Durham in his *Historia Regum*) narrates that almost all of Eadberht's army perished on its way south from Govan. This was probably as a result of an attack by the British.[40] Their king at this time was Dyfnwal son of Tewdwr (Dumnagual son of Teudebur), who died around 760.

During the next 100 years the sources are silent, except for the record of the burning of Al Clud (*Combustio Alo Cluadhe*) on 1 January 780 (*Annals of Ulster*). The perpetrators are not named, but as is clear from the fragments of history set out above, there was no lack of hostile neighbours who could have been responsible.

In about 849, the Britons were on the warpath themselves, since it is recorded that they burnt Dunblane.[41] This was in the turbulent first years of the reign of Cinaed mac Alpín (Kenneth son of Alpine), king of the Picts, when the Norse were also attacking Pictland. It is even possible that at this time the Norse and British of Al Clud were in alliance. If so, then this alliance seriously broke down twenty years later, when late in 870 the Norse kings Ólafr and Ívarr besieged the fortress of Al Clud (Dumbarton Rock) for four months, then captured and destroyed it. In 871, Ólafr and Ívarr returned to their base in Dublin 'with 200 ships, bringing away with them in captivity to Ireland a great booty of English and Britons and Picts' (*Annals of Ulster*). One casualty of the fall of the fortress of Al Clud (Dumbarton) was Arthgal king of the Britons, since it is told that in 872 he was killed, presumably by the Dublin Norse, on the advice of Custantin mac Cinaeda (Constantine son of Kenneth mac Alpine), king of the Picts, 869–77.

In the note on Arthgal's murder, which appears in one of the main sources for this period, the *Annals of Ulster*, an important name-change can be observed. He is referred to not as king of (the Britons of) Al Clud, but, for the first time, king of the Britons of Strathclyde (*rex Britanorum Sratha Cluade*). After this, the name Strathclyde completely ousts Al Clud (Dumbarton) as the name of the kingdom. This almost certainly reflects a shift in the centre of power within the north British kingdom southwards to the valley of the Clyde, centred around Cadzow (Hamilton) and Lanark. This area, as well as much of south-west Scotland, had certainly been part of the kingdom of Al Clud for centuries. Al Clud (Dumbarton) itself was, however, no longer considered to be the chief place of that kingdom. In fact, it is likely that, after the fall of the fortress of Al Clud in 871, much of the area north of the Clyde, above all that of the later earldom of Lennox, ceased to be part of this northern British polity. This is reflected not only in the change of name for the kingdom, but also in the place-names of the Lennox, which are overwhelmingly Gaelic. This is in clear contrast to the place-names in Lanarkshire, which can be seen as the successor to the heartland of the later kingdom of Strathclyde. Here, the survival of British place-names is markedly higher, reflecting the existence of this latter kingdom until the eleventh century, along with the survival of its language. It should be stressed, however, that the kings of Strathclyde belonged to the same family as those of Al Clud, and regarded themselves as their direct successors.

As this chapter is primarily about West Dunbartonshire, this is not the place to explore in detail the later history of the kingdom of Strathclyde. Its last king is usually said to be Ywain (Owen), known as the Bald, described as king of the men of the Clyde (*rex Clutinensium*), who fought alongside the king of Scots Mael Coluim mac Cinaeda (Malcolm II son of Kenneth) at the battle of Carham in 1018. It has generally been thought that he was killed at that battle, but this has recently been called into question.[42] Also, one 'Malcolm son of the king of the Cumbrians (i.e. of Strathclyde)', whom Siward, Earl of Northumbria, tried to put on the Scottish throne in place of King Macbethad (Macbeth) in 1054 or 1055, may have been Ywain's son.[43] After this, however, there is no more mention of kings of Strathclyde.

THE LENNOX

After the downfall of the kingdom of Al Clud in 871, and the shift of the British centre of power southwards into Clydesdale, there is another long silence on the part of the annals regarding the Dumbarton area. It is probably in this period that the Lennox emerged as the name for the new Gaelic-speaking polity that took the place of the British one. Also, it would have been at this time that the name Dumbarton ousted the name Al Clud, as a result of Gaelic-speakers ousting British-speakers. The name (Gaelic *dùn breatann* 'fort of Britons') may well have been used by Gaelic-speakers to refer to Al Clud long before 871. It was certainly so well established that, when the Gaels finally took possession of it, 'fort of Britons', which was of course from this time on a purely historical description, became the current and enduring name. [44]

As for Lennox, our earliest reference comes from the early twelfth-century Irish text about the wars between the Irish Gaels and the Norse, usually referred to in English as 'The War of the Gaedhil with the Gaill'.[45] Its heroic central character is the famous Irish king Brian Bóruma, who died in battle in 1014. However, it is more about the politics of Ireland and the Irish Sea world at the time it was written, about a century later, than about the time of Brian. It was commissioned by Brian's great-grandson Muirchertach son of Tairdelbhach, who dominated Irish Sea politics for many years before his death in 1119.[46] One passage purports to describe Brian's levying tribute and hostages in 1005 from peoples surrounding the Irish Sea, that is 'from the English and Britons, and the people of Lennox, that is [Lennox] of Scotland, and Argyll'.[47] This suggests that Lennox fell within Muirchertach's sphere of lordship, or at least within his sphere of ambition, around the year 1100.

It might be to this obscure period in Lennox's history that the roots can be traced of the mormaers or early earls of Lennox, as they are portrayed in a poem by the Irish poet Muireadhach Ó Dálaigh, written around 1200. This poem is written in Gaelic, and addressed to Alún or Alwyn son of Muireadhach, the first recorded mormaer or earl of Lennox, who died c. 1200. It is one of two poems by this poet that were addressed to Lennox patrons: the other being to Amhlaibh grandson of Alún I, ancestor of the MacAulays of Faslane and Gareloch, Dunbartonshire.[48] Both show not only that the language and culture of the ruling kin of Lennox was still thoroughly Gaelic in the early thirteenth century, but also that this ruling kin were proud to see their origins in terms of the mythological history of Ireland, more precisely of Munster (south-west Ireland). The family of Uí Briain (to whom Muirchertach son of Tairdelbhach belonged) originated in Munster, and these Munster connections of the earls of Lennox celebrated in poetry around the year 1200 may be an echo of close Uí Briain involvement a century earlier.

PLACE-NAMES

Given the extremely sparse historic record for the Lennox before about 1200, a key piece of evidence for early settlement, culture and language in this period is provided by names of places. As for so much of Scotland, there has never been a proper, in-depth study of the place-names of Dunbartonshire: all that has appeared in print is John Irving's *Place Names of Dumbartonshire*, published in Dumbarton in 1928. Unfortunately, this meets none of the basic criteria of a scholarly place-name study: for example it does not give early forms of names, without which no credible derivation of a place-name can be attempted, and it is full of errors, both factual and typographical. This brief survey of the place-names of West Dunbartonshire has, therefore, had to be undertaken practically from scratch, which means that conclusions drawn from the toponymic (place-name) evidence must be very tentative and provisional. However, it is very much to be hoped that the data collected for this chapter can form the core of a much more thorough-going survey of the place-names of West Dunbartonshire. There is no doubt that it will add greatly to our understanding and appreciation of the history of the area.

Three languages have contributed to the bulk of the place-names not only of West Dunbartonshire, but of the whole of the Lennox: these are British, Gaelic and Scots. Together they span the period from c. AD 500 almost to the present day. It is always a risky and problematic undertaking to fit a linguistic history into a historical-political history of a given area, especially into one so fragmented and poorly understood as that of the kingdom of Al Clud. But the general impression of a landscape dominated by names of Gaelic origin can be tentatively tied in to the decline and disappearance of the British kingdom of Al Clud after the great siege of 870–1. As mentioned above, one of the chief differences between the place-names of Dunbartonshire and those of Lanarkshire is that, in the latter, the British survival rate is significantly higher, and it was in Lanarkshire that the later British kingdom of Strathclyde was centred.

British Names

Al Clud (the modern Welsh form, with *Clud* pronounced to rhyme with English 'weed') is the name of both Dumbarton Rock and the kingdom from which it was ruled. It is a British name, meaning 'rock of Clyde'. The word *al* 'rock' has a close Gaelic cognate, *ail*, while the Gaelic for Clyde was *Cluad* (where *d* is pronounced like *th* in English *the*), so the name was easily adapted into Gaelic, appearing frequently as *Ail Cluade*, etc. The name has an exact equivalent in Auckland, Co. Durham, the earliest form of which appears in the eleventh century as *Alclit*. This means that the river that flows past Auckland, now called the Gaunless, once had the same name as the Clyde.[49]

Another entirely British name is probably Carman, the fort on the boundary of Bonhill and Cardross, discussed above (p. 15 and in endnote 6).

The parish name **Cardross** is assumed to be a British name,[50] but there are problems with this. Its earliest forms are: (church of) *Cardinros* and *Cadinros* 1208 x 1233.[51] After this, it occurs as two syllables only, starting with *Cardros'* 1325.[52] The same name (Cardross) appears also in Menteith, Perthshire. It would seem to contain **carden* and *r(h)os* 'promontory', meaning '**carden* of (the) promontory'. Scottish Gaelic *ros* 'promontory, headland' is found in many central Scottish place-names, from Ardrossan in Ayrshire, to Ardross by Elie, Fife. The name Cardross refers originally to the site of the medieval church, which lies on a well-defined promontory on the west bank of the Leven as it enters the Clyde, and is dominated by

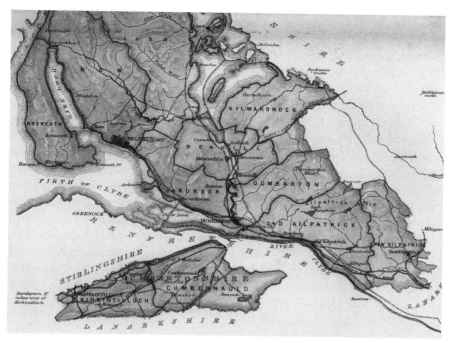

Figure 4 Map of the county in 1879 from Joseph Irving's *Book of Dunbartonshire*. Included as an inset is the detached part of the county which consisted of the medieval parish of Kirkintilloch (now Kirkintilloch and Cumbernauld). In the Middle Ages much of Rhu (*Row*) was in Cardross, while Old and New Kilpatrick formed the single parish of Kilpatrick.

Dumbarton Rock on the opposite bank.[53] Welsh *rhos* means '(upland) moor, heathland', and does not apply here. The element *carden is traditionally assumed to be a Pictish word meaning 'woodland',[54] but recently Andrew Breeze has plausibly suggested the meaning 'enclosure, encampment'.[55] Whatever the meaning, its distribution in place-names is thoroughly Pictish, even if it is sometimes combined with a Gaelic element (e.g. Kincardine). In fact, Cardross by Dumbarton is the only example of this element outside historical Pictland. It is difficult to know what to make of this, but it is unlikely to be a British survival.

Another name that looks deceptively British is **Aber**, Kilmaronock parish, on the banks of Loch Lomond.[56] This element, however, is otherwise unknown in Lennox, and it much more probably derives from Gaelic *eabar* 'pool, puddle, marsh'.[57] This would refer to the extensive bog, pitted with pools, which lies mainly to the south of the point where the Endrick flows into Loch Lomond, and immediately to the north of the lands of Aber.

The early settlement and parish name **Bonhill**, if not British, may show British influence. Early forms are (parish of) *Buthelulle* 1247 x 1259, and

Bohtlul 1274.[58] The second element is probably the same name, and perhaps even the same saint, whose name is Latinised as *Lolanus*, and whose cult was centred at Kincardine-in-Menteith, Perthshire. It was at Kincardine that both his bell and his crosier were preserved,[59] and where, at least by the early sixteenth century, it was believed he was buried, in earth brought from St Peter's in Rome.[60] There is no record of him in any of the extensive early Irish hagiographical material, and so he was fairly certainly a figure of the Pictish or British church.[61] The first element, Gaelic *both*, can be both 'hut' and 'church', in this context clearly the latter. While it is sometimes found in Ireland as an ecclesiastical element, its distribution as such in Scotland suggests a Pictish and British (i.e. p-Celtic) bias, with the underlying p-Celtic word (Welsh *bod* 'dwelling, residence') having been adapted to the related Gaelic *both*.[62] Within the Lennox, it is found in the parish names Balfron (earlier *Buthbren*, etc.) and Baldernock (earlier *Buthernok*, etc.), both in Stirlingshire. The latter contains *Ernoc*, a common saint's name, found also for example in Kilmarnock, Ayrshire and Argyll (Cowal).[63] Exactly the same elements (*both* + Ernoc) are found in Balernock, Rhu, Dunbartonshire (*Buthernock*- 1239 *Lenn. Cart.* 30), although no physical trace of a church has been found here.

Gaelic Names

In stark contrast to British names, Gaelic names dominate the toponymy of Dunbartonshire. Two of the three parishes in our area contain the Gaelic *cill* 'church', **Kilpatrick** and **Kilmaronock** (the latter containing a pet-form of the Gaelic saint's name Ronan). W. J. Watson suggests that the Ronan in Kilmaronock may have been Abbot Ronan of Kingarth, Bute, the chief church of Cowal, who died in 737,[64] and his commemoration here would be entirely consistent with the close links between Al Clud and Cowal mentioned above. Kingarth was clearly a major church centre in this period, and is the only church in the Firth of Clyde to appear in the early annals. So, whatever the nature of the political relationship between Al Clud and Cowal, it is very likely that Kingarth's influence reached to the kingdom of Al Clud. It is impossible to say when the name Kilmaronock was coined, but an early eighth-century date is quite plausible. There is evidence in eastern Scotland of *cill*-names being coined well before Gaelic became the main language of that area, under the influence of the Gaelic-speaking Church,[65] and there is no reason to think that the situation in Al Clud would have been very different.

However, most of the Gaelic place-names in our area must date from the period after Gaelic had become the main language, that is probably from the later ninth century onwards. The commonly occurring Gaelic place-name elements are dealt with first.

Auch-*names*

Gaelic 'field', it can also mean 'small farm, secondary settlement'.[66] It is found in West Dunbartonshire in the following names: **Auchincarroch** (*Hachenkerach* c. 1247 *Glas. Reg.* no. 177), Bonhill parish; **Auchenreoch** (*Auchinreoch* 1609 *RMS* vii no. 190 col. 5), Dumbarton parish; **Auchenduich**, **Auchentorlie** (*Achyntuerly* 1452 *Pais. Reg.* 250), **Auchentoshan** (*Auchintoschen* 1592 *RMS* v no. 2070), **Auchingree** (*Auchingrie* 1592 *RMS* v no. 2070), **Auchinleck** (*Auchinleck* 1592 *RMS* v no. 2070, now part of Faifley), all Old Kilpatrick parish.[67]

In various parts of Scotland, including the Ochil Hills, *achadh* can also mean 'hill-field' or 'piece of ground cleared for grazing or cultivation', occurring between c. 50 and c. 500 metres.[68] This certainly suits several *Auch*-names in the Kilpatrick Hills, such as Auchenreoch (*riabhach* 'variegated, striped'), lying at 210 metres; and Auchingree (probably containing Gaelic *greigh* 'herd, usually of horses, horse stud'). The latter was muir-land lying at a height of about 250 metres and attached to Paisley Abbey's lands of Boquhanran, although it lay more than 6 kilometres to the north.[69] It is striking that there are no names containing *achadh* in Kilmaronock parish,[70] where their place seems to be taken by *blàr-* and *gart-* (for both of which see below).

Blair-*names*

Gaelic *blàr* 'muir, field' is common in place-names practically everywhere in Scotland where Gaelic is or has been spoken, the best known being Blair (Atholl) and Blair (Gowrie), the only two *blàr*-names that became parishes. It is unknown as a place-name element in Ireland, where it has the more specialised meaning 'battlefield'. This suggests that its usage on this side of the Irish Sea has been influenced by a related British or Pictish word, but this remains to be investigated. Unlike other common place-name elements, such as *achadh*, *baile* (*Bal-*) and (with only one or two possible exceptions) *pett* (*Pit-*), it can stand entirely on its own, without a specifying element, and without a suffix. This suggests that it can at least sometimes refer to a much larger unit of land than an individual settlement. Blair Atholl and Blair Gowrie are examples of this, since the specifiers Atholl and Gowrie are never used locally, and have been introduced by outsiders to distinguish them from each other in a national context. It also suggests that there can be only one *blàr* in any given territory. The examples in West Dunbartonshire strikingly reinforce this pattern. All the *Blair*-names are found clustered together in the south-west corner of Kilmaronock parish, nine in all, and all contiguous. They are **Blairbeich**, **Blairdennan**, **Blairennich**, **Blairhosh**,[71] **Blairlinnans**, **Blairlusk**, **Blairnyle**, **Blairquhanan** and **Blairquhomrie**, suggesting that originally this whole corner of the parish was known simply as Blair, and that these nine names represent divisions thereof.

Gart-*names*[72]

Gaelic *gart* 'enclosure, farm' (modern Gaelic *gort* 'field') has an especially well-defined distribution in central Scotland. It is common right up to the border of medieval Fife on the east, but there is not a single one in Fife itself. On the west, the River Leven is the boundary, unless **Garmore**, Bonhill, NS360800, 4 km west of the Leven near Alexandria, is for Gaelic *gart mòr* 'big *gart*'.[73] In his discussion of early medieval sculpture of the Glasgow area, Derek Craig suggests that the River Leven acted as a territorial boundary at some point around the tenth century, on the basis of different sculptural traditions on either side of it.[74] Could these two phenomena in relation to the River Leven – the distribution of *Gart*-names and the change of sculptural traditions – be in some way linked? It is certainly a question that would repay further investigation.

Examples in West Dunbartonshire are: **Garshake**, Dumbarton (*Gartschavok* 1466 *RMS* ii no. 875), the second element being Gaelic *seabhog* 'hawk'; **Gartinbantrick**, Kilmaronock (*Gartpantre* 1546 *RMS* iii no. 3208), the second element probably being *bantrach* 'widow' or *bantrachd* 'company of women', and **Gartocharn**, Kilmaronock (*Garth<c>harne* 1528,[75] *Gartoquharne* 1627 x 1628 *RMS* viii no. 1222), for *gart a' chàirn* 'farm of the cairn', the cairn probably being a burial mound.

Within West Dunbartonshire, their distribution is far from even. Out of a total of seven, six are in Kilmaronock parish, and five of these cluster together in the northern part of the parish.[76] The seventh is Garshake, Dumbarton parish, for which see above. In the medieval parish of Kilpatrick, now split into Old and New Kilpatrick, the four or five examples of *gart*-names are all in the eastern (New Kilpatrick) part (and so outwith modern West Dunbartonshire).

The element *gart* would therefore seem to reflect a very particular response to the environment both chronologically and physically, perhaps indicating settlement by Gaelic-speakers at a time of population expansion in areas previously given over to other uses, such as woodland or hunting.

Pit-, Bal- *and* Both-*names*

The total absence throughout Lennox of *Pit*-place-names (containing the Pictish loan-word into Gaelic *pett* 'land-holding, farm') points to a Gaelic which had not been strongly exposed to direct Pictish influence: that is, Gaelic-speakers who settled and named Lennox were coming from the west and north-west. There is also a remarkable dearth in West Dunbartonshire of place-names containing the common Gaelic element *baile* (found in both Scottish and Irish Gaelic), with a similar meaning to *pett*. It may be the first element in **Ballagan**, Bonhill, and in **Balquhain**, Kilmaronock, but, without early forms, it remains uncertain as to whether these are Gaelic *baile* or Gaelic *both* 'hut, small dwelling; church'. There are, after all, several instances in Lennox where a modern *Bal*- name has developed from an original *Both*-: **Baldernock** (parish), Stirlingshire, **Balfron** (parish), Stirlingshire, and **Balernock**, Rhu, Dunbartonshire, have already been mentioned as examples of this (above p. 30). To them can be added **Balfunning** and **Ballat**, both Drymen, Stirlingshire, and probably **Baljaffrey**, New Kilpatrick (*Bojalga* 1654 Blaeu (Pont) Map, Lennox). Taking Lennox as a whole, there are a few genuine *baile*-names, but they are mainly in the eastern (Stirlingshire) part. In contrast, the element *both* is of relatively common occurrence. To those mentioned above can be added **Bonhill** (for which see pp. 29–30), **Boquhan** by Buchanan, Stirlingshire, **Boquhan**, Killearn, Stirlingshire, **Boquhanran**, Old Kilpatrick,[77] **Boturich**, Kilmaronock, and probably **Boclair**, New Kilpatrick and **Buchanan**, Stirlingshire. This use of *both* may have been stimulated by the existence of British settlement names containing the closely related **bod*, which in Welsh means 'dwelling, residence'. This may have been a standard way of referring to a settlement-unit (its ecclesiastical usage, relevant above all in the parish names Baldernock, Balfron and Bonhill, has already been discussed above pp. 29–30).

Other Gaelic names

There are literally hundreds of other Gaelic names in West Dunbartonshire. A few have already been discussed, in the sections 'Prehistoric Times' (Cochno, Shanacles, Dumbowie) and 'Roman Times' (Carleith, Duntocher, Cleddans). The lands attached to the church of Kilpatrick, which were given to Paisley Abbey along with the church by Earl Alwin (1182 x 1199 *Lenn. Cart.* 12 and *Pais. Reg.* 157), and over which there was such bitter dispute in the first decades of the thirteenth century, form what must have been almost a block of land occupying what is now much of the eastern part of Old Kilpatrick parish. Most are clearly of Gaelic origin: besides **Cochno** there is **Craigbanzeoch**

(*Craguentalach* 1182 x 1199 *Lenn. Cart.* 12, *Cragbentalach* 1234 *Pais. Reg.* 164); this seems originally to have consisted of Gaelic *creag* 'rock, crag', ? Gaelic *beinn*, earlier *beann* 'peak', and Gaelic *tulach* 'mound, hillock'. If it is indeed represented by modern Craigbanzeoch, then it has been re-analysed later in the Gaelic-speaking period as containing Gaelic *beannachd* 'blessing' (signifying church-land, see *CPNS*, p. 263). Others include **Drumcreve** (now obsolete) (*Drumcreue* 1182 x 1199 *Pais Reg.* 157) Gaelic *druim* 'ridge' + Gaelic *craobh* 'tree'; **Duntiglennan** (*Drumtechglunan* 1182 x 1199 *Pais. Reg.* 157) Gaelic *druim* 'ridge' + Gaelic *teach* (modern Gaelic *taigh*) 'house' + personal name Gillunan or the like (this name can be analysed either 'ridge of Gillunan's house' or 'ridge of a place called *Teach G(il)lunain'; the personal name itself is a typical Gaelic formation prefixing *gille* 'servant' to the name of a saint. The saint in question may be the famous Iona abbot Adomnán, later Èo(dh)nan, giving the Gaelic name Gilleonain; it is, however, also possible that it contains a reduced form of the name Lolan(us) of Bonhill (for whom see above pp. 29–30)); **Edinbarnet** (*Edenbernan* 1182 x 1199 *Lenn. Cart.* 12), 'open hill-side of (the) little gap' (Gaelic *aodann* 'face, open hill-side' + Gaelic *beàrnan* 'little gap'), the gap probably referring to a way through the Kilpatrick Hills; **Faifley** (*Finbealach* 1182 x 1199 *Pais. Reg.* 157), Gaelic *fionn-bhealach* 'white or holy pass or way',[78] possibly referring to the old route-way from Strath Blane by way of Tambowie across the south-east corner of the Kilpatrick Hills heading for the pilgrimage centre of Old Kilpatrick; **Kilbowie** (*Cuiltebut* 1182 x 1199 *Pais. Reg.* 157, *Cultbuthe* 1233 *Pais. Reg.* 166), Gaelic *cuilt* 'nook, corner, recess' + Gaelic *buidhe* 'yellow', probably referring to vegetation such as gorse or yellow-flag (iris).

Scots Names

The general replacement of Gaelic by Scots in West Dunbartonshire belongs to a much later period than that covered by this chapter. The introduction of Scots into traditionally Gaelic-speaking regions of Scotland is closely linked to the establishment of royal or episcopal burghs or trading centres, and the founding of the burgh of Dumbarton by Alexander II in 1222 is therefore an important date not only in the social and economic history of the area, but also in its linguistic history. However, the progress of Scots in West Dunbartonshire was slow, and it is not until the mid-fourteenth-century that Scots place-names start appearing in local documents. One of the earliest examples is the description of the boundaries of the land of Bonhill west of Leven in a land-grant made by Donald Earl of Lennox (1333 x c. 1364) to Patrick de Lindsay (*Lenn. Cart.* 51). The boundaries of this land are given as Poachy Burn (*Pocheburne*, probably containing Scots *poch* 'poach', a kind of fish), the *Blindsyke* (Scots *syke* 'small burn', with *blind* in the sense of 'hidden') and the *Halyburne* (Scots *haly* 'holy'), showing that Scots was being applied to many minor landscape features by this time.

CONCLUSION

Several millennia have been covered in this chapter, and many different types of evidence have been used, including archeological remains, linguistic remains in the form of place-names, hagiographical material, and brief annals almost entirely detached from any meaningful historical narrative. Because of this, the details in the story told here are frequently qualified by words such as 'possibly' and 'probably', while the luxury of 'certainly' is rare. Nevertheless, there emerges from this fragmentary mosaic a clear picture of a post-Roman British kingdom moving slowly and by no means surely towards incorporation as a province into the expanding Gaelic-speaking kingdom of Alba in the tenth century, the province being the direct predecessor of the medieval earldom of Lennox. Along the way we see this kingdom using both military and diplomatic strategies to maintain its political and cultural identity in the face of larger, though not necessarily always more aggressive, kingdoms surrounding it on all sides. An important strand in this process of incorporation is the growth and promotion of the cult of St Patrick, which ensured the old heartland of the Lennox around Dumbarton and Kilpatrick found an important place within the medieval Scottish Church and its network of pilgrimage and patronage.[79]

NOTES

1   'ad furcas nostras del *Cathyr' Regesta Regum Scottorum* vol. vi (*Acts of David II*), ed. B. Webster (Edinburgh, 1982) (hereafter *RRS* vi), no. 478.

2   These have now been removed to the National Museum of Scotland; see Dennison, E. Patricia and Coleman, Russel (1999), *Historic Dumbarton* ([Edinburgh]: Historic Scotland in association with Tuckwell Press), p. 9.

3   Watson, W. J. (1926), *The History of the Celtic Place-Names of Scotland* (Edinburgh and London: Royal Celtic Society by W. Blackwood [reprinted with an Introduction by Simon Taylor, Edinburgh: Birlinn, 2004]) (hereafter Watson *CPNS*), p. 512.

4   *Registrum Magni Sigilli Regum Scottorum* (*Register of the Great Seal*), ed. J. M. Thomson and J. Balfour Paul, 11 vols (Edinburgh: Scotland's National Archives 1882–1914, reprinted by The Scottish Record Society, 1984) (hereafter *RMS*) vii, no. 190.

5   It appears in its Scots form on Ordnance Survey 6 inch 1st edition (1864), but has been Englished to 'Hill of Standing Stones' on more recent Ordnance Survey maps.

6   This appears as *Carmane* 1333 x c. 1364 as one of marches of Bonhill *Cartularium*

Comitatus de Levenax ['Cartulary of the Earls of Lennox'] (Maitland Club, 1833) (hereafter *Lenn. Cart.*), p. 51. Probably a British name containing the elements **cair* (Welsh *caer*) 'fort' and **main* (Welsh *maen*) 'stone'.

7   From Gaelic *dùn buidhe* 'yellow hill-fort', *buidhe* 'yellow' probably because it was covered in gorse for at least part of the Gaelic-speaking period.

8   Dennison, E. Patricia and Coleman, Russel (1999), *Historic Dumbarton* ([Edinburgh]: Historic Scotland in association with Tuckwell Press), p. 9.

9   Rivet, A. L. F. and Smith, Colin (1979), *The Place-Names of Roman Britain* (London: Batsford), pp. 342–4.

10 Maxwell, Gordon (1989), *The Romans in Scotland* (Edinburgh: Mercat Press), p. 32, quoting from a near-contemporary Roman account.

11 Maxwell, Gordon (1989), *The Romans in Scotland* (Edinburgh: Mercat Press), pp. 138–41.

12 For details of Duntocher, see Maxwell (1989), pp. 144–5 and Fig. 7.9. For Carleith, see Maxwell (1989), p. 160.

13 Maxwell, Gordon (1989), *The Romans in Scotland* (Edinburgh: Mercat Press), p. 149.

14 Watson, *CPNS*, p. 202.

15 *Registrum Monasterii de Passelet* (Maitland Club, 1832; New Club, 1877) (hereafter *Pais. Reg.*), p. 158.

16 Dumville, David N. and others (1993), *Saint Patrick A.D. 493–1993* (Woodbridge: Boydell Press), pp. 255–8.

17 Translation, slightly modified, from Whitley Stokes (ed. and translator), *Tripartite Life of St Patrick*, 2 vols (Rolls Series 1887), p. 9. *immorro* is translated 'moreover', rather than Stokes's 'however'.

18 *Tripartite Life*, p. 404.

19 'InNem*thur* .i. cathir sen fil imBretnaib tuascirt .i. Ail Cluade.' *Tripartite Life*, pp. 412–13.

20 Watson, *CPNS*, pp. 246–7.

21 For the full text, translation and commentary, see Dumville, David N. et al. (1993), *Saint Patrick A.D. 493–1993* (Woodbridge: Boydell Press), pp. 117–27.

22 *Saint Patrick*, p. 114.

23 For a survey of different opinions on this matter, see *Saint Patrick*, pp. 107–15.

24 Ludwig Bieler (ed. and trans., with a contribution by Fergus Kelly), *The Patrician Texts in the Book of Armagh* (Dublin: Dublin Institute for Advanced Studies, 1979), p. 66.

25 Ludwig Bieler (ed. and trans., with a contribution by Fergus Kelly), *The Patrician Texts in the Book of Armagh* (Dublin: Dublin Institute for Advanced Studies, 1979), pp. 66–100.

26 *Pais. Reg.* 157.

27 Batey, Colleen (1994), 'The sculptured stones in Glasgow Museums', in Anna Ritchie (ed.), *Govan and its Early Medieval Sculpture* (Stroud: Alan Sutton Publishing), pp. 63–72.

28 *Lenn. Cart.* 97.

29 For Kilpatrick and the development of the cult of Patrick in later medieval

Scottish sources, see Macquarrie, Alan (1996), 'Lives of Scottish Saints in the Aberdeen Breviary: some problems of sources for Strathclyde saints', *Records of the Scottish Church History Society* 26, pp. 31–54, specifically pp. 44–50.

30 The names are given in their modern Welsh forms, as used by Alan Macquarrie in his chapter, 'The Kings of Strathclyde, c. 400–1018', in Alexander Grant and Keith J. Stringer (eds) (1993), *Medieval Scotland, Crown, Lordship and Community* (Edinburgh: Edinburgh University Press), pp. 1–19, where he usefully brings together references to all the kings of Al Clud and Strathclyde. In brackets are the forms of the names as they appear in the early sources.

31 Anderson, Alan Orr and Anderson, Marjorie Ogilvie (eds and trans.) (1961), *Adomnán's Life of Columba* (revised edition, Oxford: Oxford University Press, 1991), pp. 38–41.

32 Bromwich, Rachel (1961), *Trioedd Ynys Prydein: The Welsh Triads* (Cardiff: University of Wales Press), pp. 147–9.

33 See Bromwich, pp. 504–5, for an overview of Rhydderch's many appearances in medieval story.

34 Woolf, Alex (2006), 'Dún Nechtain, Fortriu, and the geography of the Picts', *Scottish Historical Review* 85, pp. 182–201.

35 'Interfectio generis Loarinn in Tirinn': Mac Airt, S. and Mac Niocaill, G. (eds and trans.), *Annals of Ulster (to 1131)* (Dublin: Dublin Institute for Advanced Studies, 1983), under the year 678; the additional information on Ferchar Fota and the Britons appears in the Annals of Tigernach, for which see Anderson, A. O. (ed.), *Early Sources of Scottish History, A.D. 500 to 1286*, 2 vols (Edinburgh, 1922; reprinted with preface, bibliographical supplement and corrections by M. O. Anderson, Stamford: Paul Watkins, 1990), vol. 1, p. 184.

36 *Annals of Ulster*, under the year 704.

37 *Early Sources*, vol. 1, p. 208. For an alternative reading of this text, placing the battle at Loch Leven near Glen Coe, see Fraser, James (2005), 'Strangers on the Clyde: Cenél Comgaill, Clyde Rock and the bishops of Kingarth', *Innes Review* 56, pp. 102–20. I am very grateful to Dr Fraser for allowing me to read this important article before publication.

38 Anderson, A. O. (ed.), *Early Sources of Scottish History, A.D. 500 to 1286*, 2 vols (Edinburgh, 1922; reprinted with preface, bibliographical supplement and corrections by M. O. Anderson, Stamford: Paul Watkins, 1990), vol. 1, p. 239.

39 Colgrave, Bertram, and Mynors, R. A. B. (eds and trans.) (1969), *Bede's Ecclesiastical History of the English People* (Oxford: Oxford University Press), p. 575.

40 For more on this incident, and on the identification of Govan as the place involved, see Forsyth, Katherine (with Koch, John T.) (2000), 'Evidence of a lost Pictish source in the *Historia Regum Anglorum* of Symeon of Durham', in Simon Taylor (ed.), *Kings, Clerics and Chronicles in Scotland, 500–1297* (Dublin: Four Courts Press), pp. 19–34.

41 *Early Sources*, vol. 1, p. 288.

42 Duncan, A. A. M. (2002), *The Kingship of the Scots 842–1292: Succession and Independence* (Edinburgh: Edinburgh University Press), p. 29. Duncan also suggests here that King Ywain who fought alongside Malcolm II king of Scots

at Carham in 1018 (and survived) may have been the son rather than the brother of his predecessor, Malcolm king of Strathclyde (died 997).

43 Duncan, *Kingship*, pp. 40–1.

44 It does not appear in writing until much later. The earliest written form of the name is *Dunbritan* 1222, printed in Irving, Joseph (1879) *The Book of Dumbartonshire* (Edinburgh and London: W. & A. K. Johnston) vol. i, p. 58 (from a late fourteenth-century copy). However, *Dunbretane* (1238 *Lenn. Cart.* 1) is more typical of thirteenth-century forms of the name.

45 Todd, James Henthorn (1867) (ed. and trans.), *Cogadh Gaedhel re Gallaibh: The War of the Gaedhil with the Gaill* (London).

46 His complicated and switchback career is well set out by Anthony Candon in Candon, Anthony (1988), 'Muirchertach Ua Briain, Politics and Naval Activity in the Irish Sea, 1075 to 1119', in Gearóid Mac Niocaill and Patrick F. Wallace (eds) *Keimelia: Studies in Medieval Archaeology and History in Memory of Tom Delaney* (Galway: Galway University Press), pp. 397–415.

47 'an cíos rioghda Shaxan ocus Bretan ocus Lemnaigh ocus Alban ocus Airer Gaoidhel uile', *Cogadh*, p. 136. Todd is surely correct in seeing 'Lemnaigh ocus Alban' as a copyist's error for 'Lemnaigh .i. Alban'. This is probably inserted to distinguish it from other places of the same name in Ireland, such as that near Cloghar, Co. Tyrone.

48 Both these poems appear in translation in Clancy, Thomas Owen (ed.), *The Triumph Tree: Scotland's Earliest Poetry AD 550–1350* (Edinburgh: Canongate, 1998) (translations and notes by G. Márkus, J. P. Clancy, T. O. Clancy, P. Bibire, J. Jesch), pp. 258–62.

49 Watts, Victor, with contributions by John Insley (2002) *A Dictionary of County Durham Place-Names* (English Place-Name Society, Nottingham), p. 10. This does not mean that, had Al Cud survived in Scotland, it would have become Auckland, since the latter was subjected to heavy Scandinavian linguistic influence (p. 10), an influence conspicuously absent from Dunbartonshire place-names.

50 *CPNS*, p. 353.

51 *Registrum Episcopatus Glasguensis* (Bannatyne and Maitland Clubs, 1843) (hereafter *Glas. Reg.*), no. 108, where *Cadinros* is presumably a miscopying of *Cardinros*.

52 *Regesta Regum Scottorum* vol. v (*Acts of Robert I*), ed. A. A. M. Duncan (Edinburgh: Edinburgh University Press, 1988), no. 279.

53 The name Cardross has shifted several kilometres westwards, where a new parish kirk was built in 1643. The famous royal residence of Cardross, where Robert I (the Bruce) died, was at or near Mains of Cardross (no longer extant), on the west bank of the River Leven and north of the town (at NS391766) (see Barrow, G. W. S., *Robert Bruce* (second edition, Edinburgh: Edinburgh University Press, 1976), pp. 440–1).

54 See for example *CPNS*, pp. 352–3.

55 'Some Celtic Place-Names of Scotland, including *Dalriada, Kincarden, Abercorn, Coldingham* and *Girvan*', *Scottish Language* 18 (1999), pp. 39–41.

56 *CPNS*, p. 459.

57 See *CPNS*, pp. 438, 459, 466 note 1.

58 *Glas. Reg.* no. 177 and *Pais. Reg.* 216 respectively.

59 *Regesta Regum Scottorum* vol. ii (*Acts of William I*), ed. G. W. S. Barrow (Edinburgh: Edinburgh University Press, 1971), no. 372.

60 Said to be St Serf's nephew, the early sixteenth-century *Aberdeen Breviary* tells the bizarre story of how he cuts off his arm (at a place called *Planum*, which may be Plean near Stirling) to send back to Rome so that a door can be opened. His feast day was 22 September, and he is said also to be culted at Broughton, Peeblesshire. See Forbes, Alexander Penrose, *Kalendars of Scottish Saints* (Edinburgh, 1872), pp. 134, 378–9.

61 For Lolan's possible survival in a local personal name, see Duntiglennan p. 134. James Fraser suggests that Kingarth in Bute was the chief church not only of Cenél Comgaill (Cowal), but also, because of the close connections between Cenél Comgaill and Al Clud, of the latter kingdom during the seventh century ('Strangers on the Clyde'). One of the bishops of Kingarth, who died in 688, is Iolan (*Annals of Ulster* 689). Through a confusion of the first letter, this may be the origin of St Lolanus. If it is his name that is embedded in Bonhill, with an initial *L*, this suggests that Lolan- is the correct form of his name.

62 For more details on this, see Taylor, Simon, 'Place-names and the Early Church in Eastern Scotland', in B. E. Crawford (ed.) (1996), *Scotland in Dark Age Britain* (Aberdeen: Scottish Cultural Press), pp. 93–110, especially pp. 96–8 and 104–6.

63 For more examples, see *CPNS*, pp. 291–2.

64 *CPNS*, p. 309.

65 See Taylor, 'Place-names and the Early Church'.

66 See Nicolaisen (1976), pp. 125–8, 140–3.

67 I have not included Auchnacraig, Faifley, in this list, as it seems to be a new coining, not appearing on Ordnance Survey 6 inch 1st edition.

68 Watson, Angus (1995), *The Ochils: Place names, History, Tradition* (Perth: Perth and Kinross District Libraries), p. 155.

69 The name has survived in Auchingree Burn, which flows into the Kilmannan Reservoir NS4877.

70 Auchenlinnhe, Kilmaronock, is the only example, and is a modern coining, as there is neither name nor settlement on this site on the Ordnance Survey 6 inch 1st edition map (1865).

71 Blairhosh is included in this number, since it lay in the parish of Kilmaronock until transferred to Bonhill c. 1650.

72 I am very grateful to Dr John Bannerman for making available to me his extensive data on this element.

73 I have found no form of this name earlier than *Garmore* 1777 ('A map of the Shire of Dumbarton', Charles Ross. National Library of Scotland Map Library, EMS.s.182). The Clyde acts as a similarly clear-cut boundary, with not a single *Gart-* name appearing in Lanarkshire west of Clyde, Renfrewshire or Ayrshire.

74 'The early medieval sculpture of the Glasgow area', in Anna Ritchie (ed.) (1994), *Govan and its Early Medieval Sculpture* (Stroud: Alan Sutton Publishing), pp. 73–91, p. 80.

75   *Registrum Monasterii S. Marie de Cambuskenneth* (Grampian Club, 1872), no. 158.
76   These are **Gargowan** NS4487 (*Gortgaund* 1654 Blaeu (Pont) Lennox), **Gartenwall** NS4486 (*Gertonwall* 1777 'A map of the Shire of Dumbarton'), **Gartinbantrick** (see above), **Gartocharn** (see above) and **Gartochraggan** NS4287. **Gartlea** NS4583, also Kilmaronock, lies fairly isolated beside the Kilmaronock–Drymen parish boundary, at the edge of Cameron Muir.
77   Boquhanran always appears in the medieval record with a first element *monach-* (*Monachkenneran* 1182 x 1199 *Pais. Reg.* 157, *Monachkennaran* 1233 *Pais. Reg.* 166). The earliest form with *Bo-* is *Boquhanrane* 1590 *RMS* v no. 1794. This is a puzzling name. The second element may be the female saint's name Cainer, found in the medieval parish name Bothkennar by Grangemouth, Stirlingshire (for whom see *CPNS*, pp. 166, 275 and Forbes, *Kalendars*, p. 361).
78   The second element in this name, Gaelic *bealach*, is also found in the chief residence of the earls of Lennox, Balloch, Kilmaronock.
79   In the preparation of this chapter I have asked for and received help and advice from many quarters. I would like to express special thanks to Thomas Owen Clancy, Steven Driscoll, Katherine Forsyth, James Fraser, Gilbert Márkus, Catherine Swift, Jeanette Whitecross and Alex Woolf. All mistakes are my own.

APPENDIX: MIRACLES OF PATRICK'S CHILDHOOD

MIRACLE 1 [not counting the miracles recounted above at his birth and baptism]: One winter his foster-mother's house is so badly flooded that the vessels and gear of the house are afloat, and the fire is extinguished. Patrick is crying for food, as babies do, and his foster-mother snaps that she has not even got any fire. On hearing this, Patrick goes to an unflooded part of the house, dips his hand into the water, and five drops flow from his fingers, from which he makes five sparks, whereupon the fire blazes up and the water disappears (*Tripartite Life*, p. 11).

MIRACLE 2: Patrick is playing with his foster-brothers in winter and gathers a lapful of icicles, which he carries home to his foster-mother. His foster-mother scolds him, saying it would have been better if he had brought firewood. Patrick replies saying that she should believe that it is possible for God to make the icicles flame like firewood, whereupon he sets them on fire (*Tripartite Life*, pp. 11–13).

MIRACLE 3: Patrick with his sister Lupait are herding sheep, when the lambs suddenly rush to their mothers, as they do, to drink milk. Patrick and Lupait run quickly to try to separate them, but Lupait falls, hits her head against a stone and is near to death. Patrick makes the sign of a cross over the wound and heals her, but the scar remains (*Tripartite Life*, p. 13).

Miracle 4: Patrick is with the sheep and a wolf carries one off. His foster-mother blames him. Next day the wolf brings the sheep back. His foster-mother is very pleased, and wants Patrick with her all the time (*Tripartite Life*, p. 13).

Miracle 5: His foster-mother goes to milk a cow and Patrick goes along with her to drink some new milk. The cow, possessed by a demon, goes mad and kills five other cows. His foster-mother tells Patrick to bring the cows back to life, which he does, curing the mad one (*Tripartite Life*, p. 13).

Miracle 6: The Britons hold a great meeting. His foster-father dies there, and his foster-mother pleads with Patrick, who runs up to him, puts his arms round his neck and says 'Arise and let us go home', which he does (*Tripartite Life*, p. 15).

Miracle 7: Children of the place where Patrick is reared would bring honey to their mothers. His foster-mother complains that Patrick brings her none. Patrick then takes a vessel to the water, fills it, and blesses the water. It turns into honey, which then heals every disease and ailment to which it is applied, 'that is, they held it as a relic (*cretraib*)' (*Tripartite Life*, p. 15).

Miracle 8: Once the reeve of the king of the Britons comes to announce to Patrick and his foster-mother that they should go to clean the hearth of the palace of Al Clud (*ind rightighi Ailchluaide*). They go; then, an angel comes to Patrick, saying that, if he prays, he will not have to do the work. He prays and the angel cleans the hearth. Patrick then says, 'Though all the firewood amongst the Britons (*im Bretnaib*) be burnt in this hearth, it will leave no ashes the next day', and this is the case (*Tripartite Life*, p. 15).

Miracle 9: At another time the reeve of the king, that is of the Britons (*Bretan*), comes to Patrick's foster-mother to seek tribute (*císsa*) of curd and butter. She has none. Then of the snow Patrick makes curd and butter, and this is taken to the king. When it has been shown to the king it is turned again into its nature of snow. The king remits the tribute to Patrick for ever (*Tripartite Life*, pp. 15–17).

CHAPTER 3

Highland and Lowland, Gael and non-Gael: West Dunbartonshire from the Thirteenth to the Eighteenth Centuries

Edward J. Cowan

As has often been noted, Dunbartonshire was a Highland county with a Lowland fringe and therein lay its fascination. When Loch Lomond was becoming a major tourist attraction in the late eighteenth century, visitors were greatly taken with the contrast between the wild, even savage, scenery around the loch and the improved landscape to the south, symbolising Nature triumphant and Nature tamed. West Dunbartonshire was truly a frontier zone, part of that hugely significant cultural contiguity and political boundary represented by the greater Clyde throughout almost all of Scottish history, from the time of the first Scots of Dalriada (modern Argyll) through to the whimsical adventures of Para Handy. This was a zone where Gael confronted non-Gael, often in a spirit of hostility and a bloody clash of cultures, but also for purposes of trade and exchange, peaceful interaction that gradually drew the folk of the Isles and Highlands into permanent settlement in the burghs of the Clyde.

The earldom of Lennox, whose seat was at Balloch, had ancient roots, still imperfectly understood, far in the Celtic past. The medieval earls were men of independent mind, fiercely jealous of their inherited rights, privileges and obligations, and yet open to the opportunities and advantages presented by new ideas gradually seeping in from the wider world via the Scottish court and the ships that arrived in Clyde waters. By the sixteenth and seventeenth centuries, there was much greater panic and suspicion, though, concerning some of the Lennox clans and about those outside the area such as the seemingly all-powerful Campbells, manipulating menacingly and remotely from beyond Loch Long, and the wild MacGregors whose very existence appeared to be predicated upon predatory activity. As contrasting examples of interaction between the Gaels and their neighbours in West Dunbartonshire, the second section of this chapter will investigate medieval Lennox, while the last section will consider the notorious sixteenth- and seventeenth-century persecution of the MacGregors that had such close implications for the area.

NURTURER AND DESTROYER

Water has always defined West Dunbartonshire, a province hugging the north bank of the Clyde estuary. There, fingers of the Irish Sea reach for the innards of the west mainland to grasp at mountains and glens, creating communities which appeared remote if approached overland, but which fit snugly and conveniently into sea routes. The bonnie banks of the most famous loch in Scotland (and possibly the world) border the district to the north, while the River Leven flows out of much-celebrated Loch Lomond, linking it to the Clyde at Dumbarton, over 5 miles away.

When King Hakon led a mighty fleet from Norway to assert his sovereignty over the Hebrides once and for all, in 1263, he sent some sixty ships across the mile of land that separates Arrochar and Tarbert (a place-name signifying a portage) where, taking once again to the water, they wasted the 'well-tilled' islands of Loch Lomond and burned the countryside around it, a feat celebrated by the Norse bards, the skalds:

> Drew boats over dry land
> For many a length;
> Those warriors undaunted
> They wasted with war-gales
> The islands thick-peopled
> On Lomond's broad loch.

Thus they raided 'almost across Scotland and slew many men'. Stirling Castle was readied in defence, but the true targets of Norwegian wrath were the earldoms of Lennox and Menteith, both loyal to the king of Scots, but both also having aggressive interests in the Inner Hebrides.

Launching his earlier expedition into Argyll in 1222, Alexander II sailed across Loch Lomond, as did Robert Bruce in 1306. One month after returning from the west, Alexander issued a charter founding a royal burgh 'at my new castle of Dumbarton'. He thus not only established a supposed bulwark of 'civilisation', pacification, law and order at the site of the ancient stronghold on Dumbarton Rock, but he also encroached on the territory of his ally the Earl of Lennox. When issuing a charter to Maoldomhnaich, or Maldowen, third earl, in 1238 confirming his possession of all the lands held by his father, the king excepted Dumbarton Castle and all the estates granted to the burgh since its recent creation. The medieval earldom of Lennox extended far beyond the present boundaries of West Dunbartonshire, of course. According to a thirteenth-century poem, it was named for Leamhainn, a Pictish princess, who drowned in the river which forever commemorated her, the Levenax or Leven. Thus water also, in a sense, defined the Lennoxes, just as it provided the crucial routes that united the earldom. Lochs, rivers and portages were taken for granted much as roads are today. A bunch of Hebrideans attacked Inchmurrin in 1439 killing Sir John Colquhoun and some of his followers. In 1506 James IV paid 84 pennies to a man who rowed him from Inchmurrin to Dumbarton following a hunting expedition. The Watergate was always the preferred and obvious option.

Yet the nurturer could all too easily become the destroyer. A local historian perceptively noted that Dumbarton itself, once the capital of the kingdom of Strathclyde, became 'a poor beggarly place, which frequently sent round the hat for aid to prevent its being swept off the face of the earth by the inroads of the waters of Leven and Clyde'. The issue was raised, as it had been before, at the Convention of Royal Burghs in 1582. Action was eventually taken in 1600 to prevent the 'waters of life' becoming the 'waters of death'.[1] In a resolution that sheds much light upon the economy of the burgh at the time, the convention recommended that the king be petitioned to permit Dumbarton to levy a toll for the space of seven years, 'to be imployit for the preservation of the said burgh fra innundations and destruction be the riveris about the samyn', on each cow and horse passing through the town. Also all merchants attending the burgh's fairs at Lammas (1 August) and St Patrick's Day (17 March) were to pay 30 pennies, stall-holders such as clothmen and smiths 12 pennies, hawkers 6 pennies, and timber ships or vessels supplying the markets 40 pennies.

Various other money-making schemes were tried, the most determined by James VI who decreed a substantial nationwide tax along with a hefty donation from the royal revenues. Measures were taken to ensure that the money was properly spent, but accounting remained an acute problem. James granted the 'drowned lands' to the burgh when new channels were cast to allow water runoff; later they became a place of recreation, as mentioned later in this book by Paul Maloney. Nonetheless, despite the building of embankments, flooding was frequent and erosion a perennial concern. Tobias Smollett was typical of many Dumbartonians in repeating the folklore that, over time, floodwaters had engulfed the greater part of the burgh.

Another concern was pollution; in 1608 Dumbarton, Glasgow and Renfrew were condemned for defiling the Clyde with carrion, corpses and other filth hurtful to the fishing. Catches of salmon and herring were valuable exports, but an enquiry of 1700 reported that Dumbarton had no harbour, no foreign trade and owned no ships save for a small bark; burgh resources were steadily diminishing while burgesses lived in the poorest of properties. There was an attempt to designate Dumbarton as the Scottish port for the importation of Irish wool, but 'the object aimed at was not hit'. Dumbarton simply could not compete with the other Clyde ports with which it was often in dispute; by the time Smollett picked up his perceptive pen its glory days lay ahead, while memories of its important role in Scottish history were rapidly fading.

THE MEDIEVAL EARLDOM OF LENNOX

There has recently been considerable debate among Scottish medievalists as to the relationship between native and newcomer during what used to be known as the Feudal Era following William the Conqueror's victory at Hastings and his domination of England. It has long been held that there was a 'peaceful Norman Conquest of Scotland', notably, but by no means exclusively, during the reign of David I. This theory suggests that David, together with his successors, Malcolm, William and Alexanders II and III, encouraged settlers of the new order to locate in Scotland, while simultaneously adapting much of value in government, administration and justice flowing from a new stream of Europeanisation. Contemporaneously, the great changes in the medieval church initiated by the Gregorian reforms were also under way. New rigorous ecclesiastical organisation required the tidy formation of bishoprics and of parishes, important adjuncts in the development of regal authority. Monarchs also recognised the potential economic and pacificatory advantages of the new monastic orders housed in their impressive abbeys, which might provide useful and welcome shelter for Scottish kings who remained peripatetic until the late thirteenth century.

Some of us have always thought that there was something wrong with this model. What, for example, happened to the people who were displaced by the incomers? Common sense would suggest that native landowners and rulers would take a dim view of foreign incursions however peaceful they supposedly were in intention. Also why were Anglo-Normans, or whatever we choose to call them, seen as so benign in Scotland when elsewhere in Europe the Normans were regarded as little better than thugs encased in steel? Why were Scottish historians at one time reluctant to take cognisance of rebellions directed against kings of Scots in Galloway, Argyll, Moray, Ross, Caithness and Orkney, many of the rebels forming alliances? The present writer has contributed to this debate, but he remains mystified as to why so many current historians apparently wish to stress assimilation at the expense of well-documented hostility, while at the same time minimising culture conflict and antagonisms. Why is it that so many wish to applaud those natives who gradually adjusted to foreign ways with reference to such basic human activities as language, religion, land-holding, government and law – to name but a few – not to mention ancient rights, obligations and assumptions that they must have been forced to surrender? The earldom of Lennox provides a fascinating case-study thanks not least to an excellent new investigation by Cynthia J. Neville devoted to native lordship in medieval Scotland with particular reference to Lennox. The author neatly states the problem(s) as follows:

> A culture that celebrated customs, practices, values, social ties, and political relationships that were alien to the indigenous hierarchy could hardly have caused anything other than tension.[2]

The earliest recorded ruler of the Lennox was the mormaer, which seems to mean something like 'great steward', a local war-leader or *dux* responsible for organising tribal or territorial armies, but possibly also having a king-like rank: MacBeth, for example, was historically *dux*, mormaer and king. During the twelfth century, these men gradually acquired the Latin title of *comes* or earl, suggesting that they were territorial rulers subordinate to a superior king. Such figures were regarded as rulers in their own regions, but may not have been so recognised by central authority. For example, Fergus Lord of Galloway was noted in one source as *rex* or king, and *mormaer* was translated as *rí* or king in Irish sources, just as later in Gaelic the *Dominus Insularum*, the Lord of the Isles, was known as *Rí Innse Gall*, 'King of the Islands of the Foreigners'. The first reference to the Lord of Lennox occurs in the 1170s when Earl David of Huntingdon, younger brother of William the Lion, was said to have received 'the gift of Lennox for life'. Quite why is obscure, but there was a precedent for royals adopting territorial titles as when David I was Prince of Cumbria. William may have been simply asserting his authority over an earldom that was dangerously close to the Lowlands. At any rate soon thereafter Ailin, Earl of Lennox is found in charters; in one he is designated as 'son and heir of Ailin, Earl of Lennox', which suggests that so far as his descendants and dependants were concerned he was *de facto* earl, whether in name or not.

The most powerful earl to emerge was probably Maoldomhnaich (c. 1217–c. 1250), but he, like his father Ailin II, appears to have kept to himself concentrating on his own extensive family, or clan, of ten brothers and a sister. His brothers had names like Dughall, Amhlaibh, Gille Criosd, Muireadhach and Corc; his son was Mael Coluim or Malcolm, his steward Mael Coluim Beg (Wee Malky!) and, as Neville indicates, he was surrounded by folk of similar Gaelic nomenclature. He granted lands to his kinsmen, but permitted the settlement of few newcomers, those being confined to the southern part of the earldom. Remarkably, eighteen of twenty-five Lennox charters surviving from the first half of the thirteenth century were granted to native men. Ironically for a culture that depended so heavily upon oral tradition, the Lennox *acta* are preserved in one of the very few surviving Scottish lay cartularies, or collections of charters.

As elsewhere in Scotland, Lennox retained the office of *toiseachdeor* usually equated with a thanage, an office closely associated with the collection of revenues and dues and thus an important enforcer of comital (earldom-wide) authority. Another crucial office was that of the steward, general manager of estates and household. Equally important was the *judex* or judge, Gaelic *breitheamh*, Englished as brieve, who was responsible for law, justice, custom, demarcation disputes, property, court business and frequently for witnessing charters. Almost all such judges in Lennox had Gaelic names, including one Gillecolman son of Domnall MacBref. Law courts much resembled provincial assemblies until the end of the thirteenth century; they must have involved an element of public attendance and observation as they did in the Scandinavian world. In all of these offices, and in others less well documented, the Lennox preference was clearly to fill them with native men who were quite often of the earl's own kindred. Fosterage, a custom that came to be closely identified with Gaelic-speaking Scotland, was practised in the medieval earldom. Usually a person would be fostered by a social superior, often forming ties that were as strong as those of blood, and acting as an important source of cohesion within the clan, or indeed outside of it, for non-clan children were sometimes involved.

Fisheries were extremely important to the economy of the Lennox, but it has been suggested that the earls were much more generous than their counterparts in England in their notions of who could fish, as they were about those who could hunt, namely their tenants. Fisheries were thus an important source of revenue and of patronage and there are some indications that earlier grants of such piscatorial facilities to the church were later regretted. The unit of land-measurement was the *arachor*, a Gaelic word that described the unit-area of land as well as its capacity; it equated with the carucate (104 acres), but generally both were measured in fractions. Many holdings must have been quite small and capacity was indicated by phrases such as 'pasturage for six cows and two horses'. The evidence suggests that the earls of Lennox were overwhelmingly protective of their earldoms, and even quite hostile to incomers, until the last quarter of the thirteenth century when they began to relax their attitudes somewhat. Already in the time of Maoldomhnaich families such as the Grahams, Galbraiths and Colquhouns were moving into the area, many of them to make a notable mark and remain. Such transition, however, is obscured by the events that transformed much of Scotland forever, and which cumulatively are known as the Wars of Independence. Some scholars despise the label, but so far no one has come up with a better one.

Almost all of those authorities who have written about the history of Dunbartonshire have dwelled upon the curious series of court cases that involved very serious and prolonged disputes with the Church. These cases came about due to disdain for, and resentment of, previous ecclesiastical endowments, conferred by the Lennox earls in a spirit of conventional piety. Donations were made to Kelso, Glasgow and Arbroath, but, above all, to Paisley Abbey. It has frequently been noted that the Lennox earls, unlike their counterparts elsewhere, founded no monasteries in their own territories. This omission can perhaps be attributed to a certain passivity so far as the new reforms were concerned coupled with a preference for the old shrines and holy places within their territories. Kilpatrick, a parish in the possession of Paisley and the traditional birth place of Ireland's patron saint, was at the centre of a case in 1233 when the rector, Dughall brother of Earl Maoldomhnnaich, was accused of forging charters. By these, he and other lay-tenants were granted church lands, among them Gille Brigte (Gilbert) son of Samuel, who had obtained the lands of Monachkenneran. The abbot of Paisley objected, producing a number of witnesses who could testify from memory to Dughall's fraud. One stated that as a child, sixty years earlier, he remembered that he and his father, although strangers, had received hospitality from an old man at Monachkenneran by the name of Bede Ferdan who lived in a wooden house and whose function was to supply food and lodging for 'persons passing by', presumably on their way to Patrick's shrine. Another recalled Bede strenuously resisting the claims of Earl David of Huntingdon over church lands back in the 1170s. A third testified that Bede was 'killed in defence of the rights and liberties of the church'. Faced with such evidence Dughall admitted his crime, but explained that it was caused 'because he did not wish to offend his father or his brother or his relations'; in other words the clan put him up to it.

That was not the end of the matter, for in 1271 Dughall's three grand-nieces, as his co-heirs, revived the claim, in the court of Earl Malcolm of Lennox, only to renounce it. That the earl may, in some way, have encouraged the action is indicated by yet another case, during the tenure of his son, also Earl Malcolm. To his court, in 1294, were summoned the abbot and convent of Paisley to answer for some of their Kilpatrick lands at the instance of Robert Reddehow and Joanna his wife. The abbot appealed to the bishop of Glasgow seeking protection and informing him that they did not wish to plead before that particular court nor were they obliged to do so. In turn, the bishop ordered Malcolm to desist from oversight of such cases and threatened Reddehow and his wife with excommunication if they did not drop the case. None paid him any attention. The vicars of various local parishes were then sent to Malcolm's court to repeat the bishop's injunctions, rejection of which would result in immediate excommunication, while twenty-seven other local worthies were warned to offer the offenders no assistance or counsel of any kind. What can be discerned in these cases is a kind of final trial of strength between church and earldom in which there could only be one obvious winner. This, nonetheless, indicates the unwillingness of the Lennox earls to submit meekly to ecclesiastical encroachment. They clearly wished to maintain local control in the face of the Church Militant and in so doing they held out longer than most and they waged a valiant fight.

Court cases apart, the history of the medieval earldom appears to be characterised by a placidity that is probably illusory. The absence of monasteries, where chronicles might have been consequently written, precludes the survival of narratives out of which a credible history of the region can be constructed. Such quietude, if such it was, ended rudely in 1333 with the death of Earl Malcolm. His son, Donald, who died in 1364, was the last of the Lennox male line, but his daughter Margaret had married Walter of Faselane and their son Duncan became eighth Earl of Lennox. Though succeeding in right of his mother, he may be thought the most successful of all the Lennoxes for he arranged a marriage contract between his daughter Isabella and Sir Murdoch Stewart, eldest son of Robert Stewart Earl of Fife, the younger brother of Robert III. The blood-royal, however, proved sadly tainted, for Robert Stewart was later Duke of Albany and Governor of Scotland during the captivity of his nephew, James I, in England. The king developed an all-consuming hatred for the kinsmen who left him to rot in confinement, particularly for Duke Robert who died in 1420. Murdoch eventually negotiated James's release in 1424 and his father-in-law Duncan of Lennox was the first to greet the king on his return. At first, all went well, but James soon demanded vengeance. Albany, his son and the eighty-year-old Duncan of Lennox were tried and executed at Stirling. Duncan left three daughters and while the title of earl and then duke survived to be borne by a number of notables – among them, James VI – the line was essentially defunct. By the early fifteenth century, the peaceful lands of Lennox were no more. Those who spoke Scots increasingly distrusted Gaelic as a language they could no longer understand, and regarded its speakers as wild caterans – members of wild Highland bands – addicted to rape, and pillage and depredation.

WEST DUNBARTONSHIRE IN SCOTTISH HISTORY

At the centre of the cross-cultural and occasionally murderous interaction of Gael and non-Gael was the essential presence of Dumbarton Castle. It was the key to the West Mainland, the Hebrides and Ireland, 'situated on the eminence of a very rugged rock, deemed by all impregnable', as well as the gateway to the Continent. As a royal stronghold, in addition to the awesome authority conferred by the nature of the site, it symbolised the presence of the monarch himself and the dispensation of justice through the sheriff – governance, law, order and obligation. The burgh created in 1222 was designed to service the castle, but so forbidding were the surroundings considered at the time that the 'kirset' – a grace and favour period free from imposts and taxation designed to encourage burgesses to settle, a kind of thirteenth-century inward induce-ment grant – was extended from one year to five. Dumbarton was marginally less barbarous than Dingwall in Easter Ross, whose kirset was ten years. In both cases, the hope was that the burgh would have a 'civilising' impact upon the surrounding countryside. When, in 1230, Earl Maoldomhnaich granted valuable fisheries on the Leven to the monks of Paisley, 'as far as the tide flowed up the river', he promised to afford them protection because it was realised that 'in going along its banks they would be led into solitary places'. If locations in the Vale could be so described, Garelochside or Arrochar, at the time, must have literally seemed like the back of beyond.

At the outbreak of the Wars of Independence, Dumbarton Castle was held for Edward I of England. There the captive William Wallace was taken in 1305, supposedly 'betrayed' by Sir John Menteith, governor of the castle and sheriff of Dumbarton. A convincing argument can be made that Menteith was simply doing his duty in performing a function of which the larger majority of the Scottish nobility would have approved, namely the removal of the upstart Wallace. It is not known for certain that Wallace was indeed actually transported from Robroyston on the outskirts of Glasgow to Dumbarton Castle where a sinister stone carving of a face is still pointed out as that of 'fause Menteith'. There is also controversy concerning the authenticity of Wallace's sword, which was kept at the castle until it was removed to the Wallace Monument at Stirling in 1888. It is on record that James IV in 1505 paid for repairs to the sword as well as binding it in silken cords. Modern opinion holds that it is not impossible that some fragments of the original still repose in the much reworked artifact. However that may be, Judas-like treachery is essential to the epiphany of all impeccable heroes and Menteith will never escape his frequently attributed, if despicable, role.

There is a story, long discredited, that Robert Bruce also almost fell into his perfidious clutches when negotiating the surrender of the castle, in return for which Menteith demanded nothing less than the earldom of Lennox. The holder of this, Earl Malcolm, was a strong and committed supporter of King Robert. In fact, if the chronicler, John of Fordun, is to be believed, the relationship between Malcolm and Bruce was that of inseparable companions in all their troubles, the earl never departing from the fealty and love he owed his king. Malcolm had been loyal to the patriots since 1296 and, though forced to submit to Edward in 1304, when he also petitioned for the return of his earldom, he was present at Bruce's inauguration in 1306. As suitable reward, Bruce, in due course, restored him to his proper inheritance and granted him the sheriffdom of Dumbarton. The king also contrived to have the church at Luss dedicated as a sanctuary, offering solace and shelter to those who had fallen foul of law and of life.

What is truly remarkable, however, is that towards the end of his life King Robert took pains to purchase some 200 acres from Malcolm of Lennox, and to exchange his lands of Montrose with the Graham family for their estate at Cardross in order that he could retire to the Gáidhealtachd. There Bruce built an unfortified manor house, probably on the site of Mains of Cardross, containing a hall, kitchen, larder, chamber for the queen and a chapel, all with thatched roofs. The king's chamber had walls of painted plaster and glazed windows. There was also a garden, a hunting park, a shelter for falcons and a fish-trap on the Leven. Some royal vessels were kept on the river including a 'great ship', which on one occasion was lifted out of the water into a burn on the royal estate. Somewhere on the premises a live lion was on display. Did Bruce by chance recall that those besieged in Stirling Castle, in 1304, had proclaimed that they held it on behalf of the Lyon, the first known abstraction of kingship or sovereignty in Scottish history? All of this intriguing detail concerning Bruce's mansion is drawn from the surviving exchequer accounts.[3] It was at Cardross that Robert Bruce died on 7 June 1329, surely the greatest person (with the possible exception of Wallace) ever to set foot in West Dunbartonshire.

During the second phase of the Wars of Independence, Malcolm Earl of Lennox was killed at the battle of Halidon Hill in 1333. Bruce's heir, David II, was sheltered at Dumbarton Castle before being sent off into protective exile at Château Gaillard in France, where he received regular shipments of Scottish salmon before his return in 1341. The garrisons of Dumbarton Castle were maintained, in part, by a commodity known as 'the watchmeal of Kilpatrick', five and a half chalders of oatmeal, paid by land-holders in the parish of Kilpatrick. As late as 1706, there was dispute over whether the meal could be compounded for a monetary payment. The vassals, who sought the latter, claimed that the meal payment was a fraud, 'nothing but dogmeal, for the maintenance of dogs that were kept in the Castle of Dumbarton for securing the country from wolves and other ravenous beasts which infested that part of the country'. To judge from the evidence, the most ravenous beast of all was the Duke of Montrose, who was, by that time, solely in charge of the Lennox, and his view prevailed.[4] His predecessor, Charles Duke of Lennox, had attempted in the 1660s to milk cattle of excessive revenues, ordering drovers from Argyll to drive their beasts by way of Dumbarton Castle where they would pay a toll of 48 pennies on each beast. Needless to say, the drovers had different ideas and they, with some powerful backing, gained full liberty to herd their cattle on the king's highways without diverting to pay Dumbarton dues. Aristocratic greed apparently had few limits.

As long as Scotland remained an independent kingdom, at least until 1603, almost all monarchs had some connection with Dumbarton Castle, though royal visitations are often as tedious to relate as they are historically uninteresting. James IV patronised a harpist and a piper while in residence. James V fitted out ships for an expedition to the Hebrides. Mary Queen of Scots, having used it as a refuge for a time, left there for France aged six in 1548. The castle figured prominently in the civil war that followed Mary's flight into exile after her deposition, a remarkable revolutionary act whose legitimacy was stoutly defended by that notable Lennox man, scholar, humanist and relentless polemicist, the incomparable George Buchanan. There were constant fears of French invasion in support of Mary, for whom the castle was held, as when Monsieur Virache 'famous ambassador and notable pirate' arrived in 1570:

> with him he brocht some oranges, some raisins, some biscuit bread, some powder, some bullet, and so, of omnigadderum, he brocht a malediction to furnish Dumbarton.

Shortly thereafter, Captain Thomas Crawford of Jordanhill captured the castle. His party ascended the rock in a fog using ropes and ladders. Famously, when one man climbing a ladder was gripped by a seizure, subsequently passing out, he was bound tightly to it before it was spun around, so allowing his fellows to climb past him. Resistance was feeble, huge stocks of weapons being seized by the victors. Crawford later presented revenues from his mill at Partick to maintain a student at Glasgow University who was to be examined by the principal and regents as to his worthiness and qualifications to study philosophy. Meanwhile, Scottish governments

Figure 5 Matthew, Earl of Lennox, grandfather of James VI.

studied the possibility of further French invasions via the Clyde and there were fears the Spanish Armada of 1588, as well as rumoured subsequent expeditions, might land at Dumbarton.

Due to the support of the Lennoxes for the Protestant cause, the Reformation took hold fairly swiftly in West Dunbarton following the parliamentary legislation of 1560, but the precise nature of the reform was to remain in doubt until 1690. The ideas of John Knox and his contemporaries were soon overtaken by the radical presbyterian notions of Andrew Melville. His views of parity, or equality, in the Kirk had dire ramifications in the secular sphere as well, leading James VI to develop his claims of divine right kingship, namely that kings were appointed by God and to resist them was blasphemy as well as treason. James gradually evolved a scheme of bishops in presbytery, while his son, Charles I, sought nothing less than the anglicisation of the Scottish Church. There must have been many folk in Scotland who knew not what or whom to believe, and some poor souls, including a few in West Dunbartonshire, fell prey to witch belief, a vicious cancer that affected the rulers as well as the ruled, but which was generally fatal to women in particular. The seventeenth century, however, was also one of climatic deterioration, famine and plague, all calamities that could make folk doubt their faith. Bitter warfare was added to the tally when Charles's blunderings became far too extreme and the very existence of the Kirk seemed threatened. Revolution broke out in 1638 with the signing of the National Covenant in Edinburgh, as Scots sought to defend their religion, but also to overhaul the constitution in opposition to Stewart absolutism. In 1639, the Covenanters took Dumbarton Castle, but during the next few years West Dunbartonshire was spared the worst of the savage and sectarian atrocities committed in the name of religion.

Following the Restoration of Charles II in 1660, significant numbers of Dumbarton ministers were outed for failing to conform to episcopalian demands. They participated in open-air services known as field conventicles and, for so doing, they were prosecuted by government troops. Local Covenanters were tortured, imprisoned (some in Dumbarton Castle), transported to the colonies, and executed, in the name of the state. In 1685, the year of the most intense persecution, Archibald Campbell, ninth Earl of Argyll, led a rebellion designed to drive James VII, a monarch with 'dangerous' Catholic sympathies, off the throne. The affair was horribly botched, but Argyll marched on the Lennox via Gareloch, Glen Fruin and Balloch. His force came to grief at Kilpatrick, while he was arrested at Inchinnan and subsequently executed at Edinburgh. One of those who fought for James was the Earl of Dumbarton, a son of the Marquis of Douglas. Dumbarton's Regiment, as it was known, later became the Royal Scots whose march-past,

Figure 6 Dumbarton Castle, c. 1685.

'Dumbarton's Drums' (also the title of a moving folk song), is named for him. He followed James (whose Latin name Jacobus inspired the word 'Jacobite') into exile where the Dumbarton title expired with his son.

While negotiations leading to the 1707 Treaty of Union were in full swing, James Stewart, Earl of Bute petitioned to be given the governorship of Dumbarton. He argued that his family would maintain and improve the castle and

> would be a check on any in that part of the nation that designed to disturb the government. As any that know the west country, we think it of the greatest importance to have that place in good hands, and the true use of it is lost when it is not in the possession of a person that has a considerable adjacent interest that would employ that and his own to serve her majesty [Queen Anne] on all occasions.

He clearly wished to play up the volatility of people in the area, though, according to him, they had always been thus. Bute recalled that in the time of his grandfather, Charles I had sent two men-of-war to take the castle, so alarming the garrison that they sank boats in the channel to prevent passage of the king's ships. In terms of the treaty of 1707, Dumbarton was listed as one of four Scottish castles that were always to be maintained and kept in repair.

Many men of West Dunbarton became involved in the hunt for the MacGregors during the '15 Rising. After the '45, a number of Jacobites were imprisoned in Dumbarton Castle under the custodianship of deputy governor Captain Robert Turnbull. The most prominent of the captives was William Murray, Marquis of Tullibardine, who had been out in the '15, now an old, exhausted individual who was captured by Archibald Buchanan of Drumnakill. Buchanan was author of a wonderful letter explaining why he did not come out for the government in 1745 in language that, we may think, admirably represents the voice of Dunbartonshire at that time:

> Though I am much at a piece with the piper's dog, who likes aye to be in good company, yet, at the same time, I'm something akin to the rotten ewes, who still lags behind, and cannot follow the flock; was it not for this last cause, I should surely have had the honours of waiting of [the Duke of Argyll] and your lordship [Andrew Fletcher of Saltoun, Lord Milton] at Inveraray; and as I'm now an old tike and cannot keep up with the pack, at least in a long chase, I have, to supply that want, and to keep up the number, sent a young one of my own breed [his son], who can, and who will muster as one of the pack when my bones are thrown over the dyke.[5] [*language modernised*]

Buchanan commented on Tullibardine's poor health, adding that he 'seems to me not only of a very crazy body, but even has made some impression on his intellectuals, so that I think of him more as an object of compassion than I could have dreamed of before I saw him'.

Turnbull thought him a polite, well-tempered person who was deserving of clemency. He then expressed an opinion remarkable for its charity and humanity at a time when elsewhere in Scotland his military colleagues were embarked upon a campaign smacking of near-genocide:

> You know I am no Jacobite; but when the King's enemies are subdued, I, according to my natural temper, compassionates every man in affliction, and then treats them as human nature and common civility dictates.

This truly sounds like the sentiment of the emerging Enlightenment, but he was less benign when two of his prisoners escaped, having repeatedly warned that he had too many to guard and that the large number of visitors made vigilance almost impossible. His instinct was to blame recruitment from

> the scum and dregs of the marching regiments, such as native Irishmen, mutineers, pardoned deserters, thieves, and common drinkers. Such are the fine men for the most part I have had to assist me during the present cursed rebellion, and you know that, as to the

defence of this important place, one ill man can doe more hurt than a hundred of our most inveterate enemies without.

THE PURSUIT OF THE MACGREGORS

An important strand of the history of the latter part of the period under discussion illustrates one of the themes of this chapter: the conflict of Highland and Lowland, Gael and non-Gael. Its wider context is worth examination here as well as its regional detail, as illustrating both an important politico-cultural issue in Scottish history and the ways in which such issues might have particular effects in and around West Dunbartonshire. This 'case-study' focuses on a particularly revealing period during the reign of James VI. It also illustrates the interaction of royal and noble interests in exploiting local historic conflicts for personal gain, whether of 'honour' or power or riches.

King James VI distinguished two sorts of people in Gaelic-speaking Scotland, the one mixed with some show of civility, the other, in the Hebrides, utterly barbarous. The present writer has argued, in fact, that the Highlands and Islands were remarkably peaceful throughout the sixteenth century.[6] With the collapse of the Lordship of the Isles at the end of the fifteenth century, it appeared that the assimilation of the Gáidhealtachd was only a matter of time. Indeed, at the Union of the crowns in 1603, the great feudal lawyer Sir Thomas Craig could confidently anticipate a time in the not-too-distant future when Gaelic would have fallen into desuetude. Several modern Scottish historians have argued that the gulf between Highlander and Lowlander was widening in the course of the sixteenth century, but contemporary commentators did not see things quite that way, rather the opposite. A clutch of brilliant Latinists, all of whom spent a good deal of their time furth of Scotland, studying in France and Spain, detected admirable values and qualities in the 'Auld Scots', as they called them: the Gaels.

Hector Boece, principal of Aberdeen University, in his *Historia* (1526) commended their physical hardiness, their ability to survive on minimal sustenance, and their moderation. They preserved values, which his countrymen had lost. Even their women demonstrated the truth of the observation made by his friend Erasmus that the breast-feeding of children was not only natural, but also beneficial! George Buchanan was actually a Gaelic-speaker from the southern end of Loch Lomond. In various tracts and a *History of Scotland* (1582) he argued that ideas about the ancient Scottish constitution were preserved within the clan system. In this, unsatisfactory chiefs could be deposed by their own followers, thus providing justification for the removal of Mary Queen of Scots by her subjects in 1567. John Leslie, the final version of whose *History* appeared in 1596, was, like Buchanan, fascinated by the fact that the Gaels had preserved their language, manner of living, and even their costume, uncorrupted for a period of over 2,000 years. Indeed, in the works of these historians – and other authorities could be cited – there seems to be a process under way that involves the sentimentalisation of the Gael almost in anticipation of the romanticisation of the inhabitants of the Highlands that took place following the defeat of the last Jacobite rising in 1745–6.

This rosy picture is, however, darkened considerably by the Renaissance fondness for neo-classicism. The historians cited were all great humanists striving to recreate in their beloved Latin, the perfection of the Ancient World. They revived the vocabulary, which the Greeks and the Romans had used to describe the Celts of their day, and applied it to their contemporary Scottish Celts, a term – Celtic – that, incidentally, George Buchanan did much to popularise. Such vocabulary was, inevitably, much concerned with such concepts as barbarism, the primitive, non-literacy, brutality and general backwardness. But if Buchanan and his fellow historians detected, like Tacitus and other Roman commentators, admirable qualities in the past that were emphatically absent in the present, believing that Scotland, like Rome, was corrupted by surfeit and luxury, there were those who drew a different moral. So far as the latter were concerned, the recycled vocabulary was not only applicable to the Celtic population of the British Isles, but was also entirely appropriate to describe the inhabitants of the New World as well as those of more familiar continents about which knowledge was yearly growing. In short, the language that would be invoked to destroy the British Celts was identical to the vocabulary of colonialism and imperialism.

The process was accelerated to some considerable extent when one of the most relentless of British imperialists inherited the throne of Elizabeth in 1603, a man who believed that he actually was the once and future king, none other than the reborn Arthur of the Prophecies of Merlin, destined to be the first to rule over all the peoples of the British Isles. James' main obsession, from his precocious adolescence until it was achieved in middle age, was his succession to the English throne. Therein lay the true origins of his Highland policies.

Elizabeth had made it known that James must act to curb the involvement of Hebridean mercenaries, known as gallowglasses, who were crossing the North Channel to aid Irish resistance against English rule. One of the clans so involved was that of Macdonald of Islay and Kintyre. James was happy to give the appearance of obliging Elizabeth, but both monarchs entertained another possibility, namely the recruitment of Scottish manpower to support the English against the Irish. In this regard, the favoured candidate was mighty Clan Campbell. An English agent opined that the best solution to the Irish situation would be to foster 'blood and feuds' between the Irish rebels and the island clans; 'my lord of Argyll may do it best of any'. The Argyll in question was the splendidly devious, unfathomable and impossible Archibald, seventh earl, known as Gill-easbuig Gruamach ('the Grim'). He was to have a massive, and unsavoury, impact upon West Dunbartonshire. The king shared Gill-easbuig's views on the fomenting of feuds in order to gain Crown objectives, and thus it was that the promise of the sixteenth century, so far as the Gáidhealtachd was concerned, was squandered. It is a sad, but sobering, reality that, when feuds in either the Highlands or Lowlands are investigated, Crown intervention is usually to be distinguished.

One clan that James had in his sights was that of MacGregor. He granted commissions to the Campbells to hunt down members of the clan in 1593, 1596 and 1601. James harboured a near-pathological hatred for the MacGregors, which perhaps defies investigation, but he may have deemed them highly culpable on at least two counts. First, they occupied lands on the Moor of Rannoch, whence they regularly raided into the Lowlands, but they were also conspicuously active in particular around the shores of Loch Lomond. Their depredations thus threatened the commerce of the Clyde. Secondly, they also claimed, like James, descent from Kenneth MacAlpin, the ninth-century king of the Picts and Scots. Their Gaelic motto translated as 'Royal is my Race'. All of this in the king's eyes must have amounted to gross genealogical impertinence, the penalty for which was eradication. Or almost so, for James declared that he would not be satisfied until he was assured that only twelve MacGregors remained alive in his entire kingdom. How this figure was to be confirmed was never divulged.

On 3 March 1601, Argyll became a privy councillor and the recipient of a commission of lieutenancy against 'the wicked and unhappie race of the Clan Gregour, quha sa lang hes continewit in bluid, thift, reif and oppressioun'. He was given sole responsibility for justice within the bounds of MacGregor territories, the king promising that he would in no way interfere, for example by granting pardons to MacGregors, but would remit all matters to Argyll himself. Gill-easbuig had not been noticeably active in carrying out two previous commissions of 1593 and 1596 against the clan, but on this occasion he made an impressive beginning by receiving within the month a bond from the MacGregor chief, Alasdair of Glenstrae, guaranteeing the future good behaviour of his people. Many others, the 'principallis and maist speciallis of the race and name of McGregour', bound themselves 'to be ansuerable for thair raceis and houssis respective for observing guid reull in tyme coming'. The 'children of the mist' had suffered persecution and harassment for close on a century, one Duncan Laudasach earning particular notoriety north and south of the Highland line before his execution in 1552. Many of them already considered themselves to be dependents of the Earl of Argyll and Alasdair of Glenstrae doubtless anticipated a more settled existence under the protection of the earl. In November 1602, the privy council ordered that Argyll should forfeit 20,000 marks surety for the good behaviour of MacGregors after it had received a complaint from Alexander Colquhoun of Luss. Argyll privately begged the king to have some thought to the great expenses and burdens his commission involved.

The waters of Loch Lomond were frequently ruffled by a series of chaotic feuds between the clans around its shores. The Colquhouns of Luss were 'at blood' with the MacFarlanes of Arrochar, the Buchanans of that ilk and the Galbraiths of Culcreuch as well as the MacGregors. Detailed inventories were compiled of Colquhoun losses at the hands of MacFarlanes and MacGregors between 1590 and 1594. Cattle, horses, oxen, sheep and goats to the total value of £155,501 0s 8d were lifted during the five-year period. All clans from the Lennox to Caithness indulged in such raids. They were an essential part of the Highland economy and they usually took place in the winter months. The settled clans in more sheltered countryside had less need to indulge in such activity, but it was very much part of the ethos of Gaelic society and the Campbells were as experienced in the practice as any. Clan Gregor was an extreme case, for their unsettled existence left them with no alternative short of starvation.

Sir Humphrey Colquhoun of Luss made a band with the Earl of Huntly, a well-known opponent of the Campbells, shortly before the MacGregors killed Luss at Bannachra Castle, and raped his daughter, in 1592. During the 1590s his successor, Alexander, achieved an uneasy truce with all of his neighbours except the MacGregors, who made a spectacular raid on Glenfinlas in December 1602. They plundered a total of forty-five houses, carrying off 300 cattle, 400 sheep, 400 goats and 100 horses. Two Colquhouns were killed. Argyll lacked the means, or perhaps the inclination, to prevent such raids on the lands of one who was associated with his enemy, Huntly.

Colquhoun's friends in Dumbarton, whose worthy burgesses were always guarding against the possibility of a MacGregor attack on the burgh itself, urged him to make an issue of the Glenfinlas episode. They advised him to stage a demonstration before the king at Stirling 'with als mony bludie sarks as ather ar deid or hurt of zour men, togither wyth als mony women'. James, predictably revolted by the display of bloody shirts, immediately granted Colquhoun a commission against Clan Gregor. On

7 February 1603, some 400 MacGregors defeated a force of Colquhouns in Glen Fruin, the long wide glen linking Loch Lomond and Gare Loch. Possibly as many as 100 Colquhouns were killed; stored cereals were destroyed and hundreds of head of livestock carried off. Some of the dead were burgesses of Dumbarton. The MacGregors may have been incensed at the heavy-handed governmental response to what they regarded as an 'honest' lifting at Glen Finlas. There is more than a suspicion, on the other hand, that Colquhoun attempted to conceal his own deficiencies as commissioner behind exaggerated losses and imaginative atrocity stories. Tradition and Sir Walter Scott would greatly embroider such tales. It was later said that a number of defenceless Dumbarton schoolboys were butchered by the MacGregors, that the chief of Colquhoun was slain, and that Argyll had deliberately orchestrated the whole affair, using MacGregors to daunt Colquhouns. On the first count there is not a shred of evidence; the second is demonstrably untrue; the third is highly improbable.

Two days before King James departed for England, an act of privy council proscribed the name of MacGregor forever and prescribed penalties for those who sheltered them. As a consequence of that 'horrible and detestable murder committed by the wicked and unhappy Clan Gregour' at Glen Fruin, the king was seized with an obsessive, pathological desire 'altogether to extirpate and root out that infamous race'. The MacGregors had deliberately flaunted Colquhoun's commission. They had also killed several burgesses of Dumbarton and elsewhere, so underlining the precarious nature of life in these outposts of civilisation so essential to the implementation of James's schemes for 'civilising' his kingdom.

Argyll regarded his commissions in a somewhat different light than did James. A commission of justiciary to all intents and purposes made the MacGregors part of Clan Campbell and so extended Argyll's clanship. Furthermore, since they were widely scattered throughout the southern Highlands, Argyll's own authority extended to all areas and jurisdictions within which they lived. The commission of 1593 indicated that a good number of MacGregors actually lived on his own estates as well as on those of the Campbells of Cawdor, Glenlyon, Lawers and Arbeith. They were to be found, however, also on the lands of the lairds of Weem, Tullibardine, Buchanan, Struan and of John Napier of Merchiston, inventor of logarithms, at Gartness near Drymen. What transformed Argyll's attitude to the MacGregors was his visit to London in the company of the king in 1603. By that time he had declared war on the MacDonalds and had made his peace with Huntly. He was now persuaded for the first time that co-operation with King James could only redound to his own advantage; he realised that MacGregor heads would purchase rich rewards.

On 20 September 1603, the king ordered Angus MacDonald of Dunyveg and Hector MacLean of Duart to surrender their fortresses to Argyll 'to whom we have given some special directions concerning the matter of the Isles'. Exactly one month later, Argyll received a commission of fire and sword to harry 'an infamous byke of lawless limmers the MacDonalds, MacLeans, MacLeods and Clanranald being specially denounced', a people 'void of the fear and knowledge of God, delighting in nothing but murder and a savage form of living'. Simultaneously, the earl moved against Clan Gregor.

Between 20 May 1603 and 2 March 1604, thirty-four MacGregors were convicted and executed for their part in the conflict at Glen Fruin. After the raid, the tenants of Campbell of Ardkinglass, at the head of Loch Fyne, had purchased cattle and other commodities from retreating MacGregors. It was therefore suspected that when Alasdair MacGregor of Glenstrae escaped from the custody of Ardkinglass by swimming ashore from a boat conveying him across Loch Lomond, there was more than a possibility of collusion. Early in 1604, Argyll persuaded Alasdair to give himself up and he was taken to Edinburgh. Imperilled Gaels had long had, and would long continue to possess, a touching, if sometimes erroneous, belief that, if they could obtain the ear of the king, all would be well. Argyll gave Alasdair a safe conduct to proceed to London, but he changed his mind when he reached Berwick and he had him returned to Edinburgh. Gill-easbuig Gruamach thus 'keipit ane Hieland-manis promes', for Alasdair was executed along with eleven of his kinsmen. 'Himself being chief he was hangit his awin hicht above the rest of his freindis', but not before he had bitterly condemned the infamy of the chief of Clan Campbell. He accused Argyll of inciting him to murder both Sir Humphrey Colquhoun and Ardkinglass, and of inspiring MacGregor attacks on the Buchanans and the Colquhouns. There is probably much truth in these assertions. What successive commentators have overlooked is that Alasdair did not specifically accuse Argyll of being behind the Glen Fruin escapade. There was further interest in the remainder of Alasdair's revelations for he claimed that Argyll had betrayed the MacGregors in return for a grant of the lands of Kintyre.

> God and men seis it is greidenes of warldlie geir quhilk causis hm to putt at me and my kin, and not the weill of the realme, nor to pacifie the samyn, nor to his Majesteis honour, bot to putt down innosent men, to cause pur bairnes and infanttis bege, and pure wemen to perisch for hunger.

The power politics of the nobles who sought land and authority by whatever means would continue to cause suffering to the poor.

Alasdair MacGregor was executed on 20 January 1604. By that date, therefore, it was already known that Argyll, presumably in conversation with James the previous summer, had set his sights upon Kintyre. Gilleasbuig was purchasing MacDonald lands in Argyll with MacGregor lives in Lennox. Alasdair's dying declaration is corroborated by the contents of an undated memorandum in the privy council register. The grant of Kintyre to Argyll would

> embark him in action against the Clan Donald, being the strongest pillar of all the broken Highland men who never in any age were civil, but have been the schoolmasters and fosterers of all barbarity, savageness and cruelty – have ever from the beginning been addicted not only to rebellion within this continent, land and isles, but always were assisters of north Irish people.

It was anticipated that Argyll would have the greatest difficulty removing 'that mischievous clan, whose actions deserve no less than their utter extirpation and rooting out'. In pursuit of the prize, he was given authority in 1606 to step up the campaign against the 'children of the mist'. The evidence suggests that, wherever possible, they were persuaded to lose their names rather than their lives. They became Stewarts, Grants and Cunninghams, while not a few called themselves Campbell. The MacGregors and the Macdonalds went down together. On 7 August 1607, the lordship of Kintyre was granted to the Earl of Argyll 'and his heirs male heritably to be held blench of the king for payment of a penny yearly'. Many contemporaries must have shared the well-expressed sentiments of the Bishop of the Isles. 'I cannot think it either good or profitable to his Majesty or this realm', he wrote, 'to make the name of Campbell greater in the Isles than they are already; nor yet to root out one pestiferous clan, and plant in another little better.'

For a few years, there was something of a lull in MacGregor persecution. When the Earl of Dunfermline reported to the king that Argyll had arrested two notable malefactors in the Highlands, he forbore to trouble the king with their 'onplesand, onworthie and ungodlie names'. There were many without a name still to be brought to book and it appears that, early in 1611, James reminded Argyll of the terms upon which he had received the grant of Kintyre: on 31 January, the king ordered a renewed assault on Clan Gregor. James, 'in his accustomed disposition to clemency and mercy', graciously allowed that any MacGregor who should 'slay another of the same name of as good a rank as himself' would be granted a free pardon. Rewards for MacGregor heads ranged from 100 marks to £1000, depending upon the rank of the victim. All males between sixteen and sixty in the Lennox and surrounding district were ordered to assemble to carry boats from Loch Lomond to attack these 'wolves and thieves [. . .] within their own den and hole', on their island refuge at Loch Katrine in the Trossachs. In granting a new commission to Argyll in April 1611, James resolved to 'lay mercy aside and by justice and the sword to root out and extirpate all of that race [. . .] that shall be found rebellious and disobedient to us and our authority'. MacGregor wives and children were to be transported furth of the Highlands after the women had been branded on the face.

Persecution continued with little abatement for two years. At court in March, Argyll informed the king that all MacGregors save for twenty-six were now slain, executed, had changed their names, or had found surety for good behaviour. James decided that those who sheltered the outlaws should be fined a total of one-fifth of the value of their property – previously reset-ters had been fined one-tenth. When the number of MacGregor survivors fell to twelve, Argyll was to be excused from maintaining a force to hunt them down. Meanwhile, he was given an opportunity to supplement an income much depleted through frequent sojourns in England by pocketing the lion's share of such fines. His scope was wide-ranging: a committee appointed for the purpose processed a list of over 100 persons from Perth to Dingwall who had been fined for resetting MacGregors. The sums varied from £1000 for Ross of Balnagowan to 20 marks each for a burgess of Inverness and Gill-Anndrais, piper in Dingwall, while Alasdair Grant in Cromdale was fined 10 marks. The total sum was about £10,000. Argyll gen-erously offered James precisely 22½ per cent of the profits. Later in July 1613, the committee listed 169 resetters from the Stewartry of Menteith, while, at the end of the month, a further batch of 120 were located in Inverness-shire. Of the latter, Rory MacKenzie, tutor of Kintail, was fined £4,000, a sum exceeded only by Grant of Freuchie who was fined a staggering £26,000 in September, in which month 200 resetters were listed from Perthshire. The following March, some 240 were noted in Dumbarton and Strathearn. It has been calculated that in 1613–14 some 920 individuals were fined a total of £110,000, although by no means all the fines were paid. The vicious acquisi-tiveness of the Crown-Campbell partnership is without parallel in the annals of Scottish history. It was not to be forgotten or forgiven. Gill-easbuig Gruamach almost single-handedly created the reputation of the Campbells as one of the most hated, if most successful, clans in Scottish history.

Many, however, must have applauded the Crown's naked policy of geno-cide towards Clan Gregor. Colquhoun of Luss, in letters to the king and in a petition to the privy council, estimated that the MacGregors had reduced some 500 of his people to beggary through their 'schamefull and cruell

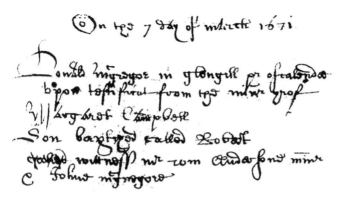

Figure 7 Rob Roy's baptismal entry in the Buchanan parish register.
It reads:
On the 7 day of March 1671
Donald Mcgregor in Glengill pr of Calendar
upon testificat from the minr yrof
Margaret Campbell
Son baptized called Robert
witness mr Wm Andersone minr
& Johne Mcgregor

murthouris, slauchteris, thiftis, reiffis and oppressionis'. He, like Black
Duncan Campbell of Glenorchy, would have strongly recommended trans-
plantation and 'the extermination of this damnable race of people'. Despite
the sickening calendar of comprehensive persecution and merciless pursuit,
the MacGregors survived, in large part because of the kin-based system of
society, but also because the measures used against them were greeted with
repugnance throughout Scotland. Equally repugnant were the instruments
of Crown policy. The rich rewards in fines and forfeitures paid doleful div-
idends in future years, when it was shown that the Campbells had few
friends in the many areas that had offered shelter to the children of the mist.
And, despite all the persecution, somehow they survived in and near West
Dunbartonshire.

In support of the 1715 Jacobite Rising, for example, the MacGregor clan
seized all of the boats on Loch Lomond and occupied the island of
Inchmurrin. From there, they launched an attack upon the Vale of Leven,
literally setting off alarm bells and inviting warning shots from the cannon
of Dumbarton Castle. This persuaded them to retreat, boats and all, to
Inversnaid. Meanwhile, 120 Paisley Volunteers were towed up the Leven in
longboats belonging to naval vessels moored in the Clyde, as others from
Dumbarton, Kilpatrick, Rosneath and Rhu marched to Luss. On arrival,
they sailed round the loch-shores, making a great din, in search of elusive

MacGregors. Having chanced upon some ropes, anchors and oars hidden in loch-shore shrubbery, they eventually found the boats drawn up quite far inland; 'such of them as were not damaged they carried off with them, and such as were, they sunk or hewed in pieces'.[7] The waterborne participants in this episode were, like their forebears, engaged in the long-term politico-cultural conflicts from the thirteenth to the eighteenth centuries between Lowland and Highland, Gael and non-Gael, in West Dunbartonshire.

The traveller Robert Heron noted that, in 1755, during the Lisbon earth-quake, the waters of Loch Lomond were extremely agitated. 'A boat, it is said, was thrown upon dry land, forty yards from its station in the lake'. These tremors were surely symptomatic of the colossal forces and changes that West Dunbartonshire was about to experience in the shape of agri-cultural improvement, the Industrial Revolution, the democratisation of politics, mass tourism and a maritime renaissance. The old, sometimes savage, conflict was to give way to a different kind of upheaval.

NOTES

1   MacLeod, Donald (1896), *Ancient Records of Dumbarton* (Dumbarton), p. 35.

2   Neville, Cynthia J. (2005), *Native Lordship in Medieval Scotland: The Earldoms of Strathearn and Lennox, c. 1140–1365* (Dublin: Four Courts Press), p. 7. Much of my discussion is drawn from this important study.

3   Barrow, G. W. S. (1988), *Robert Bruce & The Community of the Realm of Scotland* (Edinburgh: Edinburgh University Press, 3rd rev. edn), pp. 319–21.

4   Fraser, William (1874) *The Lennox*, 2 vols (Edinburgh), pp. 82, 126–7.

5   Fraser, *The Lennox*, pp. 131–2 note.

6   Cowan, Edward J. (1997–8), 'The Discovery of the Gaidhealtachd in Sixteenth Century Scotland', *Transactions of the Gaelic Society of Inverness*, lx, pp. 259–84.

7   Rae, Peter (1718), *The History of the Late Rebellion; Rais'd against His Majesty King George, By the Friends of the Popish Pretender etc*, Dumfries: printed by Robert Rae, pp. 286–7.

CHAPTER 4

Urbanisation and Industrialisation: West Dunbartonshire since 1750

Richard J. Finlay

The history of the area of West Dunbartonshire encapsulates most of the significant themes of Scottish history in the period after 1750, and indeed can be said to epitomise the key theme of urbanisation and industrialisation in the nineteenth century. Even before 1750, the area was well on its way to becoming a predominantly urban and industrial society. The growth of the textile and dyeing industries in the Vale of Leven soaked up the cheap labour made available by agricultural modernisation and a growing population. As the towns of Dumbarton and, later, Clydebank grew, so did the industry necessary to provide work for more and more people. In time, shipbuilding and engineering complemented textiles as the key drivers of the region's economy. As happened elsewhere in Scotland, urbanisation and industrialisation left a raft of social problems in its wake. Poor sanitation and housing, low wages and poverty, and bad health and pollution took their toll on the lives of ordinary working people. Not surprisingly, class-consciousness emerged as workers banded together in order to improve their lot in life. In the nineteenth century, the area was known for its political radicalism and the growth of trade unionism. Yet, the people of the region bore the burden of life's hardships with great dignity, and in the days before the Welfare State formed strong bonds of community and self-help. They had no other option.

Even at the height of the Scottish industrial economy in the latter part of the nineteenth century, when the Clyde was the world's leading producer of ships and Scottish engineering was a byword for excellence, Scottish workers in the area noticed few real improvements in their standard of living. Worse was to come. The men of the Vale, Dumbarton and Clydebank volunteered in their thousands to defend King and Country in August 1914. Many did not return and, for those who did, the area was gripped with unemployment and mounting social discontent. The goods from the industries that once propelled the global economy were no longer in demand and the region faced economic collapse. Fuelled by a sense of injustice, many turned to communism and the Vale of Leven witnessed the establishment of local Soviets: 'Little Moscows' as one historian called them.[1] Not surprisingly, the Labour Party emerged as the political champion of the region as long-term mass unemployment took its toll. Housing remained overcrowded, health suffered and things only began to improve as a result of rearmament in the late 1930s. At the end of the Second World War, government had come to the conclusion that the region's reliance on the old traditional industries had been the root cause of the area's problems in the past. Together with economic regeneration, there would be social regeneration as central government and local authorities built new houses on new estates. New hospitals and schools would be built to improve the quality of life. Yet, as happened elsewhere, post-war planning produced a mixed legacy. Economic regeneration often took the form of branch plant manufacture, while the older industries rumbled on until their collapse in the 1980s. The new housing often did not live up to peoples' expectations and new estates soon became old ones associated with social problems and bad tenants. The recession of the early 1980s plunged the area back to the bad old days of mass unemployment and poverty. Since then, the area has made a slow recovery and attracted new business and new industries. Also, new social problems such as drug addiction have complemented the older ones of poverty and unemployment. Like the rest of Scotland, West Dunbartonshire has experienced great changes in its history.

THE MAKING OF AN INDUSTRIAL ECONOMY: 1750–1914

Geography played an important part in the development of the region's economy. In the eighteenth century, the hub of the world's economy moved away from the Mediterranean to the Atlantic as trade to the New World expanded.[2] The rise of Glasgow and the tobacco trade is well known, but the area of West Dunbartonshire developed also as a result of transatlantic trade.[3] With easy access to the Clyde (as in an earlier period discussed by Ted Cowan, water was still the most effective means of transport in the eighteenth century), the area's farmers were able to take advantage of Glasgow's growing population as a market for foodstuffs. The area's main landowners, the Duke of Argyll, Lord Stonefield, the Colquhoun family and Lord Elphinstone, were keen to improve profits and promoted greater efficiency in farming, which led to farms increasing in size and maximising output. The growth of the linen industry was also a boon for the area as bleaching and printing works were established in the Vale of Leven whose population grew from about 1,200 in the mid-eighteenth century to over 16,000 by the end of the nineteenth century.

Bleaching and printing were the main industries and the area was able to make use of the River Leven which flows a distance of over 5 miles from Loch Lomond in the north to the River Clyde in the south. Before the advent of the cotton industry, linen was the main textile produced in Scotland. Until the invention of chemical bleaches based on chlorine, bleaching was done in shallow pools of water with the sun and the elements of nature used to whiten linen. On occasion sulphuric acid was also used. This made Scottish linen quite scratchy and, no doubt, this was a factor that explains why slaves in the plantations in the West Indies were the only people who could be obliged to wear the stuff.[4] Printing involved the use of primitive dyes to make patterns on the textiles and, like bleaching, this would remain dependent on the technology of the day. Linen stamped for sale in Dumbarton increased its value tenfold in the period from 1738 to 1758.[5] This boom petered out, however, as the counties of Lanark and Renfrew gobbled up the lion's share of the trade as the depth of the Clyde was deepened further upstream. In any case, linen would be replaced by cotton towards the end of the eighteenth century.

Bleaching and dyeing would remain the staple of the Vale of Leven economy into the first half of the nineteenth century. The early bleachfields were encouraged by a government subsidy supplied by the Board of Trustees for manufactures, which was formed in 1727. Much of the work carried out was unskilled, primitive and part-time. It was the advent of dyeing and calico printing that brought the Vale of Leven into the industrial era. The first print work was established at Levenfield in 1768, followed by Croftengea in 1790. These small-scale industries paved the way for the larger concerns of the nineteenth century. In 1850, amalgamating Levenfield, Croftengea and the Charlestone Engraving factory formed the Alexandria Works. By the second half of the nineteenth century, four main firms dominated the economic landscape of the Vale of Leven and all were involved with printing, dyeing and bleaching: James Black & Co., John Orr Ewing & Co., Archibald Orr Ewing & Co. and William Stirling & Sons. Each of these firms had expanded or been created by amalgamation or by absorbing smaller firms. By the end of the century, most were amalgamated under the United Turkey Red Co. (see Plate 7) and the erosion of local power was complete when James Black & Co. was taken over by the Calico Printers Association in 1899. All in all, over 6,000 people were employed in the industry.[6]

The work involved in the bleaching and printing industries was hard and debilitating and working conditions changed throughout the nineteenth century. The extensive use of chemicals created widespread pollution, and constant exposure to dangerous substances took its toll on health. Initially, the work was very repetitive and child labour was used extensively because small hands could untangle blockages and small frames could duck and dive among moving machinery. It was also dangerous: printing blocks had to be fitted by hand and dyestuff mixed and applied on site, while there was always the threat that hands would be caught by cumbersome machinery as they strove to align and move cloth. In time, a number of key changes affected the industry. Greater use of technology effectively de-skilled the workforce to such an extent that it mainly employed women by the later part of the nineteenth century. The old printing blocks were replaced by rolling machines that were powered by large steam pumps. The men took advantage of improved transportation to work on the burgeoning ship-building industry on the Clyde. A further development was the tendency for small local firms to be taken over by larger concerns that moved management away from the area. Eventually, this reduced the paternal aspect of employment, as management became more distant and remote, leading to the growth of the political discontent discussed below. The bleaching and printing industry also attracted newcomers to the area. Journeymen from Manchester moved north to make the most of their technical expertise and Highland migrants who were originally employed in casual and seasonal work in the latter part of the eighteenth century began to settle on a permanent basis. In the period after 1850, increasing numbers of Irish immigrants arrived in flight from the ravages of the famine. They tended to be used for unskilled labour, and many also found work in constructing the area's transport network.

While life was undoubtedly hard and there are plenty of examples of poverty, the Vale did not experience the same degree of social hardship that many places in Scotland experienced during the late eighteenth and early nineteenth centuries. According to the Old Statistical Account, the inhabitants of the Vale were becoming 'extravagant in the articles of dress, tea and spirituous liquors' and beginning to purchase butcher meat.[7] One key factor in its favour was the tendency for the networks of small towns to survive and retain their independent character. It did not become an urban sprawl. Small towns retained an essential number of services such as the local bank, hotel, shops and other small businesses. Also, there was extensive contact with the local farming community, which provided business for dykers, blacksmiths and the like. Indeed, Alexandria established itself as a successful market town. The presence of a local middle class provided community leadership and arguably (through self-interest as much as anything else) prevented the area from degenerating into a major health hazard. Prominent local business leaders provided public monuments and buildings and patronised local societies. In spite of the community leaders' best efforts, however, poor sanitation was a problem and contributed to the outbreak of cholera in 1866. The use of local burns and the Leven as a repository for all kinds of rubbish did little to help the situation. Yet, local authorities did try to stamp out the problem and there was considerable progress made before the First World War. Again, it should be borne in mind that much of urban Scotland experienced worse problems of poor sanitation.

Arguably housing was the biggest social problem facing Scotland in the nineteenth century, with half the population still living in two-roomed units of accommodation on the eve of the First World War. Cramped, damp and insanitary conditions dominated the home life of most Scots in this period. Comparatively, the people of the Vale were a cut above the rest of the population and, although there were squalid areas, it is important to stress that, overall, this area was not as bad as some of the inner-city areas. Most of the real problems were to come later as a result of the inter-war depression in the next century, rather than a nineteenth-century inheritance of poor housing. The strong presence of artisans and the fact that many families had both parents working meant that there was more money available for decent housing. Also, in 1906, the Argyll Motors Company opened and offered good jobs with good rates of pay to some 1,500 workers, although it closed within a decade, becoming a munitions factory. Many of the employers in the bleaching and dyeing works provided houses for their workers, which, in the initial stages, were of reasonable quality. The same could not, however, be said of Clydebank and the working-class areas of Dumbarton where most accommodation was in the form of one- or two-roomed houses in built-up tenement areas. Such houses were cramped and insanitary and were a breeding ground for disease. The population of Dumbarton more than doubled in the period from 1801 to 1861 from 5,000 to over 12,000. Squeezing more people into existing tenements accommodated most of this rise. Until 1871, Clydebank was a collection of fields. After this date it began to urbanise and industrialise at an unprecedented rate and the population grew from 5,000 in 1881 to almost 20,000 by 1901. As happened in Dumbarton, landlords took advantage of growing demand for housing to squeeze as many people as possible into existing buildings.[8]

Transport links and industrial development were intertwined. As was mentioned earlier, many in the Vale took advantage of the growing transport links to work in Dumbarton and Clydebank. Communication across the Leven was by ferry until the Bridge at Bonhill was opened in 1836. Initially, pedestrians had to pay a toll and this was a major source of grievance. In 1848, under the leadership of Chartists, a mob burst across the bridge and tore down the payment box. It was only in 1878 that bridges

Figure 8 The original 1841 suspension bridge over the River Leven, popularly the 'bawbee brig' in reference to the ha'penny toll for passengers. Alexandria is to the left, Bonhill to the right.

across the Leven were taken into public ownership. In 1858, a direct rail link was opened between Balloch and Glasgow and extended to Dumbarton, laying the foundation for the modern rail system of the area. As both Clydebank and Dumbarton were situated on the Clyde, it was perhaps inevitable that the economic tentacles emanating from Glasgow would spread along this route. Glass had been the main economic activity in Dumbarton in the latter part of the eighteenth and early part of the nineteenth centuries. At the time, it was the largest glassworks in Scotland and depended on most of its raw material, kelp, which was burned seaweed, from the Highlands. By the second half of the nineteenth century, it had almost died out, largely because the owners, the Dixon family, died out. Shipbuilding emerged as the key industry in both Clydebank and Dumbarton in the second half of the nineteenth century and both would see their populations grow in response to the success of the industry as workers piled in looking for employment. Dumbarton soon established itself in shipbuilding with the foundation of William Denny and Archibald MacMillan in the early nineteenth century. Denny's constructed the famous clipper *Cutty Sark* in 1869 and were among the first shipbuilders to build iron- and steel-hulled ships.

'Clydebuilt' was a sobriquet for excellence and Clydeside shipbuilders enjoyed an international reputation. The success of the shipbuilding industry was due to a number of key factors, some general and others particular. In general, the River Clyde was a natural harbour for the construction of ships and had easy access to the Atlantic. Further, the massive increase in transatlantic traffic after 1870 was responsible for a surge in the demand for ocean-going vessels. First among the particular factors was that the shipbuilders had a great deal of technical expertise and designers could develop blueprints to very specific specifications. Each ship was a one-off build for a specific customer for a specific purpose. The ability to tailor-make ships in this precise way gave the shipbuilders of the Clyde a major competitive advantage. Secondly, they could utilise a vast reservoir of cheap skilled labour that had the necessary expertise to construct these large-scale complex technical undertakings. It was no easy matter to construct a ship in the age before prefabrication. Every aspect of construction had to be done on site. Scaffolders had to construct a massive framework to hold the hull, riveters and welders to join the steel plates together, carpenters to construct the deck, engineers and plumbers to install the massive engines and an army of foremen to oversee the whole operation. Not only was considerable expertise needed to work to the highly detailed technical specifications, but it was also required for the necessary tinkering that was inevitably needed when plans did not quite work. Needless to say, this was all highly complex, demanding and skilled work. The final particular reason why the Clyde excelled at shipbuilding was that other industrial nations simply could not afford the wages that their skilled workers would have demanded for such work. In 1914, the output of the Clyde was equal to the combined output of the German and American shipbuilding industries.[9]

It would be wrong to claim that all involved in the shipbuilding industry were skilled workers: a huge army of unskilled workers was required to do the shifting and carrying. The specialists formed an elite of skilled workers whose status was jealously guarded and entry to the trade was protected by the apprentice scheme, which more often that not was kept for family members. The dominance of shipbuilding in Clydebank and Dumbarton can be illustrated by an examination of the occupational profile of both towns at the turn of the twentieth century. Each town had a population of around 20,000 people and metalwork (under which shipbuilding was categorised) was the single largest occupation in each town. In Dumbarton, it accounted for almost 4,000 workers, more than half the adult population. In Clydebank, it was just over 4,000, and, given Clydebank's slightly smaller population, this represented an even bigger proportion of the adult male population.

The Singer Sewing Machine Factory at Clydebank was, however, the single biggest employer in West Dunbartonshire in the period just before the First World War, drawing its workers from a wide area around. It was established in 1884 and was the largest sewing machine factory in the world for a time: in 1914, it manufactured some 80 per cent of the world's output. It employed over 12,000 people, of which 3,000 were women. The arrival of Singer at Clydebank was indicative of wider changes that were affecting the world's economy. It was an American multinational company attracted by the prospect of cheap labour and easy access to European markets. Furthermore, it brought new ways of working and production. Taylorism was the application of scientific management and rationalising the labour process. This was a change from much of the paternalistic practices that had existed in other factories where the management was usually local and the business was family run. Not surprisingly, Singers was hostile to trade unions and, in 1911, confrontation between the workforce and the employer came to a head when twelve women struck over changes in their work practice that would have led to a reduction in their wages. Within a short time, other workers joined them and the factory was brought to a complete standstill for three weeks.[10]

Work dominated the life of ordinary people in West Dunbartonshire in this period. Most lived within a reasonable proximity to the place of work, but with the building of an extensive transport infrastructure, people were able to travel further afield. The area was noted for its ethos of independent skilled working-class culture. This was reflected in the fact that the ratio of male to female workers for the region was approximately six to one. Most women were expected to stay at home and look after the children, with unmarried women making up the bulk of the workforce. In both Dumbarton and Clydebank, for example, two-thirds of all women aged over ten years were classed as 'unoccupied' according to the 1901 census. Yet, these figures can be quite unreliable as they fail to take into account part-time work and work of a temporary nature, which was exactly the type of work that most women tended to do. Among those women who worked, textiles and domestic service were the most common occupations. Clydebank was unusual in having a quarter of its workforce involved in manufacturing who were women. It was also a fairly young society with about a third of the population under the age of ten. The middle class formed a small part of the population of Dumbarton and Clydebank, the former having a slightly larger proportion, but it was numbered in the hundreds: most middle-class professionals moved out into the more rural small villages.

The skilled working class believed in independence and the ability to stand on one's own feet. In the era before the Welfare State, as noted in the introduction to this chapter, they had no other option. Some commentators criticised the 'respectable' working class for their degree of conformity, but it should be borne in mind that notions of self-betterment and self-improvement are not the preserves of the middle class. Self-improvement was a strong ethic in the community and social ties were reinforced by the creation of a variety of clubs, societies and organisations. Evidence of this notion of 'independence' can be seen in the establishment of burial societies, in which members would contribute a penny a week to ensure that there was enough money to guarantee that there was a decent burial. This was to ensure that relatives would not be encumbered with the responsibility for funeral costs, and was symptomatic of the belief that even in death there should be no debt. Building and saving societies were vital to ensure that most families had enough money put aside for a rainy day. This was more a necessity rather than a lifestyle choice. Many of the industries in which the majority of the main family bread-winners worked, such as shipbuilding, engineering, building and metalwork, were prone to short-term lay-offs as orders were completed, but new ones were not yet on the books. The tendency for orders to dry up temporarily meant that there was a cyclical nature in the local economy.

Temperance was another feature of the time. As with much of the rest of Scotland, alcohol was regarded as the main cause of social evil in the same kind of way that drugs such as heroin are regarded today. Alcoholism was part and parcel of everyday culture in the early nineteenth century and workers in textiles were notorious for their consumption of whisky. The birth of a child – the first day at work – the last day at work – the start of the week – the end of the week – a birthday – a death and a marriage were all an excuse for a drink and contemporary reports note that it was common to see both women and children lying inebriated on the streets. Easy access to illicit whisky from the Highlands also played its part. Drink took its toll on family life. Child neglect, wife abuse and domestic violence were all associated with the demon drink. Middle-class employers and the Church initially set up temperance associations. Undoubtedly, both had their own reasons as drink was associated with an inefficient and obstreperous workforce and alcohol kept people away from church and led to immoral behaviour. Yet, there was popular endorsement from many, especially women and children who were the most likely to become victims of drunken rage and the irresponsibility associated with addiction. By the latter part of the nineteenth century, working-class communities looked down on those who drank to excess and self-regulation was the order of the day.

The prevalence of teetotal, respectable and earnest values might lead one to conclude that there was no fun to be had in the area of West

Dunbartonshire. Nothing could be further from the truth. In the days before television, there was much more community activity. As Paul Maloney later discusses in some detail, there was a plethora of clubs dedicated to sports, hobbies and education. It was also a period in which the extended family was important. Most family members lived within a close proximity and could rely on one another to help during illness and provide some financial assistance. Looking after children was more often than not a communal activity. Family get-togethers were an important part of social activity and such occasions were the ideal opportunity for telling stories, jokes and playing musical instruments. The ability to do a 'turn' was an indispensable social asset. It was also an oral society in that family and local history was recounted by word of mouth. Gossip was a staple of everyday life.

The Church was an important pillar of the community and was responsible for the administration of poor relief before 1845 and education until 1872. Its presence was more important in the Vale of Leven as the parochial system survived to a greater extent in rural and small town areas than in the urban conurbations of Dumbarton and Clydebank. In the Vale, the traditional parish was Bonhill (the old name for the Vale) with the church at Kilmaronock, but in the eighteenth century there was the growth of dissent. After a dispute about using the church, a Relief church was created out of a field and a shed in 1770. A Burgher Kirk was established in Renton in 1786 that was more populist and evangelical than the established church, which at this time was dominated by moderates. Religious dissent was always a good indicator of popular independence of thought and many drew their inspiration from the Covenanters of the seventeenth century. In the early nineteenth century, a number of chapels-at-ease were established in response to the growing numbers of adherents and to accommodate the growth of small towns. One such church was established in Alexandria in the early 1840s in spite of opposition from the minister of the established church. The congregation at Alexandria reflected many of the social changes that had been taking place in Scotland in the era of urbanisation and industrialisation. The aspiring new middle class, drawn from the world of commerce and business, led its congregation. A constant gripe of this group was the issue of patronage, which was the ability of a landowner to appoint a minister to a church on his land. Chapels-at-ease were usually constructed on land where this right could not be exercised and the middle class were free to appoint a minister of their own choosing without interference from a landowner. The issue of patronage had been dividing the Church of Scotland since the late eighteenth century and things came to a head in 1843 with the Disruption, when half the Church walked out to form the Free Church to demonstrate their opposition to patronage. As with elsewhere in Scotland, the Disruption divided society and this was reflected in the Vale of Leven. On the one hand, the old church at Bonhill remained with the establishment and reflected the more traditional, rural and conservative part of the community; on the other, the church at Alexandria went with the Free Church and represented the newer industrial and middle-class part of society. Again, reflecting the significant social changes that took place in the first half of the nineteenth century, a majority of the congregation in Dumbarton joined with their minister in walking out of the Established Church.

Although the area would have a reputation for industrial militancy and support for socialism in the twentieth century, the region's politics were of a more conservative hue during the nineteenth century. There was extensive Chartist activity in the Vale of Leven in the 1840s, because of the limited franchise. Before the 1832 Reform Act, two constituencies represented the area, the burgh constituency of Dumbarton, which was shared with Glasgow, Renfrew and Rutherglen and was known as the Clyde District of Burghs, and the county constituency of Dunbartonshire. Politics was notoriously corrupt and there were only sixty-six voters in the county: as many as half of those may have been fictitious or 'faggot' votes. After 1832, Dumbarton was grouped with Kilmarnock, Port Glasgow, Renfrew and Rutherglen to create the seat known as Kilmarnock Burghs. The electorate of the constituency of Dunbartonshire remained tiny. After the 1832 Reform Act, which gave the vote to the middle class and larger farmers, and even after the Second Reform Act of 1868, which gave the vote to the skilled working class, the electorate only numbered some 2,500 souls. The smallness of the electorate in part explains why the area had a reputation for radicalism, but returned a Conservative MP from 1841 to 1892. Paternalism was undoubtedly the major factor in securing a Tory victory at the polls. Much of the housing in the area was tied to local employers. Denny's in Dumbarton created Dennystown and many of the dye-workers lived in company houses. The brothers Alexander and Patrick Smollet of Bonhill were the most influential family in the area in the early nineteenth century and were responsible for much of the civic leadership in the area.

From 1869 to 1892, Archibald Orr Ewing held the seat and again was able to exert considerable influence in the locality due to his ownership of several dyeworks. Paternalism did not only affect voting patterns; it was a common feature of that day where employers would play a much larger part in the life of employees than is the case today. Orr Ewing built and owned terraced houses in Jamestown and Bonhill for his workforce and it would be a brave employee who voted against his employer and landlord, particularly before 1872 and the introduction of the secret ballot. He also contributed to the building of the new church and school in Jamestown and erected the

Figure 9 Top: Men leaving John Brown's yard, Clydebank, c. 1905 In the background is Tamson's Toon, one of the first tenements to be built by Thomson's (the founders of the yard that became John Brown's) and among the earliest buildings in Clydebank.
Bottom: Tenement building, Glasgow Road, Clydebank, in the nineteenth century.

Jamestown Institute, where workers could attend evening classes and hold meetings of various societies and clubs. The extension of the franchise, however, worked against the Conservative Party. In 1884, the vote was extended to the rural workforce and the electorate much more than trebled, from just over 2,500 to almost 8,500 (although much of this increase can be explained by the inclusion in the constituency of Clydebank and its growing population). By the eve of the First World War, the electorate had risen to 16,000 voters.

Orr Ewing lost his seat in 1892 to the Liberal Party candidate John Sinclair, the future Lord Pentland. After Orr Ewing's retiral from politics, a Liberal Unionist candidate, Alex Wylie, represented the seat after 1895. This was a result of sharp manoeuvring by the Liberal Unionists, who put up a popular local candidate before the Tories had a chance to nominate a successor to Orr Ewing. In essence, it was a form of forced co-operation between the two parties, but they were politically moving closer together and would eventually unite in 1912 to form the Scottish Unionist Party.[11] Wylie opposed Irish home rule and this may have been a factor in securing Protestant support among the working class. This was especially the case as Orangeism was quite strong in the shipbuilding industry located at Denny's in Dumbarton, which had ceased to employ Catholics after Protestant workers rioted in 1855. Also, Wylie was known to be liberal in his attitude towards workers' rights and demonstrated a great interest in their personal welfare. The growth of the franchise and the inclusion of Clydebank into the seat meant that in the general election of 1906, after the retiral of Wylie, the Liberals won the seat and would hold it until the end of the First World War.

WAR AND DECLINE

The Clyde conurbation was the most important centre of war production in the United Kingdom. Overall, it is reckoned that the area was able to increase its industrial output by a fifth.[12] Thousands of workers flocked into the area, lured by the prospect of full employment in the munitions industries where wages were rising. The shipyards in Dumbarton and Clydebank worked at full pace in order to rebuild the ships that were being sunk by the U-boat campaign in the Atlantic. The Argyll motor works in Alexandria were converted to produce munitions. The Dunbartonshire Territorials were mobilised and became the 9th Battalion of the Argyll and Sutherland Highlanders, the regiment with which the area was most associated. Many of the engineers in the shipyards elected to serve with the Royal Navy, where their technical expertise would be of greatest value. Like other parts of the

United Kingdom, there was considerable patriotic enthusiasm for the war in its initial phase. Yet this would soon evaporate as increasing disillusionment grew with the conditions of war and the political handling of the conflict.

Workers soon found that their increased overtime was being eroded by inflation and rent rises. Furthermore, wartime changes in working practices that were designed to increase production witnessed the use of unskilled labour for work that was formerly the preserve of the skilled. Many believed that these were not emergency temporary measures, but were in fact the thin edge of the wedge that would see the skilled workers replaced by unskilled. While workers were encouraged to do their patriotic duty, it seemed that the bosses believed in business as usual. The 'Shell Scandal' of 1915 revealed that employers were putting profits above patriotism. Rack-renting landlords gobbled up overtime payments in the Clydebank area because of a shortage of accommodation. This victimised families whose main breadwinners were fighting at the front and could not afford to pay the price of rising rent. For many, it seemed as if there was one rule for them and another for those with money. Employers who had government on their side harassed trade unionists. Eventually, tempers would snap in 1915 with the outbreak of wildcat strikes and the Rent Strike of 1915 when people refused to pay rents and demanded that rents be frozen for the duration of the war. The people won and this enhanced the reputation of the Independent Labour Party and the trade unions. Increasingly socialism and the Labour Party would build up greater credibility as people lost faith in the Liberal Party, which sided with the Tories in a coalition government and backed the bosses in their endeavours to change working practices and keep wages low.

Far from being over by Christmas 1914, the war looked likely to drag on, and gung-ho gallantry was replaced by a deep sense of pessimism as the horrific casualty rates began to mount up. In an endeavour to maximise recruitment, local soldiers were kept together, but a consequence of this was that they often died together. In the small towns and villages of the Vale, for example, relatives would not only have to cope with the loss of a loved one, but often several loved ones, as brothers, cousins and friends had all joined up to serve together. An unlucky shell could wipe out a third of the young men of a small village in seconds. Some 700 men of the 9th Battalion of the Argyll and Sutherland Highlanders lost their lives during the First World War and the total for West Dunbartonshire would likely be in the region of some 6,000 fatalities. Conscription was introduced in 1916 because the supply of volunteers could not keep pace with the insatiable demand of the Western Front. Furthermore, there was rationing of food, an unrelenting demand for war production that meant long hours for workers and, to cap it all, a government increase in taxation on booze in an endeavour to stop the working class drinking too much. Against a consequent rise in discontent, the Labour Party began to make significant inroads among the electorate. Labour activists spoke at trade union meetings, while Labour women networked among the female population in the closes and gardens. Ideas of social justice, decent wages and housing, and a fairer society found a ready audience among the working class.

The First World War and its aftermath had a dramatic impact on the area of West Dunbartonshire. Very little of the Victorian and Edwardian world was able to withstand the impact of the change that followed in the wake of the Great War. The traditional industries found that demand for their goods dried up in the new world economic order. The old deferential politics was swept away by a bolder and harder politics based on class interest that squeezed out the centrist Liberal Party. Many of the social problems of the pre-war era that had been swept under the carpet in the past came into full view and, as we shall see, became worse. To the old problems of poor housing, poverty and poor health was added a new one: long-term, mass unemployment. Without a doubt, the period between the wars was one of traumatic upheaval and, sadly, it would take the impact of another World War before many of the region's social and economic problems were solved.

Shipbuilding was the single biggest employer in the area. Denny's and MacMillan's in Dumbarton and John Brown's and Beardmore's in Clydebank had all prospered during the war, as there was an insatiable demand for ships. Yet, after 1918, a number of factors conspired to bring demand to an end. Firstly, there was a glut of shipping, especially after the confiscation of the German merchant fleet, which depressed orders. Secondly, the Americans had developed prefabrication techniques, which meant that ships could be built quicker and cheaper. Finally, after the war, confidence in the world economy had suffered a blow and this depressed the demand for capital investment goods such as ships as it was believed that there would not be enough demand to warrant the building of new ones. Shipbuilding was closely related to the steel and engineering industries and the collapse in the demand for ships had a knock-on effect. The Argyll motor works at Alexandria had kept going during the war by producing munitions, but, once the war was over, it went back to being empty. The textile industries in the Vale suffered a similar fate as demand collapsed due to a depressed market at home and competition from overseas. Pre-war clothing markets had been lost during the war as employers sought to capitalise on the quick and ready profits to be made from war production. Things became even worse with the impact of the Great Depression in 1929 when struggling companies were finally pushed over the edge.

In 1930, Beardmore's closed and was joined by MacMillan's the following year. The widespread introduction of tariff barriers following the Great Depression badly hit the market for printed cloth and as a result many of the struggling factories in the Vale of Leven were forced to shut. In 1932, 64 per cent of the male and 31 per cent of the female working population were unemployed, making the Vale one of the worst-hit communities in Britain during the depression. Things were only slightly better in Clydebank where about half the insured workforce was out of work. Dumbarton was least affected, but still had about one in three of its insured workforce idle. These figures did not include those who were not insured, such as the independent tradesmen and small businessmen, many of whom would have found custom for their trade had dried up, because they were living in unemployment black spots. So, the overall figures for the jobless total in this period would have been higher. Unemployment was misery. For many skilled workers there was a psychological price to pay for being idle. These were men who were proud of their work and believed in independence, as they saw it, which meant providing for their family. Many found receiving poor relief humiliating, believing it to be state charity. The unemployed were forced to seek menial and part-time work or stand listlessly on street corners. Following the imposition of Means Testing in 1931, all family income was taken into consideration in calculating the amount of poor relief that a family was entitled to. Dunbartonshire council's endeavour to exclude war pensions from the calculation was ruled illegal by the government.[13] This meant that the unemployed family would have to exist on what was regarded by government officials as the absolute minimum money required to maintain their health. This was in spite of the fact that a number of experts disputed this calculation and pointed out that many families were living below what would be regarded as an adequate minimum nutritional value for a healthy lifestyle. Mothers tended to be the worst affected. They would go without to ensure that the family was better fed. Also, many women would take up part-time work to supplement family income, but were still expected to do the housework, as men found this demeaning to do.

Housing was arguably the most acute social problem. In Clydebank, there had been a considerable influx during the war to work in the munitions industries, and the 1917 Royal Commission on Housing showed that the extent of demand was such that all accommodation in the town was being rented out.[14] Most of the buildings were tenements that were divided into units of one or two rooms and all were in the hands of private landlords who were eager to cash in on the wartime boom. No new building work was undertaken during the war and the rise in population was accommodated by squeezing more people into the existing housing stock.

Although rents were frozen for the duration of the war, landlords maintained profits by not carrying out repairs and improvements. Similar conditions were to be found in the Vale of Leven where, in Bonhill, one street had only one outside toilet per twenty-seven people. Initial hopes that there would be 'homes for heroes' proved forlorn. In spite of the recommendation of the Royal Commission on Housing that there was an immediate need for a quarter of a million new homes in Scotland, the 1919 'Geddes Axe' curtailed the powers of local government spending. In Clydebank, for example, the local authority was only able to build 2,000 council houses in the inter-war period. Local authorities were hampered by a number of issues. Firstly, with the economy in turmoil and charged with funding much of the demand of poor relief for the unemployed, local government was strapped for cash throughout the inter-war period. Secondly, land in built-up areas in Clydebank and Dumbarton was expensive in precisely the areas where new housing was most needed. Thirdly, central government constantly reduced the subsidy to council housing, which meant that rents were comparatively expensive, and so it was only the better-off who could afford them. Those in the worst housing remained there. Finally, private landlords failed to make repairs and improvements and conditions actually got worse.

The impact of social and economic change was translated into political change. In 1918, the franchise was extended to include all men over the age of twenty-one and all women over thirty. The hardships engendered by the war had a radicalising effect on society in the area, and the victory of the Rent Strike in 1915 had convinced the working class that they could look after themselves politically. The news of the Russian Revolution in 1917 was a further factor in radicalising the working class and it also had the effect of making the middle class swing more to the right out of fear that revolution could happen in Scotland. In the Vale of Leven, worker militancy led to the establishment of local Soviets and the dominance of the Communist Party in local politics. The Vale was especially hit hard following the end of the war. The munitions factory at Alexandria closed in 1918 and left 2,000 unemployed. The United Turkey Red Company closed at Levenbank in the same year. The extent of the radicalisation in the Vale can be shown by the way in which many skilled workers who had belonged to various voluntary societies banded together to form a branch of the National Unemployed Workers Union. Working-class solidarity peaked in the local elections of 1922 when an alliance of Communist, Independent Labour Party and Labour Party candidates won a majority of seats and set about improving conditions for the unemployed. This solidarity did not last and the disintegration of the alliance meant that the working-class vote was split: in 1925, the 'moderates', in reality Conservatives, took control.

In national politics, Labour made a breakthrough in 1922 when it became the largest political party in Scotland in terms of the number of seats won at the general election. David Kirkwood won the seat of Dumbarton Burghs for the Labour Party. Dumbarton Burghs was made up of the urban areas of Clydebank and Dumbarton town and, at this time, the former had about twice the population of the latter. Increased voter registration, extensive trade union links and good organisation by the Labour Party were critical ingredients in Kirkwood's success. Kirkwood was a popular MP and would retain his seat until his elevation to the House of Lords in 1951 as Lord Kirkwood of Bearsden. His credentials had been forged during the war when he emerged as the leader of the trade unions at the Parkhead munitions factory and had been imprisoned for his activities. A passionate and powerful speaker, he was also one of the early Labour proponents of Scottish home rule. Down to earth, with a love of Burns and an irreverent sense of humour, his passionate outbursts in Parliament made him one of the best known of the Clydesiders and he even won the praise of Winston Churchill.[15] Kirkwood's popularity can be demonstrated by the fact that following Ramsay MacDonald's split with the Labour Party and his decision to form a National Government, Kirkwood was one of only seven Scottish Labour MPs to retain his seat in the 1931 general election. Labour did not make the same progress in the more rural constituency of Dunbartonshire, which stretched out east to take in places such as Kirkintilloch and Cumbernauld. William Martin won the seat in 1923, only to lose it again in 1924. Thomas Johnston, the wartime Secretary of State for Scotland, came close to winning the seat in a by-election in 1932, and would have won it had it not been for the intervention of a nationalist and a communist candidate. In a by-election in 1936, a Falkirk lawyer, Thomas Cassells, won the seat for Labour and the party would hold on to it until the seat was abolished in 1950.

The Second World War marked an important turning point for the area. The problems that had dogged the region in the inter-war era would have to be addressed by government in order to prosecute the war with maximum efficiency. The Clyde estuary became once again an important centre of munitions production and, in the period after the Fall of France, was a vital lifeline for the Atlantic convoys that had to bring in desperately needed supplies from the United States. Strategically, the importance of the area cannot be overemphasised. A whole range of vital war materials was produced in the area. The old Argyll motor works in Alexandria was reopened in 1936 to produce torpedoes for the Royal Navy. Singer's factory was converted to produce parts for aircraft. Ships were constructed in Dumbarton and Clydebank. Shells, parts, engineering components, machine guns and engines were also manufactured, and the area was important for storing munitions and fuel. Flying boats were constructed in Dumbarton. Because of the area's strategic significance to the British war economy, the Luftwaffe targeted it in March 1941.

The Clyde estuary was a highly visible target on account of its distinctive coastline, which bombers would be able to follow straight to the target. Government had expected an attack and Clydebank was designated as a high priority for the evacuation of children in the first months of war. An official delegation from the German Navy had been given a tour of the area in 1938 and could see for themselves at first hand the important concentration of industry. Decoy lights were employed to try to steer night bombers out into the surrounding countryside. The strategy of the Luftwaffe was to cause maximum disruption to the war effort and it believed that the best way to achieve this was to attack civilian areas to spread terror and destroy the homes of workers, so affecting industrial production. In many ways, this strategy made sense. The population of Clydebank was densely packed together in tenements and an easier target than the factories that were widely distributed. Also, because tenements contained so many people, the effect of bombing would be very destructive and indeed had a much greater impact than in English industrial cities where the population lived in 'back to back' houses. In one direct hit on a tenement in Clydebank, eighty-eight people were killed as a result of living together in such close proximity.

On 13 March 1941, 236 German bombers left their bases to attack Clydebank, Govan and the industrial estate at Hillington. During the night, a total of 270 tons of explosives would be dropped on the intended targets. The authorities were not prepared for the scale of the attack. The fact that there had been no significant raid on Scotland had led to a degree of complacency: many of the children who had been evacuated in the initial stages had, for example, drifted back to their families. Some 7,000 children were in Clydebank when the Luftwaffe struck. The concentrated attack on Clydebank overwhelmed the rescue services. One of the first buildings to be hit was the public library, which acted as the command centre for the emergency services. Gas and electricity supplies were cut and the local authorities were forced to call on outside assistance. One feature that hampered rescue attempts was that the fire brigades from outside the area had incompatible equipment and could not use their hoses. Furthermore, the water supply was cut and this meant that the canal had to be used as a water source, but the pumps were of insufficient strength to reach homes built on the higher ground. These were simply allowed to burn themselves out. The Luftwaffe tended to attack the same targets two nights in a row, so most of the population simply fled into the surrounding countryside and, sure enough, the Luftwaffe came back for a second attack. When the residents returned in the morning, they found a scene of utter devastation. There were only seven buildings left intact; 35,000 people were left homeless and had to be relocated around the country. In the immediate aftermath of the raid, the population of Clydebank dropped to 2,000. As a result of the raids, 1,200 were killed and a similar number seriously injured, and about half of those were from Clydebank town itself. Clydebank suffered the most concentrated bombing of any British urban area during the Second World War. In May, a further attack took place, but by then there were few workers living in the area.

RECONSTRUCTION: 1945–2006

The Second World War witnessed a revolution in British politics. The necessity of conducting total war meant that the people could no longer be taken for granted, especially those in the industrial areas that had suffered most during the depression and were now so vital to the war effort. It was agreed that, following the war, the state would assume responsibility for the social and economic well-being of all citizens from the 'cradle to the grave'. This idea was enshrined in the 1942 Beveridge Report that laid down the blueprint for the Welfare State. Grandiose plans were laid for the reconstruction of society following the war and the area of West Dunbartonshire was encompassed within Sir Patrick Abercrombie's Clyde Valley Plan. It was recognised that many of the region's problems were down to an overdependence on the traditional heavy industries of shipbuilding and engineering, and that a downturn in demand for these goods had led to the high unemployment of the past. High unemployment had been responsible for much of the area's poverty and attendant social problems such as poor housing. It was argued that by encouraging new lighter industries to the area, the local economy would be modernised and have a greater economic diversity that would be better able to weather a downturn in the global economy. It was the sort of plan that promoted the idea of not having all one's economic eggs in one basket. To help with the new economy, there would also be an ambitious programme of social reconstruction that would build new houses, schools, hospitals and transport infrastructure.

In many ways, this ambitious vision for a new Scotland was handicapped from the start. The British government was strapped for cash and had undertaken a costly programme of welfare reform. In any case, few seemed perturbed that the dominance of the old industries continued after 1945. The main objective in promoting industrial diversification was to ensure full employment, but with European reconstruction in full swing, British

Figure 10 The *QE2* under construction before her launch in 1967.

industry's order books were full, as there was a huge demand for machinery, engineering plant, ships, steel and coal. The shipyards of Clydebank and Dumbarton took advantage of the fact that they were among the few operating yards in the aftermath of the war that could construct ships for the post-war European economy. They did not, however, modernise. They stuck to old-fashioned types of production, and with small yards were unable to compete in the market for super tankers and large cargo ships. Prefabrication techniques and deep-water yards were essential for this type of construction. Instead, Clyde shipbuilders stuck to small-scale construction. Also, the yards were very inefficient in completing orders on time and had inadequate methods of marketing their wares. By the early 1960s, they were running into problems and unable to compete with the growing shipbuilding industries in Japan, Germany and Scandinavia. By 1963, Denny's of Dumbarton had gone into liquidation. In response to the recommendations of the 1967 Geddes Committee, Brown's was merged with other shipyards to form the Upper Clyde Shipbuilders. It was argued that merger would enable greater economies of scale and ensure that the Scottish yards were competitive. Also, the industry received a considerable amount of government subsidy for modernisation, which instead went to hold up profits, and in 1971 the company went into liquidation, despite a workers' occupation for a time. After the last ship was launched in 1972, the yard continued for a short period with work constructing North Sea oil platforms. One successful spin-off from the debacle of shipbuilding was that the engineering section of John Brown's was formed into a separate company that manufactured turbines. It fared much better and was able to secure orders and, although it has had a number of close escapes, has managed to continue manufacturing to the present day.

The industrial giant Singer did not fare well in this period either and many of the same factors that contributed to the downfall of shipping worked against the sewing machine factory. By the early 1960s, the company was facing increasingly stiff competition from cheaper Japanese machines. Like the shipbuilding industry, the factory laboured under poor management and old machinery. Also, Singer, as a multinational, directed more of its investment to the Far East where low-cost labour produced new and cheaper sewing machines. In spite of investment in Clydebank, the numbers employed there dwindled from 16,000 to 6,000 in the period from 1960 to 1970 and further reductions took place thereafter until the factory closed in 1980. The torpedo factory that was housed in the old Argyll motor works continued production after the war, but closed in the early 1970s. Textiles in the Vale did not fare any better. The last of the dyeworks closed in 1960 and the silk factory that had been established in Balloch between the wars closed down in 1980.

Post-war government strategy called for the diversification of the economy and hoped to attract new lighter industries. Most of the industries established in the region were foreign owned and 'branch plant manufactures' became a staple of the economy in the 1960s. Most of these industries were lured to the area with government grants and subsidies. Burroughs, Wisemans, Westclox and Polaroid established factories in the Vale. The production of adding machines, lenses, clocks and sunglasses added to the diversity of the economy and provided employment. Westclox, for example, arrived in the Vale in 1949, was soon producing 10,000 clocks per week and had managed to produce over a million by the end of 1950. Yet 'branch plant manufacture' was not without its problems. Most of these firms were highly mobile and would move to other parts of the world if it suited them. Burroughs closed in 1977 and Wisemans followed suit in 1978. Although Polaroid remains, its production has become more specialist and scaled down. Evidence of the fragility of relying on 'branch plant manufacture' can be demonstrated by examining the takeover of the Argyll works by Plessey in 1970. The firm had given an undertaking that it would open a machine shop and base its numerical control operations in the factory. It was claimed that it would eventually employ over 2,000 people. By the middle of 1971, Plessey announced that it would close the factory, which led to an occupation by the workforce. More disconcerting was the fact that the company had bought the works for a knock-down price and was quite happy to make a profit by asset-stripping the plant. In spite of the best efforts of government intervention, unemployment in the Vale was consistently higher than other parts of Scotland throughout the 1960s and 1970s.

Housing was the greatest social problem facing the post-war administration. The destruction of so many homes in Clydebank, together with dilapidation, meant that there were significant housing black spots in the area. In the Vale, it was reported in 1946 that out of the 5,500 houses, 3,500 were considered to be substandard. By 1966, a total of 14,000 new houses were built in the county of Dunbartonshire, with 6,000 built in Clydebank. Much of this was achieved by the use of tower blocks, especially in Clydebank. Tower blocks were a favourite with local government because they attracted a higher government subsidy, although they did not prove so popular with local residents who wanted houses on the ground. Although there has been much criticism of council housing, it is worth remembering the enormity of the problems that the region faced. After the Second World War, many in Clydebank were housed in prefabs; there were extensive slum areas and considerable overcrowding. The construction of new housing in estates was a massive operation and most believed that the new houses were a considerable improvement on what they had had before. As a result of the housing programmes of the 1950s and 1960s, most people now had access to an indoor toilet and a bath. Yet the biggest problem facing local government was keeping pace with the demand for housing and the SNP was able to exploit Labour's difficulties on the issue in the early 1970s and won control in Clydebank and pushed the Conservatives into third place in the Vale.

The economic recession of the early 1980s had a dramatic impact on the region. The traditional industries collapsed and many of the branch plant manufacturers closed. Unemployment in the region soared and even surpassed the levels of the inter-war period. Yet by the 1990s there were signs of recovery. Redevelopment of the Clyde that focused on retail and services began to provide employment. The extensive development of private housing in the area brought in new blood. The development of the commuting society brought additional wealth into the area and newer lighter industries were established. Local authorities used their extensive powers to promote the development of business and retail parks that provided much-needed employment. Central government also used government incentives to attract new business. One major change with the economic development of the area in the 1990s has been the growth in small business and the fact that the area now has few large employers, with the exception of local government. In this way, the development of West Dunbartonshire has mirrored other areas in Scotland. Although the prosperity of the area has improved, pockets of deprivation still exist and, as is common elsewhere in the western world, some local communities have been ravaged by the new social plague of drug addiction. In part, the expansion of local government services can be explained by phenomena that are part of the post-industrial world such as an older population, isolated and vulnerable communities that have failed to be absorbed by the new economy and the breakdown of traditional family structures. Again and again, developments in West Dunbartonshire continue to reflect and feed into developments in the world at large.

NOTES

1 MacIntyre, Stuart (1980), *Little Moscows: Communism and working-class militancy in inter-war Britain* (London: Croom Helm).

2 Cain, P. J. and Hopkins, A. G. (1993), *British Imperialism: Innovation and Expansion, 1688–1914* (London: Longman).

3 Devine, T. M. (1990), *The Tobacco Lords: a Study of the Tobacco Merchants of Glasgow and their Trading Activities c. 1740–90* (Edinburgh: Edinburgh University Press [Originally published, Edinburgh: John Donald, 1975]) and Devine, T. M. and Jackson, G. (eds) (1995), *Glasgow vol. 1: Beginnings to 1830* (Manchester: Manchester University Press).

4 Durie, A. J. (1979), *The Scottish Linen Industry in the Eighteenth Century* (Edinburgh: John Donald), pp. 65–95.

5 Slaven, Anthony (1975), *The Development of the West of Scotland 1750–1960*, (London: Routledge & Kegan Paul), p. 83.

6 Gallacher, Roddy (1982), 'The Vale of Leven 1914–1975: Changes in Working Class Organisation and Action', in Dickson, Tony (ed.), *Capital and Class in Scotland* (Edinburgh: John Donald), p. 187.

7 Old Statistical Account of Scotland, vol. 9, 'Bonhill'.

8 See Rodger, R. (ed.) (1989), *Scottish Housing in the Twentieth Century* (Leicester: Leicester University Press).

9 Campbell, R. H. (1980), *The Rise and Fall of Scottish Industry, 1707–1939* (Edinburgh: John Donald).

10 Ballantine, Ishbel (ed.) (1989), Glasgow Labour History Workshop, *The Singer Strike, Clydebank 1911* (Clydebank: Clydebank District Library).

11 Hutchison, I. G. C. (1986), *A Political History of Scotland 1832–1924: Parties, Elections and Issues* (Edinburgh: John Donald), p. 210.

12 Lee, Clive (1999), 'The Scottish Economy and the First World War', in Catriona M. M. Macdonald and Elaine McFarland (eds), *Scotland and the Great War* (East Linton: Tuckwell Press), pp. 11–36.

13 Levitt, Ian (1988), *Poverty and Welfare in Scotland 1890–1948* (Edinburgh: Edinburgh University Press), p. 136.

14 *Report of the Royal Commission on the Housing in Scotland* (Cd. 8731) (Edinburgh: HMSO, 1917), p. 237.

15 Kirkwood, David (1935), *My Life of Revolt* [foreword by Winston S. Churchill] (London: George G. Harrap & Co.).

Chapter 5

Enlightenment, Arts and Literature in West Dunbartonshire

Alan Riach

The triangular territory from Glasgow north-west to Loch Lomond, south-west towards Helensburgh, then east along the Clyde back to Glasgow, encompasses one of the richest and most varied literary and artistic histories in Scotland. It is a terrain of rich natural resource: river, loch, forested hills and urban development independent of, but connected to, the merchant city, looking north-east to central Scotland, north-west to the Highlands and Islands, the heartland of Gaelic Scotland and ancient Celtic identities, and south across the Clyde to the industrial yards of shipbuilding in Port Glasgow and Greenock. The boundaries of West Dunbartonshire have shifted in history and this chapter will look on them as open to the surrounding areas, especially since travellers have so frequently passed through the county and its neighbouring territories and its natives have often travelled widely furth of its borders.

All the major writers of Scotland – at least since Burns – have associations with the area, some well-known and celebrated like Tobias Smollett, the great eighteenth-century novelist, some less closely linked, like the poet Iain Crichton Smith, who lived in Dumbarton in the early 1950s. There are significant writers whose visits to the area are memorably recorded, such as the Wordsworths and Coleridge in 1803; there are others who have lived here, including C. Day Lewis and W. H. Auden at different times between 1928 and 1932. There are major writers from just over the area's boundaries whose vision reaches into the territory: from Greenock, John Davidson and W. S. Graham, or from Ardoch and Gartmore, Robert Graham and his grandson R. B. Cunninghame Graham. Neil Munro, James Bridie and George Blake all have links with the area. Before the First World War, Munro's Para Handy captained *The Vital Spark* in Clyde waters between Bowling, Dumbarton and Greenock and further west, while during and after World War II, Hugh MacDiarmid was to work on the same stretch of river. Neither got quite so close to it as Dumbarton-born Charles Joseph

Kirk, who composed his 'Ode to the Clyde' while floating in the cage of a buoy moored just off Cardross. All speak of the spirit of the place, or the various places contained by the territorial boundaries of West Dunbartonshire. And in the work and lives of Burns, Scott and the first National Poet Laureate of Scotland, Edwin Morgan, there are notable connections and moments of vivid evocation. This chapter will trace some of these connections and associations and discuss the qualities in literature, enlightenment and art that West Dunbartonshire has given rise to.

Perhaps the best place to begin is with the iconic painting *The First Steamboat on the Clyde* (c. 1820) by John Knox (1778–1845), to be seen in the Glasgow Art Gallery and Museum at Kelvingrove (see Plate 2). Here the different elements that characterise the area are held in balance at a particular historical moment. The painting appears at first to be of a classical landscape, trees, hills, river and sky in Arcadian compositional harmony. Yet, a tinge of wildness touches the scene. The wind in the leaves comes from a wilderness of mountains and the Clyde estuary runs past the ancient mechanics of sail towards the future of industrialisation still to come: at the centre of the work, from a small, dark, shadowy ship, a ragged plume of smoke trails up. The painting commemorates the maiden voyage in 1812 of the first commercially run steamship, the *Comet*, designed by Henry Bell. The voyage – a three-and-a-half hour trip from Glasgow to Greenock – was a triumph for Bell, David Napier, who constructed her boiler, and John Robertson, who built her engine. With her double set of paddles, high funnel and single sail, the *Comet* was the herald of the shipbuilding industry. The painting portends the whole story of shipbuilding on the Clyde and the industrialism that accompanied its development. In the foreground, isolated people are depicted in a sylvan glade – pastoral figures perhaps, but also foreshadowing the workers who would seek the hills and countryside as recreation from the factories, workshops and warehouses of the built-up industrial towns. In the distance, Dumbarton Rock can be seen, reminding the viewer of a more ancient past and carrying the eye to the imagined west beyond the furthest depth of the canvas: the further reaches of the Clyde estuary, the islands of the west and Ireland. The viewer stands in the east, looking westwards; the Highlands encroach from the north and the south stretches off to the left of the canvas. The theatrical space of the painting sets a comprehensive, encompassing scene that might be described as characteristic of the area, from modern times to the ancient past.[1]

Early Celtic stories, legends and songs tell of heroes travelling freely between Ireland and Scotland. One of the earliest and most beautiful songs known is 'Deirdre's Farewell to Scotland', composed, it is presumed, after her nine-year residence in Scotland, the happiest years of her life with

Naoise, her lover. Also, Cuchulain, the great hero, learned his skills in the arts of combat from Scathach, the woman who was his teacher, in Scotland. While the Ossianic tales have frequently been claimed as purely Irish, it is worth insisting that Scotland has equal claim to these heroic and tragic stories. The eighteenth-century 'versions' by James Macpherson have often been dismissed as 'forgeries', as if not only those specific texts but also the stories themselves were 'false' and not to be associated with 'authentic' Scottish identity. But it is surely clear that the stories have much to do with ancient Scotland and a social context that carried over between Ireland and Scotland, and may still exert powerful creative influence, as they did, for example, on the ultra-modernist Scottish composer Erik Chisholm (1904–65), in his 'Night Song of the Bards' composed in 1944–51. Dunbartonshire, along with Argyll and the ancient kingdom of Dalriada, is centrally located for any literary understanding of the ancient imaginative commerce between the peoples who lived and travelled in these places.[2]

Dumbarton was the capital of the Cymric kingdom of Al Clud, later Strathclyde, from the fifth century AD to 1018. In the anthology *The Triumph Tree: Scotland's Earliest Poetry AD 550–1350*, Thomas Owen Clancy notes that *The Gododdin*, while known as the oldest Scottish poem (sixth century), must be read with many questions in mind:

> How did the text survive, how was it transmitted, how much was it changed in the course of transmission? While it seems certain that the poem was preserved in some form in the kingdom around Dumbarton, the other questions are more difficult to answer.

It seems clear that the territory occupied by the Gododdin was the Lothians with Din Eidyn (Edinburgh) as their main fortress and that the poem describes murderous military conflict between them and the English at Catraeth (Catterick), but it is worth noting that the preservation and transmission of the poem owes something to the provenance of literary culture in Dunbartonshire.[3]

The terrain of Dunbartonshire, especially around Dumbarton Rock and the Clyde estuary, is memorably described in two of Nigel Tranter's novels depicting the early years of Scotland's history. *Druid Sacrifice* (1993) tells the story of Thanea, niece of King Arthur, sister to Gawain, daughter of King Loth and mother of the child who would become St Mungo or St Kentigern, the founder and patron saint of Glasgow. Glasgow in its early days was known as Cathures, and Thanea gave her other name to the surviving St Enoch underground station at the foot of Buchanan Street. The novel vividly recounts the story of her life (much of it inevitably 'fiction') and notes that Dumbarton Rock was Mordred's stronghold. Equally vivid is Tranter's description of a visit to the occupied fort on Dumbarton Rock some decades later in the novel *Columba* (1987), written before *Druid Sacrifice* but coming later in the historical chronology. Tranter's writing is generally workmanlike but there is no gainsaying his love of Scotland, and the geographical descriptions of the country in his fiction are sometimes enhanced by the inherent dramatic power of what he is describing. This is certainly true of the depictions of Dunbartonshire in these two novels.

The historian Nennius (fl. AD 796), in his *History of Britain*, identifies a number of stories associated with Arthur and Merlin and Loch Lomond (which was called Loch Leven). The earliest document referring to Dumbarton Rock is apparently a letter from St Patrick to the soldiers of the king, Ceredig of Alcluith or Al Clud (or, Rock of the Clyde – Dumbarton Rock), reproaching them for a raid on his Irish converts. A document of 1367 refers to Dumbarton as *Castrum Arthuri* (Arthur's Castle), while another story calls it the birth place of Mordred. Legend tells that one of the kings who stayed on the rock, Rhydderch Hael, welcomed Merlin to his court on the recommendation of Glasgow's Saint Mungo. Rhydderch's peaceful death, 'at home on his own pillow', was prophesied by Columba, in Adomnán's biography of the saint.[4]

The literary significance of all this is that it indicates the transitional moment when ancient figures and legends overlap with the established historical Christian saints: Kentigern (or Mungo), such legend proposes, knew and respected Merlin. Writers of many kinds, from poets to historians, for various reasons, might have made such stories up, or they may have heard stories from others that link back to some undocumented actuality. Similarly, legend has it that Old Kilpatrick was the birth place of St Patrick of Ireland (though Oliver St John Gogarty repudiated this); when the Devil got wind of this potential enemy he summoned a company of witches who hunted Patrick along the Clyde. They were frustrated at not being able to cross the river's running water to get him, so they ripped out a great rock and hurled it after him: Dumbarton Rock. The association of Scotland and Ireland in these stories and legends is of deep and lasting literary significance, especially for the Dunbartonshire area. It reminds us of a very different geography of commerce – and more importantly, a different geography of the imagination – than that which pertains in later dispensations of British/Irish bipolarity.

One problem here is that 'literature' normally refers to writing, whereas many of the stories mentioned come from, and are carried through, oral transmission. Storytelling is orature – but it co-exists alongside and informs literature and literary sensibility, as readers might infer from various modern novels, pre-eminently Meg Henderson's *The Holy City*, which we will discuss later. The parallels and overlaps between the oral arts of storytelling and the narrative arts of the written novel are enriching and destabilise the security of categories or genres. Similarly, the kingdoms of Strathclyde and Dalriada were much more closely associated with Ireland – and indeed with the Welsh-speaking Lothians – than modern political boundaries would encourage us even to imagine. In the twentieth century, recognising the significant work of the modern Irish literary revival both in terms of its literary and aesthetic accomplishments and its historical revisioning, Hugh MacDiarmid was keen to indicate the ancient precedent of the commerce between the two countries. The literary heritage of Dunbartonshire, with Dumbarton Rock as a key location, exemplifies it permanently.

John Barbour (c. 1320–95), in *The Bruce* (1375–6), Blind Harry (fl. 1470–92), in *The Wallace* (c. 1490), and Nigel Tranter (1909–99) in his popular, interconnected series of novels about both figures, retell stories associated with these Scottish heroes in the area. Wallace finds a safe retreat in the castle at Balloch, on the run from English enemies. After his capture at Robroyston, betrayed by Menteith, he is held in Dumbarton Castle before being removed to London. Bruce shelters in a cave by Loch Lomondside (now known as Rob Roy's Cave), a mile from Inversnaid. He spent his last days in Cardross, just over from Dumbarton Castle, happily, with his beautiful young second wife, his lion, hawk, hound and fool, and, when he died (of leprosy), instructed Sir James Douglas to carry his heart from here to battle against the Saracens, though it was returned to be buried in the grounds of Melrose Abbey.[5]

Sir David Lyndsay of the Mount (1486–1555) remains famous for his great play, *Ane Satire of the Thrie Estaits* (c. 1540), but in his poem 'The History of Ane Noble and Valliand Squire William Meldrum, umqhyle Laird of Cleish and Binns', he depicted an adventure of the gallant sixteenth-century warrior Squire Meldrum taking place at Boturich Castle, in the parish of Kilmaronock, east of Balloch. Apparently the story was based on fact: in 1515, widow Marion Lawson living in Strathearn got wind that her lands at Boturich were being raided by MacFarlanes; Squire Meldrum (who was wooing her) set off with her men to right the situation. They lay siege to the castle and Squire Meldrum brings the Chief MacFarlane to his knees, but spares the lives of his defeated enemies. He returns to the widow Lawson and the poet coyly relates how he is happily received:

Howbeit the chalmer door wes closit,
They did bot kis, as I suppoisit.
Gif uther thing was them betwene,

Let them discover that luiferis bene,
For I am not in lufe expart
And never studyit in that art.

Nevertheless, a little further on, '[. . .] this ladie fair / Ane dochter to the squyer bair [. . .]'. Thus, the rewards of his courage in defending her property and his generosity in sparing the defeated usurpers were found in Marion's physical charms and their domestic consequences. The poem may be based on medieval conventions of Romance, but it is knowingly playful and ironic with them, engaging a healthily sceptical comedy while lively metre and a gleeful pace keep the action taut.[6]

Literary – as opposed to historical – associations between Mary Queen of Scots and Dunbartonshire have less to do with Dumbarton Castle as a Marian stronghold than her entrancement by Lord Darnley, son of the Lennox family (substantial Dunbartonshire landowners), who apparently wooed her with poems. Mary's own small corpus of extant poems are sophisticated and heightened by their immediate contexts, but none we know of are explicitly addressed to Darnley. They had not been married for two years before he was killed in Edinburgh in 1567 (see Plate 1). In so far as their son was to become James VI and I and his accession to the 'united' kingdom in 1603 heralded the transition from the Elizabethan to the Jacobean era, to some extent prompting the production of Shakespeare's greatest tragedies, one might stretch the literary provenance of Dunbartonshire to lead into the work of the great age of Jacobean drama – but it *is* a stretch!

We are on more certain ground with Daniel Defoe (1660–1731), who, in his *A Tour through the Whole Island of Great Britain* (1724–6), described his progress beside Loch Lomond to Dumbarton thus:

This lake or loch is, without comparison, the greatest in Scotland, no other can be called half so big; for it is more than twenty miles long, and generally eight miles in breadth, though at the north end of it, 'tis not so broad by far. It receives many rivers into it, but empties itself into the firth of Clyde, at one mouth; near the entrance of it into Clyde, stands the famous Dunbarton [*sic*] Castle, the most ancient, as well as the most important castle in Scotland; and the gate, as 'tis called, of the Highlands. It is now not much regarded, the whole country being, as it were, buried in peace, yet there is a garrison maintained in it; and the pass would be still of great import, were there any occasion of arms in time to come; 'tis exceeding strong by situation, being secured by the river on one side, the Firth of Clyde on the other, by an unpassable morass on the third side and the fourth is a precipice.

Defoe's eye for military potential was sharp and his role in Scotland as a spy for the English government to support and foster the move towards union in 1707 perhaps underlies these later observations of Scotland and his sense of what might be noted as a precaution for the future, 'were there any occasion of arms in time to come'.[7]

Auguries of the aftermath of the Jacobite rising point forward to one of the most famous of all Scottish songs, 'The Bonnie, Bonnie Banks of Loch Lomond', with its chorus:

> Ye'll tak' the high road and I'll tak' the low road,
> And I'll be in Scotland afore ye –
> But I and my true love will never meet again
> On the bonnie, bonnie banks o' Loch Lomond.

This refers to the idea that the spirit or soul of a Scot who dies in a far land will return home by 'the low road'. The words are supposed to be uttered by a captured Jacobite soldier to his friend, who had been freed. While his friend would walk home by the 'high road', the singer's spirit, after his own execution, will return more quickly by the 'low road' and be there first. Sentimentalism may exaggerate the emotion, and the song has been milked to exhaustion in popular renditions, but there is a real poignancy in the paradox of faith in a spiritual return to a home and hard recognition of a love – not so much for a woman or a particular place as for a lost or broken nation – that might never be fulfilled.[8]

Popular as that song might be, however, Dunbartonshire's most eminent literary figure is unquestionably Tobias George Smollett (1721–71), born in the parish of Bonhill (reputedly Gaelic *bogh-n-uill* 'the foot of the burn', but see Simon Taylor on p. 29) at the old house of Dalquhurn. (His family was a Whig one and his Hanoverian middle name was a pointed baptismal statement in the years after the Union and the '15 Rising.) The main occupation of the people around him was farming and the whole view in his childhood was of pastoral country. He was educated at Dumbarton Grammar School and studied medicine at Glasgow University, leaving for London in 1739, carrying a play with which to achieve theatrical success and metropolitan fame. It was not to be. (Garrick declined *The Regicide*, though it was published in 1749, its preface loaded with conspiracy theories about why it had not been produced.) Smollett went to sea in 1740 as a surgeon's mate, returning to England in 1741, but travelling widely for the next few years. He was in the West Indies before setting up as a surgeon in Downing Street, London, moving later to Mayfair. Yet in all his international travels and London-centred ambitions, Dunbartonshire was home. His love of

Scotland was real. If his experience of it gave him a deeper sense of what he encountered in his own travels, then his international travelling allowed him to review his native country as if with freshened eyes, as one of the first literary tourists (he revisited Scotland in 1753, 1760 and 1766, thus predating Thomas Gray in 1764, Thomas Pennant in 1769, Samuel Johnson in 1773 and William Gilpin in 1776). James Hogg, on his northern tours of 1802, 1803 and 1804, seems to have skirted Dunbartonshire, though he certainly travelled up the Clyde estuary, coming 'within a little of being run down by a brig that was coming up the Firth, full before the gale'.[9]

His ties to his homeland recur in his writing. When Smollett heard news of the slaughter at Culloden, without subscribing to Jacobitism, he wrote an intensely bitter, patriotic poem in six stanzas, 'The Tears of Scotland'.

> The wretched owner sees afar
> His all become the prey of war;
> Bethinks him of his babes and wife,
> Then smites his breast and curses life.
> Thy swains are famish'd on the rocks,
> Where once they fed their wanton flocks;
> Thy ravish'd virgins shriek in vain;
> Thy infants perish on the plain.

This was Smollett's first published work. Friends suggested that the poem's sentiments were too strong and might be considered treasonable and he immediately added a seventh stanza, defiantly emphasising his position:

> While the warm blood bedews my veins,
> And unimpaired remembrance reigns,
> Resentment of my country's fate
> Within my filial breast shall beat;
> And, spite of her insulting foe,
> My sympathizing verse shall flow:
> 'Mourn, hapless Caledonia, mourn
> Thy banish'd peace, thy laurels torn'.

In his greatest work, *The Expedition of Humphry Clinker* (1771), he wrote:

> I have seen the Lago di Garda, Albano, De Vico, Bolsena and Geneva, and, upon my honour, I prefer Loch Lomond to them all, a preference which is certainly owing to the verdant islands that seem to float upon its surface, affording the most inchanting objects of repose to the

Figure 11 Portrait of Tobias Smollett from Cameron House, reproduced by kind permission of Mrs Georgina Smollett.

excursive view. Nor are the banks destitute of beauties which even partake of the sublime. On this side they display a sweet variety of woodland, cornfield and pasture, with several agreeable villas emerging, as it were, out of the lake, till, at some distance, the prospect terminates in huge mountains covered with heath which being in the bloom, affords a very rich covering of purple. Everything here is romantic beyond imagination.

And he wrote with great affection of the Vale of Leven, the 'charming stream' of the Water of Leven, the outlet for Loch Lomond, which pursues for over 5 miles a winding, murmuring course 'over a bed of pebbles, before it joins the firth at Dumbarton'. It was a pure, 'transparent, pastoral and delightful' stream in his boyhood, but was transformed in the nineteenth century as bleaching and dyeing industries took over. As those industries declined, however, the stream recovered its clarity.

Smollett's first novel, *Roderick Random* (1748), sets the precedent for his career of achievement as an innovator in the comic novel. It is a picaresque story, but is also distinguished as one of the great novels depicting life at sea – and his description of sea-battle is recognised as classic – through its measured account of shipboard life and its judgement on the shortcomings of those in charge. In his preface, Smollett explained that his hero is a Scot because 'the disposition of the Scots, addicted to travelling, justifies my conduct in deriving an adventurer from that country'. If the description of Scottish schooling which is given in *Roderick Random* is accurate, there is little wonder about Scots' addiction to travelling. The sadistic teacher in the novel represents the worst alternative to Smollett's own teacher, John Love, whose enlightened attitudes led him to abjure corporal punishment. Picaresque adventures of naïve travellers in a recently united kingdom is Smollett's mode, similar to that of the English novelist Henry Fielding in *Tom Jones* (though Tom's travels do not take him north of the border). He was considered the peer of the great foundational writers of the novel genre: Fielding, Daniel Defoe and Laurence Sterne. Scott, Thackeray, Dickens and Joyce all thought highly of him and enjoyed his work. He visited Paris and the Low Countries in 1750 and *Peregrine Pickle* (the title suggests the method succinctly – unpredictable peregrinations in which the 'hero' finds himself in various 'pickles') appeared in 1751.

As a novelist, Smollett's method opens up the possibilities of exploring the social habits and political prejudices of people throughout the country, as the travellers wander in various stages of planned and accidental peregrinations, encountering others, incidents, different priorities and cultural dispositions. Smollett was a voluminous writer, however: his multi-volume *History of England* was the most substantial example of his work as a 'jobbing' writer. He was a historian, a travel-writer (his most famous book in his own lifetime was *Travels through France and Italy*, published in 1766), a pamphleteer and journalist. In 1752, he published 'An Essay on the External Use of Water' – a medical study of the use of spa resorts. In 1756, he launched *The Critical Review* and continued as its editor until 1763. A literary aristocrat once asked him for a complete set of his works to add to his personal library and was suitably dismayed when the books arrived by cartload with a matching heavy bill for transportation. Smollett employed a team of helpers with this 'hack' writing, translating, editing and abridging work which Smollett would then recommend for publication. However, one of his major achievements in the literary world was the translation of Cervantes's *Don Quixote* (a major work of seventeenth-century Spanish literature, which only began, however, to exert a powerful influence in English-language literature in the eighteenth century, spurred partly by Smollett's translation). He was especially admired by Dr Johnson, who quipped noxiously, 'A scholarly man, Sir, although a Scot.'

Smollett was highly sensitive to perceived libel or insult and sometimes responded with malicious self-righteousness when his vanity was ruffled. His friend, the philosopher David Hume, said, 'He is like a cocoa-nut, the outside is the worst part of him.' He was imprisoned for three months in 1760–1 for political libel, having published a scathing attack on Admiral Knowles in *The Critical Review*, a magnificently sustained piece of literary invective that is a fine precedent for the more scabrous vilifications in the journalism and letters of Hugh MacDiarmid in the twentieth century. Knowles, Smollett tells us,

> neither has, nor ever had any friend at all; and yet for a series of years, he has been enabled to sacrifice the blood, the treasure and the honour of his country, to his own ridiculous projects. Ask his character of those who know him, and they will not scruple to say he is an admiral without conduct, an engineer without knowledge, an officer without resolution, and a man without veracity. They will tell you he is an ignorant, assuming, officious, fribbling pretender; conceited as a peacock, obstinate as a mule, and mischievous as a monkey; that in every station in life he has played the tyrant with his inferiors, the incendiary with his equals, and commanded a squadron occasionally for twenty years without having established his reputation in the article of personal courage.[10]

The extravagant critical dexterity of this writing suggests also that bitterness and resentment were in Smollett's character. Was this linked to his position as a Scot? One argument runs that his foundational role in the history of the English novel came about as a self-consciously British writer, a new kind of trans-nationalised Scot, engaging the literary culture of post-Union Britain. Another might insist on Smollett's singular position as an author of the Enlightenment, whose language, choice of literary form, authorial posture, self-importance and ambition were all in a complex relation with his quick-witted attunement to the energies of vernacular life, the language of illiterate people, his sense of the value of the small community beyond the social mores of the metropolis, a vigorous sense of humour and a grasp of the absurdity of pretentiousness that remains immediately effective with readers today. He cannot subscribe to or support the pretensions of the Enlightenment pose without leavening it with the experience of vital, vibrant, unenlightened life, in touch with darker energies. As a doctor, a seaman, an international traveller and theatre-man, he knew a much wider world than that of the salons and debating clubs. And this breadth of knowledge was rooted in Dunbartonshire and Scotland. In 1760, he began work on *The Present State of All Nations*, which included accounts of Dunbartonshire and was finally published in 1768:

> The little town of Dumbarton, which stands in the neighbourhood of the castle, on the banks of the Leven, was of old a flourishing city, capital of the Cumbrian kingdom of the Britons, and for a considerable length of time under the immediate protection of the Roman Camp, maintained to defend the wall of Antoninus, which ends or begins at Kilpatrick, within three miles of Dumbarton. The ancient inhabitants called that place Alcluith, from the castle standing on the bank of the Cluith or Clyde; but the Scots and Picts gave it the name of Dunbritten, or the castle of the Britons, from which it was corrupted into Dumbarton.[11]

From 1765 to 1768, Smollett lived in Bath, visiting Scotland and following the itinerary of *Humphry Clinker*. His novels – especially *Humphry Clinker* – include wry, critical but affectionate descriptions of Scotland, the crude sanitation in Edinburgh, the pleasing prospect of Glasgow, proto-industrialism (he wrote of the Carron ironworks and plans to build the Forth and Clyde Canal, not completed till over twenty years later) and the pastoral Loch Lomond. He is also sharp, funny and intensely prophetic about some of the icons of Scottish identity that were to become over-familiarised clichés: haggis, oatcakes, whisky and bagpipes. In later years, health declining, Smollett hoped for a consulship in Italy and David Hume tried to help him in this. But nothing came of it and Smollett spent the last six years of his life in voluntary exile in the warmer climate of Italy and produced his masterpiece, *Humphry Clinker*, in the year of his death. Had he lived longer, the Dalquhurn estates and financial security would have been his, but he died at Antigniano, near Leghorn, in September 1771.

Smollett depicted the Vale of Leven as an Arcadian paradise, which links his vision of Scotland's natural beauty to the pre-Romantic depictions of classical beauty that the Enlightenment endorsed and enjoyed. In the year of

Smollett's death, the travel-writer Thomas Pennant confirmed the novelist's view: 'The vale between the end of the lake and Dumbarton is unspeakably beautiful [. . .]'. Smollett's 'Ode to Leven Water' addresses the scene:

On Leven's banks, while free to rove
And tune the rural pipe to love,
I envied not the happiest swain
That ever trod the Arcadian plain.

Pure stream, in whose transparent wave
My youthful limbs I wont to lave;
No torrents stain thy limpid source,
No rocks impede thy dimpling course,
That sweetly warbles o'er its bed,
With white, round polished pebbles spread;
While, lightly poised, the scaly brood
In myriads cleave thy crystal flood;
The springing trout in speckled pride,
The salmon, monarch of the tide;
The ruthless pike, intent on war,
The silver eel and mottled par
Devolving from thy parent lake,
A charming maze thy waters make,
By bowers of birch and groves of pine,
And edges flowered with eglantine.

Still on thy banks, so gaily green,
May numerous herds and flocks be seen,
And lasses, chanting o'er the pail,
And ancient faith, that knows no guile,
And Industry, embrowned with toil,
And hearts resolved and hands prepared
The blessings they enjoy to guard.[12]

Smollett's association of stainless and transparent purity with his childhood in Dunbartonshire is clearly a literary conceit as well as an autobiographical self-representation. But the powerful salmon, aggressive, malevolent pike and slippery eel suggest the denizens of a more untrustworthy adult world for which the Vale of Leven may also have helped prepare him.

The Smollett Monument is a Tuscan column erected in 1774 beside the road near Dalquhurn, in Renton, an industrial village established by the novelist's sister for workers in the bleaching industry. The Latin inscription ('miserably bad' Latin, commented Coleridge to Dorothy Wordsworth), to which Dr Johnson contributed, was approved by Boswell, who noted in his journal that the inscription would only be of interest to learned men. He was wrong. An English translation can now be read engraved in a sheltering arc of stone surrounding the monument, set back from the road:

Stay, Traveller! If elegance of taste and wit, if fertility of genius, and an unrivalled talent in delineating the characters of mankind, have ever attracted your admiration, pause awhile on the memory of Tobias Smollett, MD, one more than commonly endowed with those virtues which, in a man or a citizen, you would praise, or imitate.

Who, having secured the applause of posterity by a variety of literary abilities and a peculiar felicity of composition was, by a rapid and cruel distemper snatched from this world in the fifty-first year of his age.

Far, alas, from his country, he lies interred near Leghorn in Italy. In testimony of his many and great virtues this empty monument, the only pledge, alas, of his affection, is erected on the banks of the Leven, the scene of his birth and of his latest poetry, by James Smollett of Bonhill, his cousin, who would rather have expected this last tribute from him.

Try and remember this honour was not given alone to the memory of the deceased, but for the encouragement of others. Deserve like him and be alike rewarded!

Little trace remains of Smollett's birth place, Dalquhurn House, but on the site of the family home of the Smolletts and their successors, the Telfer-Smolletts, Cameron House, on the shores of Loch Lomond, there was built a baronial mansion of the later Victorian period that later housed a Smollett museum, with portraits of the author, a photograph of the plane tree at Dalquhurn House, under which he was supposed to have been born, and the papers of Lewis M. Knapp, author of *Tobias Smollett* (1949). The Place of Bonhill was the family home of the Smolletts of Bonhill from 1684 to 1763, including Tobias's grandfather Sir James, who was also his guardian; it was demolished in 1964. In Dumbarton, the Grammar School was held in the old Parish Church.[13]

James Boswell and Samuel Johnson were received at Cameron House on 27 October 1773 by Smollett's cousin James, whom Boswell described as 'a man of considerable learning, with abundance of animal spirits; so that he was a very good companion to Dr Johnson'. Boswell recollected that Johnson delivered 'an able and eloquent discourse on the Origin of Evil', showing 'how it arose from our free agency [. . .] Mrs Smollett whispered me, that it was the best sermon she had ever heard'. On their return from the Hebrides, Boswell and Johnson coached past Luss on their way to stay the night with Sir James Colquhoun at Rossdhu. 'Had Loch Lomond been in a happier climate,' Johnson complained tellingly:

> it would have been the boast of wealth and vanity to own one of the little spots which it encloses, and to have employed upon it all the arts of embellishment. But as it is, the islets, which court the gazer at a distance, disgust him at his approach, when he finds, instead of soft lawns and shady thickets, nothing more than uncultivated ruggedness.[14]

The comment predisposes the reader to favour the wonderful praise-poem of such uncultivated ruggedness by Gerard Manley Hopkins (1844–89), 'Inversnaid' (1881), evoking the small 'darksome' burn and water-fall, the 'rollrock highroad roaring down' – on the far side of Loch Lomond (but clearly seen from the Dunbartonshire side):

> Degged with dew, dappled with dew
> Are the groins of the braes that the brook treads through,
> Wiry heathpacks, flitches of fern,
> And the beadbonny ash that sits over the burn.
>
> What would the world be, once bereft
> Of wet and of wildness? Let them be left,
> O let them be left, wildness and wet;
> Long live the weeds and the wilderness yet.[15]

Inversnaid is, of course, near, but not in, Dunbartonshire, but its truth is universal, and, despite Johnson, vital. Similarly, it is worth noting that it was near here that William Wordsworth listened uncomprehendingly to 'The Highland Girl' and asked, 'Will no one tell me what she sings?' This is a key poem about the distance and difference between the prevailing Anglocentric culture and the mystery of Gaelic language and identity, which opens up a number of painful and deepening questions about cultural assumptions, the superiority that attaches to the combination of ignorance and authority, the plangent helplessness of the individual (singer and listener) in this cultural impasse, and the value of a sense of one's own limitations confronted with the fact of difference. Perhaps this is another law of nature confirmed by Scotland's varied and unpredictable terrain, in West Dunbartonshire as much as anywhere else.

The attractions of spontaneous and unpredicted energies were engaged by no one more eagerly, at times, than Robert Burns (1759–96). In 1787, on his second Highland tour, he was returning from Inveraray by Arrochar:

> I write you this on a tour through my country where savage streams tumble over savage mountains, thinly overspread with savage flocks, which starvingly support as savage inhabitants. My last stage was Inveraray – tomorrow night's stage, Dumbarton [. . .]

Next day he 'fell in with a merry party at a Highland gentleman's hospitable mansion' (Cameron House) where the company danced 'till the ladies left us at three in the morning':

> [. . .] we ranged round the bowl till the goodfellow hour of six; except for a few minutes when we went out to pay our devotions to the glorious lamp of day peering over the top of Benlomond. We all kneel'd: our worthy landlord's son held the bowl; each man a full glass in his hand; and I, as priest, repeated some rhyming nonsense, like Thomas a Rhymer's prophecies I suppose. – After a small refreshment of the gifts of Somnus, we proceeded to spend the day on Lochlomond, and reached Dumbarton in the evening. We dined at another good fellow's house, and consequently push'd the bottle; when we went out to mount our horses, we found ourselves 'No vera fou but gaylie yet'. My two friends and I rode soberly down the Loch side, till by came a Highlandman at the gallop, on a tolerably good horse, but which had never known the ornaments of iron or leather. We scorned to be out-galloped by a Highlandman, so off we started, whip and spur. My companions, though seemingly gaily mounted, fell sadly astern; but my old mare, Jenny Geddes, one of the Rosinante family, she strained past the Highlandman in spite of all his efforts, with the hair-halter: just as I was passing him, Donald wheeled his horse, as if to cross before me to mar my progress, when down came his horse, and threw his rider's breekless arse in a clipt hedge; and down came Jenny Geddes over all, and my bardship between her and the Highlandman's horse. Jenny Geddes trode over me with such cautious reverence, that matters were not so bad as might well have been expected; so I came off with a few cuts and bruises, and a thorough resolution to be a pattern of sobriety for the future.[16]

From Dumbarton he went on to Paisley and returned to Mossgiel, 'a certain gloominess' seeming to hang around his countenance. It was from Mossgiel that he wrote the letter just quoted (probably on 30 June) to his old

Mauchline chum Jamie Smith, which continues: 'I am, just as usual, a rhyming, mason-making, raking, aimless, idle fellow.' Shaking off his gloom with such self-reassurance, Burns set off for Edinburgh and travels in the North-east shortly afterwards.

'For well over a century it was believed in Dumbarton that Burns had been made an honorary burgess in 1787; but no record of this existed and the Revd James Oliphant was blamed for this omission', writes Burns's 1992 biographer, James Mackay. Oliphant, previously minister at Kilmarnock's High Kirk, had been lampooned by Burns in 'The Ordination' in 1786. As Mackay notes, one of Burns's companions, George Grierson, wrote that

> the magistrates did them all the honour of conferring the freedom of their city; and Oliphant preached next day, being the Fast-day, against the parties foresaid, and found great fault [with] the magistrates for conferring honours on the author of *vile*, *detestable*, and *immoral* publications.

Mackay writes that the conferral of 'honorary burgess tickets' was not worth the trouble of entering in the Burgh records as they were dispensed with such profligacy so that the town clerk could charge a fee from the Burgh revenue. However, Burns's ticket came to light in 1911. So, he was indeed thus honoured and a number of subscribers to the Edinburgh edition of his works resided in the area. John McAuley, the town clerk, seems to have helped with these subscriptions and it was at McAuley's residence, Levengrove House, on the night of 28 June, that Burns was entertained. He seems also to have visited the Freemasons' Lodge.[17]

Sixteen years later, in 1803, William and Dorothy Wordsworth, the Lakers out for a jaunt with a rather glum and sickly Coleridge, visited Luss, with its straggle of Highland black houses and stone kirk. Dorothy's journal records that the houses had 'not a single ornamented garden' and that she 'first saw houses without windows, the smoke coming out of the open window-places; the chimneys were like stools with four legs, a hole being left in the roof for the smoke, and over that a slate being placed upon four sticks'. William and Dorothy spent a cold, sunless day wandering by the lochside while Coleridge, under the weather, stayed indoors. They admired Ben Lomond, the loch and its islands, but compared everything unfavourably with their own Lakes. They received rather reticent hospitality, Dorothy having to insist upon a fire being lit:

> I had seen the landlady before we went out, for, as had been usual in all the country inns, there was a demur respecting beds, notwithstanding

the house was empty, and there were at least half a dozen spare beds. Her countenance corresponded with the unkindness of denying us a fire on a cold night, for she was the most cruel and hateful-looking woman I ever saw. She was overgrown with fat, and was sitting with her feet and legs in a tub of water for the dropsy – probably brought on by whisky-drinking. The sympathy which I felt and expressed for her, on seeing her in this condition – for her legs were swollen as thick as mill-posts – seemed to produce no effect; and I was obliged after five minutes' conversation, to leave the affair of the beds undecided [. . .] It came on a stormy night; the wind rattled every window in the house, and it rained heavily. William and Coleridge had bad beds, in a two-bedded room in the garret, though there were empty rooms on the first floor, and they were disturbed by a drunken man, who had come to the Inn when we were gone to sleep.

The Wordsworths had been abandoned by Coleridge by the time they were descending to Loch Long from Arrochar, but Dorothy still noted that

the stillness of the mountains, the motion of the waves, the streaming torrents, the sea-birds, the fishing-boats, were all melancholy [. . .] I thought of the long windings through which the waters of the sea had come to this inland retreat, visiting the inner solitudes of the mountains [. . .] From the foot of these mountains, whither might not a little barque carry one away?

However unfortunate some aspects of their journey were, Dorothy's journal preserves a vivid sense of her own engagement with the character of the place: 'Wherever we looked, it was a delightful feeling that there was something beyond.'[18]

(The mystery of the loch is conveyed in a modern anecdote. Alasdair Gray, the novelist, once described to the present writer the curious phenomenon of his having discovered, in the course of some research, maps in which one small island in Loch Lomond seemed to be in different locations at the different periods in which the maps were made. He speculated, given the nature of the soil with which it was constituted, and the vegetation and its roots that grew on it and went through it, it was conceivable that this was indeed a floating island. This might have relocated in the course of time, putting down new roots in different parts of the loch then, eventually, moving off again.)

Sir Walter Scott (1771–1832) visited Ross Priory a number of times, gathering material for *The Lady of the Lake* (1810) and *Rob Roy* (1818), and there is a designated 'Scott Room' there. *The Lady of the Lake* helped set the fashion for the Romantic landscapes and lochside views by Loch Lomond that became the subject of innumerable paintings partly intended for the escalating market among tourists and exiles. In 1817, when he was still not publicly known as the author of the *Waverley* novels, his visit to Rob Roy's Cave prompted speculation about what sort of interest he might have in Rob Roy, if not a novelist's (though in fact he did not use the location in the novel).

One of the most essential qualities of Scott's writing was the work of reconciling differences – Highland and Lowland, Jacobite and Hanoverian, progressive and reactionary allegiances all figure sympathetically in his fiction. In *Rob Roy*, this is most vividly seen in the relationship between the eponymous hero and the shrewd Glasgow man, Bailie Nicol Jarvie, who travels north from the city to the wilderness country and, it is revealed, is in fact Rob Roy's first cousin. Just as Nicol Jarvie and Rob Roy are related by blood and Scott's intention is to demonstrate their connectedness, the country they travel through together holds its contrasting elements in a crucible of inter-relations. West Dunbartonshire itself retains the ethos of both Highlands and Lowlands: thus the hinterland of Scott's novel draws on this interconnectedness and the sense that differences may be understood within a broader family structure. The proximity of Highlands and Lowlands in Dunbartonshire also gave Scott historical precedent for the novel's adventures: Highlanders were close enough to exercise careful observation of Lowlanders' cultivation of cattle and crops. Raids from the north could be very well-timed and the MacGregors, as Ted Cowan has noted in his chapter, were notorious.

A significant conflict is highlighted in many of Scott's novels, one that lies at the heart of the Enlightenment in Scotland. This is the conflict between, on the one hand, inherited wealth, the property of landed gentry, and, crucially, linguistic propriety in the prioritising of English over vernacular Scots and, on the other, the values and speech – whether Scots or Gaelic – of honest families of modest means. Often, too, as with Rob Roy, Scott sees the value in lives lived well beyond the scope of the Enlightened world of happy resolution his novels often encompass. Yet, such conflicts are central to Scott's work as a whole. An entire study could be developed into the question of how far Scott recognises the difficulties they present as ultimately irreconcilable, or whether by presenting them as he does, he is bringing to the attention and care of his readers not only the differences between his characters, but their connectedness. These complex questions play themselves out in a landscape of coastal waters, forests and cliffs, a geography of abrupt transitions the characters explore at their peril. Scott's aspiration towards reconciliation is inescapable, even if he does not avoid the difficulties and irreconcilable elements.[19]

The linguistic variety and different motivations of Scott's characters are complex, but the pictorial aspect of his writing and his ambiguous political position (patriotic, conservative, progressive, unionist) are evident links with clear qualities in the national school of painting developing in the nineteenth century. There is a definite desire to preserve the past pictorially and glorify 'safe' or proprietorial 'views' of landscape in perspectives intended to please and gratify, rather than challenge, the viewer. Innumerable paintings of Loch Lomondside and the Clyde estuary illustrate this. Among the finest are *View of the Clyde from Faifley and Duntocher, looking South-West towards Dumbarton Rock* by John Knox, *View of the Clyde from Dalnottar Hill* (1823) by John B. Fleming (1792–1845) and *The Clyde from Dalnottar Hill* (1858) by Horatio McCulloch (1805–67). The first-named suffuses Dumbarton Rock in golden light and presents the Vale of Leven firmly in the classical landscape tradition ultimately derived from the work of Claude Lorrain. The latter two take the same point of view as John Knox's *The First Steamboat on the Clyde* (with Dumbarton Rock centre-left and the Clyde estuary winding in tranquillity towards the west) and depict the scene in conventional perspective. Fleming's painting includes a number of steamboats and, in the foreground, another major innovation of the industrial revolution, the Forth and Clyde Canal, opened to navigation in 1790 from Grangemouth to Bowling. *Autumn, Loch Lomond* (1893) by Arthur Melville (1858–1904) is more radical in technique, with a special watercolour 'blottesque' approach developed into abstractions (which still keep connection with landscapes) by William Johnstone (1897–1981). Melville's paintings, with their vibrant sense of colour and seasonal precision, retain their brilliance.

The Dumbarton Yards of Archibald McMillan (1855) by Samuel Bough (1822–78) captures the transitional moment when the countryside scenes familiar to Smollett and Scott – the shores of the Clyde estuary, Dumbarton Rock, the hinterland of the Leven valley – are being overgrown by massive man-made constructions: ships of different sizes and buildings for the shipbuilders, manufactories and warehouses on the shorefront. McMillan's Dumbarton yards produced over 500 ships. The Dumbarton-built *Cutty Sark* (now permanently berthed in Greenwich, London) is perhaps the most famous ship with a literary association in its name (from Burns's 'Tam o' Shanter'). Bough is an important landscape painter, still undervalued and neglected. Directly and significantly influenced by Turner, his paintings of seaports and sky form a crucial connection between the picturesque work of McCulloch and the more radical innovations of William McTaggart (1835–1910).

International travel in the late nineteenth and early twentieth centuries exerted an influence seen in new techniques and ideas in landscape painting. The more conventional work of the nineteenth century was overtaken by new sensibilities, realising qualities of form, light and colour that might be taken from disparate locations and refashioned in a native Scottish landscape. This might not be a direct influence, but rather a contemporary development running parallel to developments in France or elsewhere. Thus, McTaggart prefigures Impressionism and develops his own painterly style independently of the French movement, but is clearly related to it. Similarly, John Quinton Pringle develops a technique similar to Pointillism, but seems not to be directly connected to the painters involved in that movement. Perhaps their work is best understood in an independent Scottish context, from which artists might journey and to which they would return. In this way, E. A. Hornel was among the very first British painters to bring his visual experience of Japan and the Far East back to Scottish landscapes. George Leslie Hunter (1879–1931) – one of the group named 'The Scottish Colourists' – discovered Loch Lomond in the 1920s. He brought to it a sense of light and colour he had grown up with in California: a Pacific light and intensity that combined with the intensities and varieties of colour and form he found in West Dunbartonshire. He was intensely self-critical: one story recollects him standing on the bridge in Balloch, angrily dissatisfied with his work, throwing canvases into the water for the tide to carry them away. Yet his paintings of Loch Lomond are evanescent and remarkable. *Reflections, Balloch* (1930) is unmistakably Balloch, yet it breathes the sunshine brightness and colour of the south of France. *Houseboats on Loch Lomond* or *Houseboats, Balloch* (c. 1930; Plate 5) also catch a world of playful movement in water and in the colourful living-quarters of the houseboats themselves. Returning to the same subject allowed for continual variations and freshening familiarity. These paintings speak of a daily engagement with elemental realities of colour, climate and weather that anyone might share and find exhilarating. Perhaps this is the lesson the Scottish Colourists – Hunter, F. C. B. Caddell (1883–1937), S. J. Peploe (1871–1935) and J. D. Fergusson (1874–1961) – all brought to their work: light and colour are as freely available for eyes to see as air to breathe, and any reductive idiom that stuck with hodden grey and the nondescript was not for them. Loch Lomondside, especially for Hunter, was inspirational. The influence of the Colourists persisted fruitfully through the twentieth century and is evident in such paintings as *Loch Lomond* (1974) by David Donaldson (1916–96) and some of the work of John Cunningham (1926–98), whose landscapes of Gartocharn, Ben Lomond, Balmaha, Strathendrick, Drymen, Gartness, Croftamie and the River Endrick were painted from 1963 well into the 1970s (see Plate 4). Donaldson and Cunningham are both artists of great panache and free brushwork, rich with colour and brightness, equally capable of capturing the incessant activity of sky, clouds, water and reflections as much as the calm and natural loveliness of their locations.[20]

Something of the contrast between the scenic and industrialised aspects of the character of the nineteenth century can be seen in the examples of two literary visitors to the area. In 1847, Hans Christian Andersen toured the Trossachs, Inversnaid, Loch Lomond and by steamer and coach to Balloch and Dumbarton, in the company of a family named Hambro. From Dumbarton, he travelled to Glasgow by steamer and then to Edinburgh by train. He had carried with him a walking-stick which, he told the young son of the Hambros, would return with him to Naples, where he had purchased it, and where it might tell of the magical land of mists and heather it had seen on its travels. But he left it behind at Inversnaid. Andersen arrived in Edinburgh and was awaiting the London train, when a Glasgow train pulled in and a guard rushed over to him and handed him back his stick. He remarked that the walking-stick had travelled quite well under its own steam, the label attached to it, 'Hans Christian Andersen, the Danish poet', being sufficient address for it to have been passed from hand to hand till it reached him. Something of the benign, perambulating pace of the curious tourist is part of that story and suggests a world inhabited by good fortune and the picturesque. By contrast, Jules Verne visited Scotland in 1859 and wrote two novels set in the country, *The Green Ray* (1893), which depicts the Hebrides, and *Child of the Cavern* (1877), which responds to the social dystopia of industrialisation with a vision of a labyrinthine network of coal mines in a subterranean world underneath Loch Lomond. This novel is essentially popular science fiction, spectacular, lucid, punchy and tense, but, saturated in the works of Walter Scott as Verne was, it is nonetheless an antidote to the merely picturesque aspect of Scotland Loch Lomond was coming too easily to represent.[21]

There are a number of West Dunbartonshire connections, too, with the architect and artist Charles Rennie Mackintosh (1868–1928, and now internationally perhaps the most famous of all Scottish artists). When the publisher W. W. Blackie moved to Helensburgh in 1902, he commissioned Mackintosh to design his family home on a hilltop overlooking the town. The resulting Hill House (owned by the National Trust for Scotland) is one of Mackintosh's finest architectural works, along with the Glasgow School of Art itself. On meeting 'Toshy', Blackie noted, 'I myself was not terribly old, but here was a truly great man who, by comparison with myself, I esteemed to be a "mere boy" '. Blackie specified 'grey roughcast for the walls and slate for the roof [. . .] any architectural effect sought should be secured by the massing of the parts rather than adventitious ornamentation'.

Mackintosh combined Scottish Baronial with contemporary features, suggesting old Scottish towers or keeps while using wide glass for the bay window and a modern flat roof. The details of the house interior were closely supervised by Mackintosh and Blackie approved: 'Every detail, inside as well as outside, received his careful, I may say loving, attention; fireplaces, grates, fenders, fire irons.' Consequently, the complementarity of traditional Scottish architectural forms (or structures evocative of them), innovative modern features and designs, and the comprehensive attention to interior details and décor (including geometrically patterned chairs and carpet) strikes a uniquely distinctive balance. The library, where Blackie considered manuscripts submitted for publication, is now an information centre, with a desk Mackintosh originally designed for the editor of the *Glasgow Herald*.[22] Further, Margaret Macdonald, born in Bowling and a distinguished artist in her own right, met Mackintosh at the Glasgow School of Art and went on to marry him. They were known, with her sister Frances and Herbert MacNair, as 'The Four' and fashioned an entirely distinctive movement in the applied arts known as the 'Glasgow Style', which contributed famously to the Art Nouveau movement in continental Europe.[23]

The last three years of the life of Neil Munro (1864–1930) were spent at Craigendoran, just south-west of Helensburgh. Munro's short stories about Para Handy and *The Vital Spark*, the Clyde puffer plying an unpredictable trade through the Clyde estuary and out to the nearer Hebrides, are perennial favourites. In his descriptive account *The Clyde* (1907, beautifully illustrated by Mary Y. Hunter and J. Young Hunter), Munro describes the industrial towns:

> Whiteinch, Yoker, Clydebank, Kilbowie and Dalmuir, all on the north side of the Clyde between the Kelvin and the Kilpatrick Hills, are towns whose origin is of yesterday; they are the homes of men who work in the shipyards or in the huge factory of the Singer Sewing Machine Company whose clock tower dominates the smoky valley [. . .] With the towns named we have no pastoral associations now; their mention brings to the mind but thoughts of shrieking and insistent sirens heralding wet winter morns, the clatter of toilward feet on muddy pavements, a manner of life strenuous and unlovely.[24]

This industrial world was acknowledged by Munro, but the pastoral seascape inhabited by Para Handy and the crew of *The Vital Spark* was described with lucid warmth and real affection, and it is for this evocation of the Clyde estuary (re-enacted in the popular television series and the 1953 film of a similar character, Alexander Mackendrick's *The Maggie*) that

Munro is most fondly and widely read and remembered. *The Clyde*, nevertheless, contains splendid descriptive writing about Helensburgh, the Rosneath Peninsula and the whole stretch of Dunbartonshire beside which the river's estuary flows. It is a remarkable momentary depiction of how that area must have appeared in the early years of the twentieth century, when the pastoral and industrial worlds were in a unique balance, before the onset of twentieth-century wars, the priorities of wartime industrialism and the post-industrial era to follow.

Another important Scottish novelist with personal connections with the area was George Blake (1893–1961), who, from 1932 until his death, divided his time between Glasgow and Helensburgh. The Clyde estuary is the central 'character' in his book *Down to the Sea: The Romance of the Clyde, Its Ships and Shipbuilders* (1937). This tells the story of Clydeside shipbuilding from the launch of the *Comet* in 1812 (which we noted in John Knox's painting at the beginning of this chapter) to that of the *Queen Mary* in 1936 (about which Hugh MacDiarmid wrote a poem and a short story, as we shall see). In Blake's fiction, 'Garvel' stands for Greenock and he provides a comprehensive account of the whole area from the days of sail to the onset of the Second World War, writing seriously in the 1930s and 1940s about the consequences of industrialisation and the urbanisation of Scotland. *The Constant Star* (1945) and *The Westering Sun* (1946) follow the fortunes of the Oliphant family, who build and then lose a great shipbuilding industry. Perhaps Blake's best book is *The Shipbuilders* (1935), in which the end of the shipbuilding era is described with a great sense of its magnitude and the pathos of the epic effort it called into being.

The results of earlier industrialisation on the Clyde was the subject of one of the most famous poems of one of the most popular nineteenth-century poets, Thomas Campbell (1777–1844), 'Lines on Revisiting a Scottish River':

And call they this improvement? – to have changed,
My native Clyde, thy once romantic shore,
Where nature's face is banish'd and estranged,
And heaven reflected in thy wave no more;
Whose banks, that sweeten'd May-day's breath before,
Lie sere and leafless now in summer's beam,
With sooty exhalations cover'd o'er;
And for the daisied green-sward, down they stream
Unsightly brick-lanes smoke, and clanking engines gleam.[25]

Half a century later and the effects of industry had darkened the river further. Yet a comic perspective on this dark vision was found by Charles

Joseph Kirk, whose 'Ode to the Clyde' was allegedly composed, as was noted at the beginning of this chapter, while he was sitting in the cage of a buoy moored in the Clyde off Cardross. It was published in the *Glasgow University Magazine* and later collected in *Glasgow University Verses 1903–1910* and his *Clyde Ballads* (1911):

> Hail, great black-bosomed mother of our city,
>   Whose odoriferous breath offends the earth,
> Whose cats and puppy dogs excite our pity,
>   As they sail past with aldermanic girth!
> No salmon hast thou in the jet-black waters,
>   Save what is adhering to the tins.
> Thus thy adorers – Govan's lovely daughters –
>   Adorn thy shrine with offerings for their sins.[26]

Nevertheless, Kirk apostrophises splendidly at the poem's end: 'Yet thou art great!' Despite the smells that have holiday-makers holding their noses, the Clyde's 'exiled sons' would give up 'tons of roses' if they could 'smell thy sweetness in the desert air'.

The Irish-born poet Cecil Day Lewis (1904–72) was principally associated with the 'English leftist poets' of the 1930s, particularly W. H. Auden (who later became an American citizen) and Louis MacNeice (who, like Day Lewis, was born in Ireland). But Day Lewis and Auden both have important links to Helensburgh. In July 1928, Day Lewis was offered a teaching position at Larchfield Academy, Colquhoun Street (which had been a preparatory school since 1919). Among Larchfield's former pupils were Sir James George Frazer (1854–1941), author of *The Golden Bough* (1890), one of the most influential books of the nineteenth century, and the pioneer of television John Logie Baird (1888–1946). Day Lewis began work there on 12 September 1928, teaching English and games; he called Helensburgh 'the Wimbledon of the North'. While living there he worked on his *Transitional Poems* (1929). When he married Mary King (his first wife) at Sherborne on 27 December 1928, Auden sent him an 'Epithalamium' with the lines 'The corridors are still / Within the empty school'. The newly married couple moved to 128 West Street, a council house on an estate overlooking the Clyde to Greenock, on 10 January 1929 and on 27 February Auden visited them, coming to Scotland from Berlin. By June, however, Day Lewis had had enough; he was writing to L. A. G. Strong: 'I don't think we can stand more than another year in this hole [. . .] the parents and the directors at this place make life a positive misery.' Still, he collaborated with Larchfield's music master E. W. Hardy at

Christmas 1929 to produce the school song, dedicated to the headmaster, T. T. N. Perkins:

> School of the mountain and the lochside
> School of the white and the blue,
> Make our hearts as bright and brave
> As the mountains and the wave
> So Scotland may be proud of you.

The song was no longer used after the headmaster retired. Day Lewis left Larchfield on 3 April 1930, recommending W. H. Auden as his successor. This was accepted by the school and Auden arrived at Easter 1930, the same year that Faber and Faber accepted his *Poems* (1930) for publication: the beginning of the most significant decade in his career. In 1931, the novelist Edward Upward stayed at Larchfield with Auden in the school staff living-quarters and Auden completed Book One of *The Orators* (1932) that summer. But by October he had tired of the place, writing in a letter to Gabriel Carrit:

> The school gathers mildew. Numbers down, the headmaster partially blind, his wife growing gradually mad in a canvas shelter in the garden. I spend most of my time adjusting the flow of water to the lavatories.

In 1932, his last year there, his poem 'The Watchers' describes the town:

> Now from my window-sill I watch the night,
> The church clock's yellow face, the green pier light
> Burn for a new imprudent year;
> The silence buzzes in my ear;
> The lights of near-by families are out.
>
> Under the darkness nothing seems to stir
> The lilac bush like a conspirator
> Shams dead upon the lawn, and there
> Above the flagstaff the Great Bear
> Hangs as a portent over Helensburgh.

In 1972 Larchfield amalgamated with St Bride's School to become Lomond School, establishing a different ethos from the private fee-paying boys' school known to Day Lewis and Auden.[27]

One of the most under-researched authors of a slightly older vintage who also lived in Helensburgh when it was part of west Dunbartonshire was David Bone (brother of Muirhead Bone, the artist whose work we will note shortly). A professional master mariner and friend of Joseph Conrad, Bone was the author of a number of exceptional books, including his finest work, the quasi-documentary 'novel' *The Brassbounder* (1910), accounts of experiences of life at sea including *Broken Stowage* (1915), *Merchantmen-at-Arms* (1919) and *The Lookoutman* (1923), a collection of poems and songs, *Capstan Bars* (1931), the novel *The Queerfella* (1952), and his autobiography *Landfall at Sunset: The Life of a Contented Sailor* (1955). He is an author well worth rediscovering as, like Conrad, his reports on experience represent a world rarely captured in literary writing of any kind.

Though primarily a novelist of Caithness, Neil M. Gunn (1891–1973), one of the giants of modern Scottish literature, sets *Wild Geese Overhead* (1939) mainly in Glasgow, with the main character Will finding a place to live in the country outside the city. No location is specified but the relation between what the city does to its inhabitants and the renewal of perception and strength that comes from the vision described in the title, as provided by the country even a short bus-ride away, is at the heart of the novel's sense of conflict. The conflict portended in the novel's date of publication implicitly weighs on Gunn's struggle to find affirmation in an increasingly dehumanised and violent ethos. In a similarly multilayered way, *The Lost Chart* (1949) is ostensibly about a search for an actual missing chart, but the human allegory thickens the texture of what might have seemed a thriller plot to a much more potent accomplishment.

Clydebank grew into an important shipbuilding centre and suffered badly in the slump between the World Wars and then again in the air raids of the Second World War, especially in two raids in 1941, after which only a few houses in the whole burgh escaped damage. One of the most memorable descriptions of the Clydebank Blitz in Scottish fiction was provided by Robin Jenkins (1912–2005) in his novel *Fergus Lamont* (1979). Fergus, the first-person narrator of the novel, after complex adventures and experiences as a working-class radical, an upper-class snob, a soldier and a poet, returns to his home town of 'Gantock' in 1941 and meets his old schoolteacher, Calderwood, who had been a socialist idealist and is now drawn into himself and twisted with disillusionment.

Yet any of his pupils in Kidd Street school nearly thirty years ago would have recognized him at once. Even the least sensitive of us then had been aware that though he wanted to love us he could not: not because of our academic shortcomings, or because some of us stank through not washing often enough but because he had seen us developing into eager conformism, indolent and cowardly acquiescers in the iniquities and inequalities of society.[28]

As they drink whisky, Calderwood tells Fergus that the best thing for their old town would be for a few bombs to fall on it and that he would never have been able to write his poetry if he had thought things through to their hollow conclusion. The bombs suddenly do begin to fall and the discussion intensifies as Calderwood insists on the paradox that Fergus should feel that, for the sake of the future, it would be better if the bombs missed the shipyards, even if that meant they killed innocent people and children. Fergus finally gets out of the house and stands shaking his fist at the air, feeling no hatred of the young German airmen doing their 'loathsome job' and, for the people of Gantock, 'only pity and love'. The bitter contradiction Jenkins depicts here is the climactic moment of Fergus's story, for although he survives the Blitz and lives till 1963, he retreats into silence and bitterness and engages no more with Scotland's modern history. For Fergus, and perhaps for Jenkins, the Clydebank Blitz signals a climactic moment in Scotland's history, after which neither local idealism based on notions of community, familiarity and respect, nor international socialist idealism based on global awareness of exploitation and political hope for a better future, could be maintained in any realistic sense. *Fergus Lamont* is a contradictory, unresolving, unsatisfying novel, yet its sense of want registers very clearly the poignant, unrequited social and personal desires of its central character and the caustic irony and unsentimental compassion of its author.

No such difficult ambiguities troubled Hugh MacDiarmid's sense of the unjustified work of the London-based authorities who, he alleged, allowed the bombing of Scotland to go ahead to decoy the Germans away from London bombing raids. In 'The German Bombers' he describes an air raid on Edinburgh while the warning sirens were being blown 'only in London'. What he calls 'the blackguardly, and, indeed, murderously unscrupulous, attitude towards Scotland of the English government' inspired his vision of the London Blitz as a potential cleansing of 'Earth's greatest horror':

Death and destruction has gone out from London
All over the world. It has sat
Like a gorged spider in the ghastly centre of the web
In which all human hopes like flies are caught.[29]

In his short story 'Here's How: A Glasgow Story' and his poem 'Die Grenzsituation' MacDiarmid refers to the building and launch of the *Queen*

Mary. During its construction, the name of the ship had been unannounced until, at its launch, the royal imprimatur was delivered. The short story, mainly a monologue by one of the riveters who worked on the ship, violently turns on the hypocrisy of the class system whereby the skills, toughness and intelligence of the workers is put to use, then relegated by the aristocracy and by the excessive sensationalising of the popular press:

> It wasn't so bad while the work was going on (though calling it by a number gave a sort of convict or Army effect to the whole thing) – but once the job was nearly through and the Royalty boosters got busy . . . My God! All the infernal fuss about naming it. Columns and columns of twaddling speculation and suggestion in all the papers [. . .] And the Queen got up on the platform – the whole world hanging on her lips, breathlessly waiting for the momentous declaration. And it came! You bet your life. The biggest anti-climax in history. Mary, says she, as bold as brass and as proud as Punch. I can't understand why the whole crowd didn't burst out laughing. Talk about a sell! But no, they all took it seriously and the whole world swallowed it like a butter-ball and said how splendid it was – what a divine inspiration![30]

The poem is even more bitter:

> Was this the face that launched a thousand ships?
> No! But it frightened one right smartly down the slips
> When – while the whole world held its silly breath –
> She gave it her own holy name – as sure as death!
> Deeming that the greatest compliment that she,
> After a profound spell of Queenly secrecy,
> To duty nobly yielding her notorious modesty,
> Could pay this miracle of Clydeside industry.[31]

MacDiarmid's political certitude and unambiguous condemnation of the shameful self-satisfactions of aristocracy and establishment media are as refreshingly pertinent in the twenty-first century as they were mid-twentieth century. His own associations with Clydebank went back to 1913, when in his early 20s he found employment as a journalist with the weekly *Clydebank and Renfrew Press*. He lived at 8 Bon-Accord Street and it was while staying at Clydebank that he first heard of the pioneering socialist teacher John Maclean, of whom he later planned to write a biography. In a context of heavy industrialism, MacDiarmid – or C. M. Grieve – renewed his connection with the Independent Labour Party and became an active propagandist with James

Plate 6

Left: Clydebank Theatre, Monday 29 December 1913. Opened in 1902 as the Gaiety, the theatre was owned by A. E. Pickard between 1908 and 1917, and later became the Bank Cinema. Scottish Theatre Archive, Glasgow University Library.

Right: The Empire Theatre, Alexandria, known as the Vale Empire, opened in 1910. This poster for a benefit concert for the Vale of Leven Ornithological Society dates from either 1925 or 1931. West Dunbartonshire Libraries.

Plate 7
Label for Turkey-Red cloth produced in John Orr Ewing's Alexandria Works, colloquially the Croftengea or Craft. John Orr Ewing also donated the building now used by Alexandria Library.

Plates 8
Above and opposite page: Dalmuir Parish Church Junior Musical Association's Grand Kinderspiel, *Dan, The News-Boy*, was performed at Clydebank Town Hall in December 1912. Kinderspiels were a sort of children's musical play popular before the First World War. As the cast-list indicates, some of the children shown in the photographs had roles in the production. Those identified are: opposite page, top centre: Charlie Ross; top right: Jenny Buchanan; centre: Jessie Buchanan; and centre left: Agnes Black. The items come from an album donated to West Dunbartonshire Libraries by Mrs M. McNeill, a relative of Jenny Buchanan.

PRINCIPALS.

Mistress Jean, the housekeeper at Claver's Ha',	Miss Tina Embelton
Jeanie Gray, Sister to Duncan	Miss Jessie Buchanan
Jenny Nettles, Keeper of a fruit and flower stall,	Miss Jeanie Edmond
Leezie Lindsay, Keeper of a fancy goods stall,	Miss Nettie Glendinning
Bessie Lee, a domestic servant,	Miss Rachel Coulter
Polly, Duncan's little sister,	Miss Janet Buchanan
Britannia,	Miss Bella Robertson
Laird o' Cockpen, Principal partner in the firm of Massey, Wattie, & Co., wholesale tea dealers,	Miss Agnes Black
Dan, an orphan,	Master Jack Menzies
Duncan Gray, nephew to the Laird o' Cockpen and cashier to the firm,	„ James Johnston
Iuky M'Quill, a clerk in the office of the firm,	„ Chas. Davidson
Pedy Legit, a traveller for the firm,	„ Robt. Johnston
Jing Bang, the manager of a strolling company,	„ Willie Ross
Charlie, Duncan's little brother,	„ Robert Wishart
Policeman A1, a well-known constable in Enitown,	Mr Jack Terence

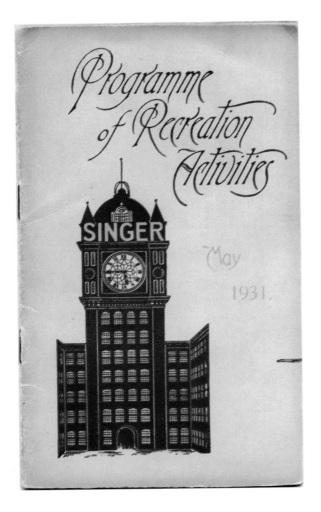

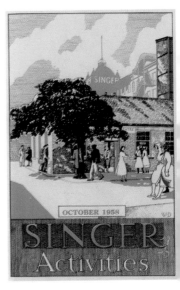

Plates 9
Recreation Activities booklets
Clockwise from above:
Programme of Recreation Activities, May 1931
Singer Recreation Activities, January 1938
Singer Activities, October 1958.

Maxton and others. His socialism was grounded in much of what he found here as he approved Maxton's declaration that he could 'ask for no greater job in life [than to transform] the English-ridden, capitalist-ridden, landlord-ridden Scotland, into a Scottish Socialist Commonwealth'.

John Maclean himself has been the subject of poems, elegies and eulogies by many of the major poets of twentieth-century Scottish literature. Hugh MacDiarmid, Sydney Goodsir Smith and Edwin Morgan all wrote stunning poems in praise of him, and Hamish Henderson's 'John Maclean March' is still a popular song in many quarters. MacDiarmid's poem calls passionately for justice to be delivered on the brutish officials who sentenced him to jail, effectively his 'murderers'. Morgan's poem, considering the courageous self-determination and independent spirit Maclean embodied in terms of the value of education for the Scottish working class, finally comes to a marvellous affirmation quoting Maclean's own words:

'We are out
for life and all that life can give us'

was what he said, that's what he said.

The tough spirit of working-class determination to demand and fight for a better way of life persisted in the area and its legacy was vibrant in the 1970s, when the nine-month work-in at Upper Clyde Shipbuilders in 1971–2 made Jimmy Reid (b. 1932) a household name. Reid's autobiographical writings and speeches, collected in *Reflections of a Clyde-built Man* (1976), are a literary encapsulation of that fierce and undaunted spirit and a record of a key moment in modern history. As Paul Maloney discusses in chapter 8, the highly influential musical play *The Great Northern Welly Boot Show* (1972), with script by Tom Buchan and music by Tom McGrath, was based on the UCS work-in. Inspired by this show, John McGrath set up a Scottish version of his 7:84 Theatre Company and this soon presented his popular play *The Game's a Bogey: 7:84's John Maclean Show* (1973). This combined stark and plainly quoted statements by Maclean from the early decades of the twentieth century with a harsh satirical presentation of the exploitation of a working-class couple in the 1970s idiom of mass-media commercialised sensationalist 'entertainment'. The play remains an indictment of the capitalism with which it was contemporary and, simultaneously, a testament to the enduring value of Maclean's position as he stood against the entrancements of the capitalism of his own era.[32]

Tom Buchan, author of *The Great Northern Welly Boot Show*, was also, incidentally, a fine poet and author of 'The Low Road', a stunning short poem from the late 1960s. In this, his persona, Walter Bohannan, is depicted: 'he held onto a birch branch / by yon bonny banks and looked down', imagining the lochside mountains 'drilled with caves' and describing the effect of an 'underwater burst' of nuclear weaponry upon the entire area. No boundaries are secure in such a scenario.[33]

A beautifully crafted saga of Clydebank taking in the range of another war-shadowed historical context is Meg Henderson's novel *The Holy City* (1997). This takes its central character, Marion Katie MacLeod, from the horrors of the Clydebank Blitz, when, as a young girl, she loses all her immediate family, through to the early 1970s. It is a stunning evocation of the divisions and loyalties brought about by class and religion, the human value of such loyalties and the bitter waste occasioned by their cost and exclusivity. The characters are memorable and brilliantly drawn, the great scenes (including the descriptions of the Blitz itself) are tense and fraught with suspense and depth, and, if the ending risks appearing wishful, one feels nevertheless that it has been earned. Some of the most horrific passages relate to the cynicism with which the working people were treated by their managers and by the Ministry of War in Westminster. Henderson describes the effects of asbestosis on Marion's husband without sentimentalising. The police are seen obeying orders by removing innocent Italians as 'alien' threats, but are also sensitive enough not to intrude on a woman's grief, standing beside her in sympathetic solidarity as she weeps in grief after the bombs have dropped. Henderson also describes dispassionately the way in which the RAF saw Clydebank as 'bait': 'As the uniformed men were cannon fodder, the civilians were bomb fodder.'

> With precise co-ordinates the Germans were able to send out a radio-navigational beam to the target area for their bombers to follow. The boffins on our side could not only pick it up, but they could 'bend' the beam [. . .] Hindsight is a wonderful thing, but no matter how many times Marion considered it over the years since, it seemed incredible, unforgivable, that no one thought Clydebank would one day get hit. There was all that important industry, the shipyards and the munitions factories in the Clyde, and by 'bending the beam' away from English cities, like London, Liverpool, Manchester and Birmingham, the Luftwaffe had a clear run to Clydeside. Why did no one spot it?[34]

The previous year, when 'the beam was on' for Liverpool, the population, forewarned and fleeing the city, were forced back by the military and police setting up roadblocks. Clydebank was not forewarned. The 'We can take it' myth was born, while the reality was that 'the people took it because they were forced to take it'. *The Holy City* burns with indignation equal to the compassion Henderson sustains for her characters, their resourcefulness, strengths and the pathos of their lives.

Similar qualities can be seen in the art of Muirhead Bone, Stanley Spencer and Hugh Adam Crawford. Bone (1876–1953), in his paintings and etchings of industrial Glasgow, delivered perhaps the major nineteenth-century artistic engagement with city life. In 1916 he became a war artist, working on the Western Front, registering the terrible anonymity and ephemerality of human lives in *British Troops Marching on the Somme*, for example. When he worked in the Clyde shipyards in 1917, his drawings and lithographs were collected in three sets: 'Building a Ship', 'On the Clyde' and 'With the Grand Fleet'. These were a significant influence on Stanley Spencer, who, possibly directly prompted by Bone, began work on Clydeside during the Second World War.

Spencer painted a major series of studies of Clydeside tradespeople at work in the period, including *Burners* (1941). These striking figures are depicted actively, intensely and attentively at work, working with great slabs of iron and steel in the process of shipbuilding, their faces masked by protective eye-guards, their hands and arms moving with precision and weight, experts in the use of machinery, familiar with the industrial world which would seem inimical to their own health, even as they create the great ships designed for more publicly celebrated acts of massive destruction. Appointed by the War Artists' Advisory Committee, Spencer threw himself enthusiastically into producing a series of pictures celebrating the activities of the shipyard workers through the early 1940s. By 1943, though, he began to turn his attention to Port Glasgow, and the later canvases in the 'Shipbuilding' series begin to show his interest moving more towards the semi-abstract formalities and shapes to be found among shipyard objects: human engagement represented in the almost religious intensities of the activities of *Burners* gives way to less urgent presence in *Plumbers* and *Riggers*. Nevertheless, the whole 'Shipbuilding' series is arguably the major sustained achievement of a war artist intent on bringing the lives and efforts of these people to full artistic presence. Spencer presents their pathos, strenuous effort, physical strength and sheer determination without caricature or exaggeration of their vulnerability. Their fragile place in the expendable human economy of war is weighed against their courage. Yet the paintings themselves remain determined in their distance, objectifying the heat of human effort with a cold, measuring eye, at the same time as they record the emotional commitment of a whole generation of working people. By contrast, in the paintings of Ian Fleming, images of Glasgow and Clydebank streets after the Blitz are poignantly and unequivocally elegiac expressions of the epic resources of people whose struggle to survive amid such devastation remains potently haunting.

Hugh Adam Crawford (1898–1982), in his *Homage to Clydebank* (1941, also known as *The Stretcher Bearers*; see Plate 3), shows the stretcher-bearers carrying a covered body through crowds of helmeted soldiers, broken buildings and fallen planks. In the angle of their heads, the determination in their shoulders and necks, these men are intent on saving lives in a context of dehumanising obliteration. The ability to represent the social consequences of such devastation, along with such qualities of individuated human dignity, is a powerful statement about what survives such horror. Crawford was a significant influence on Joan Eardley, whose figurative paintings, and later seascapes, are always attentive to that same quality of individuated humanity in the context of the inimical elements of the world, both natural and man-made. Crawford joined Glasgow School of Art in 1925 and taught 'The Two Roberts', Colquhoun and MacBryde. The interest he held in the work of Piero della Francesca and Cézanne delivered a blend of understated dignity and the energy of momentary activity that remains particularly moving in such paintings as *Homage to Clydebank*.

A different kind of intensity is conveyed by Tom McKendrick (b. 1948) in *Terrace* (1986), which depicts the terraced buildings, the homes of the people of Clydebank, going up in flames at the time of the Blitz. It is a vision of hellish destruction, dazzling and horrific. Under the night sky, leaning down as if showering its darkness on the dwellings below, the middle band of the canvas is blistering with yellow flame, red heat and black smoke. A line of terraced houses can be seen on the horizon, broken up by fire, while another line in the foreground shows the chimneys supported only by the frames of the buildings, the windows gaping, opening into the white heat of the flames. McKendrick has said that when he was growing up in Clydebank,

> it was impossible to avoid the fact that this small town had been sub-jected to a sustained and brutal attack. Only eight houses out of twelve thousand remained intact after the raids, which lasted two nights. There was still plenty of evidence lying around in the fifties and well into the sixties [. . .] and Friday afternoon siren practice when the whole town stilled [was] haunted by the horror of a memory fresh in the minds of many.[35]

A. J. Cronin (1896–1981) was born on 19 July at Rosebank Cottage, Cardross. His father, an insurance agent and travelling margarine salesman, was Irish Catholic; his mother, Scots Protestant, a travelling saleswoman and the first woman public health visitor with Glasgow Corporation. When his father died, Cronin was still a child and he and his mother moved to Willowbrook, near Miller's Farm on the Roundriding Road, Dumbarton. Torn between the different faiths of his parents, he was known as the 'Wee Pope' at Dumbarton Academy (Church Street). He studied medicine at Glasgow University (like Smollett), then married fellow student Agnes Mary Gibson (1925) and became a general practitioner in Harley Street, London (1926–30). He started writing after his own health began to give way with a duodenal ulcer in 1930. On 15 August 1930, he wrote to Dumbarton Library:

> I am an old Dumbarton Academy boy and enclose my card. At present I am on holiday [he was recuperating at Dalchenna Farm, near Inveraray, Argyll]. I am engaged at the moment on a piece of writing and require some information regarding conditions in the Dumbarton shipyards fifty years ago. Would it be possible to get any details from books in your library? If so, I would come down and consult them if you would be kind enough to let me know a suitable time.[36]

He was working on the book which brought him considerable fame – or notoriety – the neo-Gothic *Grand-Guignol* tragedy *Hatter's Castle* (1931), about the rise and fall of a small-town commercial tyrant. Set in Levenford (a thinly disguised Dumbarton), the main character is James Brodie, the town hatter and a patriarchal monster cruelly dominating his family. It is worth noting that Cronin's maternal grandfather, Archibald Montgomerie, owned a hatter's shop at 145 High Street and was considered the model for Brodie. The book alienated Cronin from his mother's family permanently. Other 'Levenford' novels include *The Green Years* (1945) and *Shannon's Way* (1948). *The Green Years*, set in 'Levenford' and 'Drumbuck', was filmed (MGM, directed by Leon Gordon) in 1946. The American writer James Agee commented,

> It has been described in the ads as 'wonderful' by everyone within Louis B. Mayer's purchasing power except his horses, so I hesitate to ask you to take my word for it: the picture is awful.

It came in for more detailed, even more scathing, criticism from Hugh MacDiarmid in his essay 'Films and the Scottish Novelist' especially for its 'atrocious falsity' in Scots pronunciation, while the novel on which it was

Figure 12 A. J. Cronin.

based displays 'what is wrong with the majority of Scottish novelists' (of whom Cronin is 'the worst'):

> They are all forced to distort the content of Scottish life in order to make it conform to some desperate personal wish-fulfilment, or flee from it entirely – into the past, into fantasy, or some other reality-surrogate.

In MacDiarmid's opinion, Cronin's work was 'valueless' and the film 'devoid of verisimilitude and false to the actualities of our country': a 'witless parody due to sheer incompetence'.[37]

Cronin went on to write numerous stories about Dr Finlay, the fictional GP of the equally fictional small Scottish town of Tannochbrae, which were adapted into an internationally popular 1960s television series (a revised version, set later in the century, was televised in the 1990s). Thus, his writing career was related to – if not based on – both the anti-kailyard austerities of George Douglas Brown's *The House with the Green Shutters* (1901) or John MacDougall Hay's *Gillespie* (1914) and the sentimental vision of small-town Scotland promulgated in the 'kailyard' fiction of the ministers S. R. Crockett and Ian Maclaren, immensely popular in the 1890s and the early twentieth century. Far from suffering from 'belatedness', however, Cronin's writing career was a commercial success-story. He was one of the most highly paid Scottish writers of his era. Other best-selling novels included *The Citadel* (1937), *The Stars Look Down* (1941) and *The Spanish Gardener* (1950). When he died on 6 January 1981, he was a tax exile in Switzerland.

Born in Dunbartonshire in 1934, Tom Gallacher was recognised first as an important playwright. He entered theatre through his connection with Dumbarton People's Theatre (founded in 1945 in succession to the Scottish People's Theatre). This company nurtured his developing talent, and he wrote and directed a number of times in the 1950s and 1960s for it. His serious-minded but gamesome, often funny, stage-plays began to be professionally produced with *Our Kindness to Five Persons* in 1969 and he attracted considerable critical praise in the 1970s. *Mr Joyce is leaving Paris* (1970, published 1972) is set in two acts in Trieste and Paris and significantly predates Tom Stoppard's more famous *Travesties* (1974, set in Zurich and having Joyce as a main character). Gallacher's play is a biography-based study of the value of art measured against the cost of personal well-being and family priorities. Its portrait of a Joyce whose ability to turn adversity into creative opportunity and whose ruthless exploitation of the loyalty of others did not cancel or invalidate an almost superstitious sense of trust, blends with a Joyce whose wit, charm and engaging brio lift the spirit from guilt-wrack and despondency. The play's familiarity with its literary contexts and its dramaturgic self-confidence remain impressive and the vicissitudes of self-pity, self-doubt and self-laceration Joyce experienced give way finally and justly to the resolution of his closing lines: 'I was equipped to explore . . . And it's explorer I'll make of every man in the crew before I'm done.'

Revival! (1972) and *Schellenbrack* (1973) were published together in 1978 and share similar themes. *Revival!* is set in a studio in an old London theatre where a retired actor-manager, having been told he has only a month to live, plans a final production of Ibsen's *The Master Builder*, which will climax in his own on-stage suicide. Intensely clever and admirably twisted in plot as the story unfolds, it is a complex, positive pleasure: nothing morbid can be trusted, as the exclamatory title suggests. The title-character in *Schellenbrack* is another reclusive thinker in a domestic situation, surrounded by intellectual subordinates who are both distracting and necessary. Gallacher's attempt to present the literary intellectual on stage is rare, courageous and unusually successful. His many other plays showed similar originality and verve.

His trilogy in prose fiction, *Apprentice* (1983), *Journeyman* (1984) and *Survivor* (1985) amount to a brilliant triptych, told in a first book of inter-related short stories and two full novels, each of which deepens and helps to explain the others. The central figure is Bill Thompson, working in the Clyde shipyards in the 1950s. But he is an outsider and his unfamiliarity with the people, language and culture of the place help the reader into a more respectful and intimate understanding of the world in which Bill finds himself. But the trilogy is more than social portraiture and industrial working-class cityscape. The second book takes us to Montreal at the time of the garish 'Expo 67' where large crowds hide intimate secrets about family past failures, inadequacies and hopes. Thompson has jumped ship and is hiding out from his father's ambitions for him, but the friends he makes in his small bed-sit accommodation lead him to a realisation about how there is an inescapable need to face things that no evasion can answer. Part mystery-story, part social portrait, part psychological analysis, the light, strong way that *Journeyman* picks up the threads of *Apprentice* and weaves them cleverly into a completely compelling narrative remains memorable.

Survivor carries the story through to a resolution as Bill returns to Britain after his ship has gone down with the loss of five lives. He finds himself forced to confront his own sense of trust, his professional integrity, the authority of his father and the opportunity of love. As the investigation into the sinking of the ship progresses, a compelling new character emerges who helps guide the novel to its conclusion: Howard Murray, a playwright and undefined-as-such detective, brings a new charisma to the trilogy and Gallacher carried him forward to be the central character in *The Jewel Maker* (1986), another book of interlinked short stories set in Dublin, London, a Highland cottage, New York and Copenhagen.

Working largely outside of conventional genres and dealing with mater-ial beyond familiar expectations, Gallacher's work is exceptionally good. The writing is lucid, calm, beautifully judged in its knowing precisely what to reveal, what to withhold, as the reader moves delightedly through the complex layers of the stories, becoming more deeply familiar with the characters as they are disclosed. Again, these are very clever works of writing – clever in the best sense: neither condescending nor elitist in their attitude – generous in sympathy but diffident in expression. Gallacher is a singular, constantly engaged and under-rated writer who never loses con-nection with the matter-of-factness of reality, but is still committed to exploring its subtleties, its sometimes dark corners, its complexities and waywardnesses. A further novel, *The Wind on the Heath*, was published in the late 1980s. Throughout his lifetime, Gallacher remained a member of Dumbarton People's Theatre, to which he donated part of his royalties for his first professional play, *Our Kindness to Five Persons*, and for whom he directed in 1989 a revival of his *Halloween* (1975). Gallacher, who died in 2001, clearly retained close contacts with his artistic roots and is one of West Dunbartonshire's most distinguished writers.

Douglas Dunn (b. 1942), though more frequently associated with Renfrewshire and Tayside, has a number of poems that connect with Dunbartonshire's industrial work places and their post-industrial consequences. In 'Ballad of the Two Left Hands' he laments the unemployment delivered to working men:

> At noon the work horns sounded through
>   The shipyards on Clyde's shore
> And told men that the day had come
>   When they'd work there no more.

But in 'Clydesiders', the work of the shipbuilders becomes a metaphor for how a poem should be made – 'My poems should be Clyde-built, crude and sure' – and Dunn tells us that he would like to write 'A poetry of nuts and bolts, born, bred, / Embattled by the Clyde, tight and impure'. He evokes something of this masculine Clydeside world effectively:

> Fag-ends in the urinal, Navy Cut
> Of yellow leaf, little boats of Capstan
> Along the trough, blue-bottles on a crust,
> And down the drain, grey ash of smokers' silt.[38]

Even in the secure knowledge that he does not have to live in this world permanently and will go 'back to London', he takes vicarious pleasure in thinking that his 'place' will follow him and dog his footsteps even there.

More deeply haunting and powerful evocations of nearby Greenock are to be found in the poetry of W. S. Graham (1918–86) and John Davidson (1857–1909), while Port Glasgow was the birth place that haunted the memory of James ('B. V.') Thomson (1834–82), author of *The City of Dreadful Night* (1874, a crucial influence on Eliot's *The Waste Land*). These poets are not essentially of Dunbartonshire, but their work is proximate and their favoured places are visible from Dunbartonshire: they are not entirely foreign and are certainly worth noting. In the same way, the poets collected in Tom Leonard's ground-breaking anthology *Radical Renfrew: poetry from the French Revolution to the First World War by poets born, or sometime resident, in the County of Renfrewshire* (1990) should be noted here. This is partly because their work is related to that of Dunbartonshire writers, but, even more importantly, Leonard's rediscovery of their writing was done from Paisley Central Library. It is more than possible that a similar job might be done through assiduous research in Dumbarton, Clydebank, Helensburgh and in local libraries throughout West Dunbartonshire. Who knows what might turn up? Certainly, Scottish literature remains the most under-researched area in modern scholarship and the writing of working-class women and men is perhaps the least-examined part of it.

There are few Dunbartonshire writers anthologised in the voluminous collections of prose and poetry from the late nineteenth century. However, Moira Burgess, in her study *The Glasgow Novel*, lists a number of works that are primarily set in Glasgow, but include episodes set in Dunbartonshire. Among these, worth noting are George Mills's *Craigclutha: a Clydesdale story* (1849) set mainly in Dunbartonshire; *A Prophet's Reward* by Euphans H. Strains (1908), a fine curiosity about the radical reformer Thomas Muir; Elizabeth Taylor's *Blindpits* (3 vols, 1868), which may have been inspired by the Madeleine Smith murder; and J. J. Bell's *Whither Thou Goest* (1908). John Buchan's *Mr Standfast* (1919) includes a vivid description of Clydeside politics at the time of John Maclean and suggests how seriously threatening such politics were to the establishment. *Gael Over Glasgow* (1937) by Edward Shiels is about a young Clydebank-Irish engineer growing up during the depression and includes vivid shipyard scenes. Hugh Munro's *The Clydesiders* (1961) is a novel of the Glasgow shipyards; his *Tribal Town* (1964), *The Keelie* (1978) and his 'Clutha' series about a Glasgow detective are also worth noting, while Douglas Scott's *Die for the Queen* (1981) is about shipbuilding, particularly the building of the *Queen Elizabeth*.

James Kelman's novel *A Disaffection* (1989) centres on a week in the life of Patrick Doyle, a 29-year-old schoolteacher facing up to his own extremes of disillusionment, memory and desire. Early on, Doyle's middle-class angst takes him 'driving along Dumbarton Road in the direction away from the city centre' and reflecting with a hollow snarl that

> Dumbarton was the kind of town you passed through without paying any heed and no doubt it would prove to be the brightest spot in West Central Scotland. Plenty of whisky of course. That was one thing about it, the capital of whisky.

The narrative brings us through Yoker and Clydebank (where Doyle had his first teaching post) to 'the swimming baths at the foot of Kilbowie Road' where 'he used to go for a swim when he was in the middle of a strong get-healthy period'. West Dunbartonshire is a key co-ordinate on the map of Kelman's excursion through the culture of class faultlines, social and personal dystopia and professional collapse to a fragile, precious reckoning of the risks of human vulnerability. It is an austere and grim-minded novel with serious intention and a hard focus.

Kelman is renowned, of course, but other writers, from in and around West Dunbartonshire, or writing about it, are perhaps unjustly neglected. Joe Donnelly's novel *Bane* (1990) is a supernatural thriller set in the ironically named town of 'Haven' (amalgamating Cardross, Helensburgh, Rhu and Garelochhead). The landscapes and setting – including Dumbarton Rock – are crucial, as journalist Nick Ryan discovers the site of an ancient source of evil (in the Rock) and has to find a way of defeating it as he did once before in his childhood. His role is recognised and understood by the local gypsies and the novel sustains a powerful balance of universal conflict and specific localities. An earlier writer now often seemingly forgotten is R. B. Cunninghame Graham (1852–1936), whose ancestral home was at Gartmore. His book *Doughty Deeds: An Account of the Life of Robert Graham of Gartmore, Poet & Politician, 1735–1797, drawn from his Letter-books & Correspondence* (1925) is another example of a neglected writer of considerable interest who borders on the territory of West Dunbartonshire.

More centrally, the poet, critic, broadcaster, anthologist, journalist, conservationist and 'unashamed populariser' Maurice Lindsay (b. 1918) moved to Milton, in 1976, to a wooden box-house on stilts overlooking the Clyde and Renfrew Hills and in the lea of the Kilpatrick Hills. His poem, 'On Milton Hill' begins:

Since I moved up to live among the birds,
gathering round my house their shawl of woods,
trees have turned staves where notes and dotted wings
measure the movements each new season brings,
phrasing the round of fields and sky, the moods
that seas and clouds whip up, or fleck like curds.[39]

Lindsay is guilty of overwriting sometimes but there is a memorable truth in his description of the renewing joy to be experienced after a miserable attempt to get a caravan into its position in a field by Ross Loan by Loch Lomond on a day when torrential rain had made all fields and roads quagmires of mud. Later, walking down to the lochside, a drizzling mist rolls down and obliterates everything:

Figure 13 Maurice Lindsay (in centre).

The air seemed to hang about me, soft and humid, the resinous smell of the damp trees giving off a fine, fragrant sweetness. Raindrops sat upon the spikes of the burgeoning blackthorn hedges, like tiny crystal blooms; the barks of the trees gleamed eagerly; the brown earth drank in the muddy gurgling moisture. Suddenly a blackbird burst out singing, as if Time itself depended on his song. No one who cannot enjoy the varied pleasures of wet weather can ever really hope to appreciate Scotland.[40]

Lindsay's associations with the old county of Dunbartonshire go back further, however, both ancestrally and in his own time, as he also lived in the area in the 1950s. He reports that Milngavie in the early 1950s boasted a remarkably healthy musical life:

Six times or so every year, the Parish Church Hall takes in three hundred people who have come to listen to chamber music performed by the leading ensembles of the day. Although the setting is by no means ideal – the chairs are as peculiarly uncomfortable as the seats of music-lovers, by Victorian tradition, ought to be; and the steeple clock has a habit of interrupting the sublimest utterances of the world's greatest musical minds with its mundane pronouncements of the hour – nevertheless, the achievement is astonishing. Glasgow, for all its millions, cannot raise an audience half that size for similar concerts, and I doubt if the position is very different in any English city furth of London.[41]

Lindsay's poems often describe his Dunbartonshire homes, and his autobiography, *Thank You For Having Me* (1983), devotes a full chapter to his life in the area in the 1950s. In his collection *Worlds Apart* (2000), a sequence of poems entitled 'Clyde Built' recollects the shipyard-workers, when Lindsay travelled at four each afternoon by steam train from Balloch to Clydebank to write for the daily press, but then moves forward to a more contemporary scene in which he asks, 'Does no one harbour any sense of guilt / in making unemployed that phrase – *Clyde Built*?' In his autobiographical poem, 'A Net to Catch the Winds' (1981), he writes:

My richest years were spent at Gartocharn;
Loch Lomond jagging distance blue with hills
endlessly ripping clouds that winds re-darn,
and gathering burns from winter's former chills.
Down battered rock and brackened ridge they churn,
hanging a silence white on distant rills,
shouldering thickened valleys far below,
their journey's breathing born of frozen snow.[42]

The autobiography itself gives details of Lindsay's Dunbartonshire ancestors and offers an amusingly anecdotal self-ironising account of his own family life at Gartocharn. His visitors included the poets George Bruce, George Barker and Dom Moraes; his domestic animals included the basset hounds written about amiably by Edwin Morgan in his poem, 'An Addition to the Family'. In his years there, Lindsay wrote voluminously, not only poetry but his *Burns Encyclopedia*, a great deal of journalism and a successful verse play in Scots, based on the James Macpherson version of the Ossianic legend of *Fingal and Comala*, broadcast twice by the BBC and staged in 1953.

A more transient resident was the playwright James Bridie (O. H. Mavor, 1888–1951). After he retired from medical practice in Glasgow, he lived at Rockbank, near Helensburgh, and was a near-neighbour of Lindsay at Gartocharn when he bought the estate of Finnich Malaise. He later moved to Craigendoran, his home at the time of his relatively early death in 1951.

Someone with much closer, even if apparently similarly transient, links to the area is Iain Crichton Smith (1928–98). Best known as a poet associated with the Isle of Lewis in the Outer Hebrides, where he went to school, he was, nonetheless, born in Glasgow. After schooling in Lewis, a degree from Aberdeen University and teacher-training at Jordanhill, he completed two years of national service before rejoining his mother and younger brother and for three years, from 1952 to 1955, he lived in Dumbarton and commuted by train to work as a schoolteacher in Clydebank. It was in West Dunbartonshire that some of his most famous early poems were written, collected in his first substantial book, *The Long River* (1955). In his essay 'Between Sea and Moor' he talks about the intense, complex images of Lewis that surfaced in reminiscence and led to the poetry of this period:

Some days were running legs and joy
and old men telling tomorrow would be
a fine day surely: for sky was red
at setting of sun between the hills.[43]

In 1986, Crichton Smith published a book of retrospective autobiographical poetry, *A Life*, in which his experience in West Dunbartonshire is evoked in four poems. He describes the humdrum ordinariness of his teaching 'adjective clause, the adverbial and the noun', and his urban context, 'In pale neon / where tenements sag brokenly: or at noon / where they burn like cages', and contrasts the girls shining with lipstick to idyllic images of the classical world. In the classroom, 'he superimposed / the texts of Greece, the scholars' monotone' while 'Beyond his window a cloud snottily flows'. His memory snapshots images:

The unpredictable flashes of girls' knees,
the curves of football that transcend all rule,
the poetry of the Clyde so silvery cool –
down sudden avenues green crowns of trees.

The nocturnal cityscape of the industrialised world is memorably held in contrast with the imagery and intellectual apprehension of the ancients:

Cloth-capped Glaswegians with their spotted hounds –
Great Homer and his pride

The vested hairy-chested boilerman
soaping his body in the kitchen sink –
The libraries and tomes.

Crichton Smith is adept at moving in for close-focus shots then pulling back to balance them in the context of his remembered geography:

> Seen here from green Argyll, the city is
> A yellow labyrinth where each winking house
> Composed a bracelet of pure randomness.

The 'scholarly lamp-posts' watch with 'viperish light' while the 'trains sang / and whined like wolves along predestined rails' and the poet, alienated from his surroundings and feeling his solitary spirit fail among 'garish ads' and 'The watery twilight of a million souls', asks himself finally, 'Where is home?' and answers:

> Not in this place with its tubercular bloom.
> The city is a painted yellow room
>
> for actors without denouement. I stand
> inside the Underground. There's a hollow sound.
> The whooshing train casts papers to the wind.

In 'Luss Village', the material reality of Crichton Smith's world seems to permit no visionary or mythic component. (It is worth noting, though, that Ken Russell's flamboyant, flippant, visionary 1974 film biography *Mahler* was filmed near Luss.) He writes in contrast to the Romantic visions of Scott and the nineteenth-century artists, in which the landscape was imbued with metaphoric import, castles, cliffs, stormy lochs and forests betokening wilderness and the frailty of social conventions. For this post-Second World War poet, reality is diminished to bleak and undisturbed parameters. Old people 'are happy / in morphean air like gold-fish in a bowl' and 'roses trail their margins down a sleepy / medieval treatise on the slumbering soul',

> And even the water, fabulously silent,
> Has no salt tales to tell us, nor makes jokes
> About the yokel mountains, huge and patient,
> That will not court her but read shadowy books.

This is 'A world so long departed!' in which Crichton Smith's disengagement is gentle, ironic, perhaps fond, but certainly untempted by excess. In 'Dunoon and the Holy Loch' the social causes of such depression are clear enough:

The huge sea widens from us, mile on mile.
Kenneth MacKellar sings from the domed pier.
A tinker plays a ragged tune
on ragged pipes. He tramps under a moon
which rises like the dollar. Think how here
missiles like sugar rocks are all incised
with Alabaman Homer. These defend
the clattering tills, the taxis, thin pale girls
who wear at evening their Woolworth pearls
and from dewed railings gaze at the world's end.

There is nothing sublime or exalted in this vision.

From Dunbartonshire, Crichton Smith moved to Oban, where he continued working as a teacher from 1955 to 1982, when he took retirement to continue to write full-time until his death in 1998. In 2001, Stewart Conn edited a collection of his quasi-autobiographical stories, *Murdo: The Life and Works*. In his introduction, Conn describes how the creation of the character of Murdo allowed Crichton Smith to distance himself from the painful experiences of depression, illness and disillusionment that he suffered in the early 1980s. 'Murdo' became the character by whom Crichton Smith could write about himself and his Scotland with the assurance of a quizzical eye, strengthened by a sense of surreal absurdity. *Murdo* appeared in 1981, *Thoughts of Murdo* in 1993, and in *Murdo: The Life and Works*, the previously unpublished, posthumous 'Life of Murdo' was added to the collection. This is a lucid, gently edged and compassionate autobiography. Here, Crichton Smith describes his experience in West Dunbartonshire clearly:

> Murdo and his mother and his younger brother moved into a new Council flat on the outskirts of Dumbarton on the Helensburgh road. It was the top flat and it was new. Never had they had a house like this. It was even on the edge of the country.
>
> Murdo's mother was happy. She went to her Free Church and she had friends. Murdo became a teacher at Clydebank High School, travelling thereto by train every day.
>
> Was he happy there? Not really.[44]

Crichton Smith describes himself as Murdo attempting to teach in a geography lesson the story of the fishing industry:

> Mackerel, he would say knowledgably, are surface fish and cod are ground fish (or the other way round). Leafing through one of the

answers he found the following: 'Mackerel and herring are surface fish; ground fish are cod, haddock and fillet'. (Thus does the fish and chip shop take revenge on academe.)

His frustrations at teaching parallel his gathering of the poems that were to go into *The Long River*. Increasingly, however, he felt ill-at-ease in Dumbarton and the move to Oban was, for him, a return to the Highlands and the sea, a leavetaking from the industrialised city and a reoccupation of more breathable air.

A bleak vision of the industrialised and increasingly post-industrialised areas around and near Dumbarton and Greenock, which Crichton Smith would have recognised, is presented in Peter McDougall's play for television, *Down Where the Buffalo Go* (broadcast 1988). Starring Harvey Keitel as a US serviceman whose marriage to a local woman has broken down, the play depicts American ships and submarines with their nuclear weapons in the 1980s in the context of alienated Scots and Americans, families and individuals, including naval and military officers. It presents a deeply depressing assessment of the human cost and the massive futility of such weaponry.[45] But, beyond the historical particulars of military occupation and the ethos of warfare, literature, poetry and the arts offer timeless moments of celebration and commemoration. Two examples demonstrate this conclusively.

A Journey down the Clyde, written and illustrated by Scoular Anderson, is a charming children's book, beginning in the Lowther Hills, where children on a family picnic lose a little red ball into the river. By the end of the book, it is floating past the Heads of Ayr and Ailsa Craig is on the horizon. As it passes down through Glasgow, we see the shipyards, lighthouses, notable buildings and the paddle-steamer *Waverley* cruising by Dumbarton Rock. The coastal seascape of West Dunbartonshire is beautifully captured and seen as part of the river's story. The particular places and the universal image of the river's course from source to sea are lovingly evoked in Anderson's words and pictures.[46]

Similarly, the first National Poet of Scotland, Edwin Morgan (b. 1920), in the love poems of his book *The Second Life* (1968), reaches beyond the specifics of any individual love affair and any actual location to affirm feelings and convictions recognisable to anyone who has ever been in love. 'The Unspoken', 'From a City Balcony', 'When You Go' and 'Strawberries' are poems of this kind. The latter begins:

There were never strawberries
like the ones we had
that sultry afternoon
sitting on the step
of the open french window [. . .]

And at the end of the poem, the reference to Dunbartonshire's hills as they overlook the Glasgow that was Morgan's favoured place throughout his writing and life, sharpens the poignant sense of human immediacy and transience:

let the sun beat
on our forgetfulness
one hour of all
the heat intense
and summer lightning
on the Kilpatrick hills

let the storm wash the plates[47]

It is a conclusive reminder of the complementarity of specific reference and universal significance: the named place has a universal resonance heightened in the memory by the virtue of art. The triangular territory of West Dunbartonshire certainly has encompassed, as we began by noting, one of the richest and most varied literary and artistic histories in Scotland. It still continues to encompass and inspire some of the very best contemporary writing and art.

NOTES

1 See MacMillan, Duncan (1990), *Scottish Art 1460–1990* (Edinburgh: Mainstream), pp. 145–7.
2 See Purser, John (1992), *Scotland's Music* (Edinburgh: Mainstream), pp. 73–4 and *Scotland's Music* (2 CDs), Linn CKD 008 (Disc One, Track 7); Macpherson, James (2002) *The Poems of Ossian and Related Works*, edited by Howard Gaskill with an introduction by Fiona Stafford (Edinburgh: Edinburgh University Press); Gregory, Lady [1904], *Gods and Fighting Men: The Story of the Tuatha de Danaan and of the Fianna of Ireland* (Gerrards Cross: Colin Smythe, 1976); Gregory, Lady [1902], *Cuchulain of Muirthemne* (Gerrards Cross: Colin Smythe, 1976); Heaney, Marie (1994), *Over Nine Waves: A Book of Irish Legends* (London: Faber & Faber); Chisholm,

Erik, 'Night Song of the Bards', on *Erik Chisholm: Piano Music*, Olympia OCD639.

3   Clancy, Thomas Owen (ed.) (1998), *The Triumph Tree: Scotland's Earliest Poetry AD 550–1350* (Edinburgh: Canongate), pp. 46–78 (p. 46).

4   See Admonán of Iona, *Life of St Columba*, translated by Richard Sharpe (London: Penguin Books, 1995); Ashe, Geoffrey (1983), *A Guidebook to Arthurian Britain* (Wellingborough, Northamptonshire: The Aquarian Press); MacIvor, Iain (1981), *Official Guide to Dumbarton Castle* (Edinburgh: HMSO).

5   For references in the preceding paragraphs, see Lindsay, Maurice (1979), *The Lowlands of Scotland: Glasgow and the North* (London: Robert Hale); Barbour's *Bruce* and Blind Harry's *Wallace* are published in modern editions by Canongate and Nigel Tranter's historical novels were paperbacked by Hodder Fawcett.

6   Lyndsay, Sir David (2000), 'Squyer Meldrum', in *Selected Poems*, ed. Janet Hadley Williams (Glasgow: Association for Scottish Literary Studies), pp. 128–74 (pp. 161–2).

7   Defoe Daniel [1724–6] (1979), *A Tour through the Whole Island of Great Britain*, ed. Pat Rogers (Harmondsworth: Penguin Books), pp. 677–8.

8   For reference to 'The Bonnie, Bonnie Banks of Loch Lomond', see Lindsay, Maurice (1979) *The Lowlands of Scotland: Glasgow and the North* (London: Robert Hale), p. 95.

9   Hogg, James (1981), *Highland Tours*, ed. William F. Laughlan (Hawick: Byway Books), p. 125.

10 For references to Smollett and Dunbartonshire I am particularly indebted to Dr Gerard Carruthers, who supplied me with a copy of Stott, Louis (1981), *Smollett's Scotland: An Illustrated Guide for Visitors* (Dumbarton: Dumbarton District Libraries,), as well as other valuable suggestions. Good editions of Smollett are easily available from Oxford University Press and other publishers.

11 Stott, Louis (1981), *Smollett's Scotland: An Illustrated Guide for Visitors* (Dumbarton: Dumbarton District Libraries), p. 15.

12 Stott, Louis (1981), *Smollett's Scotland: An Illustrated Guide for Visitors* (Dumbarton: Dumbarton District Libraries), p. 10.

13 Stott, Louis (1981), *Smollett's Scotland: An Illustrated Guide for Visitors* (Dumbarton: Dumbarton District Libraries), p. 30.

14 Lindsay, Maurice (1979), *The Lowlands of Scotland: Glasgow and the North* (London: Robert Hale), p. 90.

15 Hopkins, Gerard Manley, 'Inversnaid', in *Selected Poems*, ed. James Reeves (London: Heinemann, 1975), p. 51.

16 Cairney, John (2000), *On the Trail of Robert Burns* (Edinburgh: Luath Press), pp. 60–2.

17 Mackay, James (1993), *Burns: A Biography of Robert Burns* (London: Headline). See esp. pp. 324–7.

18 Wordsworth, Dorothy [1804] (1973), *A Tour in Scotland in 1803* (Edinburgh: James Thin at the Mercat Press), esp. pp. 55–75.

19 Riach, Alan (2004), 'The Whistler's Story: Tragedy and the Enlightenment Imagination in *The Heart of Midlothian*', *Studies in Scottish Literature*, vols xxxiii–xxxiv, ed. G. Ross Roy (Columbia, South Carolina: University of South Carolina), pp. 308–19; and Riach, Alan (2005), *Representing Scotland in Literature, Popular Culture and Iconography: The Masks of the Modern Nation* (London: Palgrave Macmillan), pp. 75–87.

20 See Smith, Bill, Smailes, Helen and Campbell, Mungo (1995), *Hidden Assets: Scottish Paintings from the Flemings Collection* (Edinburgh: National Galleries of Scotland); Bilcliffe, Roger (1989), *The Scottish Colourists* (London: John Murray); MacMillan, Duncan (1990), *Scottish Art 1460–1990* (Edinburgh: Mainstream).

21 For the Andersen story, see Ransom, J. G. (2004), *Loch Lomond and the Trossachs in History and Legend* (Edinburgh: John Donald), pp. 7–9. Verne's novel is entitled *Child of the Cavern*, or *The Underground City* or the *Black Indies* [or, *Strange Doings Underground*], translated by W. H. G. Kingston (London: S. Low, Marston, Seattle & Rivington, 1877) and is available from Project Gutenberg, website http://promo.net/pg/

22 Bold, Alan (1989), *Scotland: A Literary Guide* (London: Routledge), p. 170.

23 Hackney, Fiona and Isla (1989), *Charles Rennie Mackintosh* (London: The Apple Press).

24 Munro, Neil (1907), *The Clyde: River and Firth* (London: A. & C. Black), pp. 96–7.

25 See Gifford, Douglas and Riach, Alan (eds) (2004), *Scotlands: Poets and the Nation* (Manchester and Edinburgh: Carcanet and the Scottish Poetry Library), p. 104.

26 See Whyte, Hamish (ed.) (1983), *Noise and Smoky Breath: An Illustrated Anthology of Glasgow Poems 1900–1983* (Glasgow: Third Eye Centre and Glasgow District Libraries Publications Board), pp. 19–20.

27 Bold, Alan (1989), *Scotland: A Literary Guide* (London: Routledge), pp. 171–2.

28 Jenkins, Robin (1979), *Fergus Lamont* (Edinburgh: Canongate), pp. 287–93; see also Calder, Angus (1992), *The Myth of the Blitz* (London: Pimlico), pp. 170–2.

29 MacDiarmid, Hugh, 'On the Imminent Destruction of London, June 1940', pp. 42–3; 'The German Bombers', p. 45, in *The Revolutionary Art of the Future: rediscovered Poems*, ed. Manson, Grieve and Riach (Manchester and Edinburgh: Carcanet and the Scottish Poetry Library, 2003).

30 MacDiarmid, Hugh, 'Here's How: A Glasgow Story', in *Annals of the Five Senses and Other Stories, Sketches and Plays*, ed. Roderick Watson and Alan Riach (Manchester: Carcanet, 1999), pp. 246–8.

31 MacDiarmid, Hugh, 'Die Grenzsituation', in *Complete Poems* (2 vols) vol. 2, ed. W. R. Aitken and M. Grieve (Manchester: Carcanet, 1994), p. 1331.

32 Morgan, Edwin, 'On John Maclean', in *Collected Poems* (Manchester: Carcanet, 1996), pp. 350–1; MacDiarmid, Hugh, 'John Maclean (1879–1923)', in *Complete Poems* (2 vols), vol. 1, ed. Grieve and Aitken (Manchester: Carcanet, 1993), pp. 485–7; Henderson, Hamish, 'The John Maclean March', recorded on

Freedom come all ye: the poems & songs of Hamish Henderson (Claddagh Records, 1976); Goodsir Smith, Sydney, 'John Maclean Martyr' and 'Ballant o' John Maclean', in *Collected Poems* (London: John Calder, 1975), pp. 44–6; McGrath, John, *The Game's a Bogey: 7:84's John Maclean Show* (Edinburgh: EUSPB, 1975).

33 Buchan, Tom (1969), 'The Low Road', in *Dolphins at Cochin* (London: Barrie & Rockliff at The Cresset Press), pp. 48–9.

34 Henderson, Meg, *The Holy City* (London: Flamingo, 1997), see esp. pp. 59–61.

35 See Bell, Keith et al. (1980), *Stanley Spencer RA* (London: Royal Academy of Arts and Weidenfeld & Nicolson); McKendrick, Tom, quoted in *Scotland's Art* (Edinburgh: City of Edinburgh Museums and Galleries, 1999), p. 106.

36 See Bold, Alan (1989), *Scotland: A Literary Guide* (London: Routledge), pp. 71–2.

37 MacDiarmid, Hugh, 'Films and the Scottish Novelist', in *The Raucle Tongue: Hitherto Uncollected Prose*, ed. Calder, Murray and Riach (Manchester: Carcanet, 1998), pp. 107–9. See also Halliwell, Leslie, 'The Green Years', in *Halliwell's Film Guide*, ed. John Walker (London: HarperCollins, eighth edition, 1991), p. 465.

38 Dunn, Douglas, 'Ballad of the Two Left Hands', p. 126; 'Clydesiders', p. 83, in *Selected Poems* (London: Faber & Faber, 1986).

39 Lindsay, Maurice, *Collected Poems 1940–1990* (Aberdeen: Aberdeen University Press, 1990), p. 108.

40 Lindsay, Maurice (1979), *The Lowlands of Scotland: Glasgow and the North* (London: Robert Hale), p. 96.

41 Lindsay, Maurice (1979), *The Lowlands of Scotland: Glasgow and the North* (London: Robert Hale), p. 80.

42 Lindsay, Maurice, *Collected Poems 1940–1990* (Aberdeen: Aberdeen University Press, 1990), p. 152.

43 Smith, Iain Crichton, ' "Some days were running legs" ', p. 2; 'Luss Village', pp. 19–20; poems from *A Life*, pp. 259–61, in *Collected Poems* (Manchester: Carcanet, 1992).

44 Smith, Iain Crichton (2001), *Murdo: The Life and Works*, ed. Stewart Conn (Edinburgh: Birlinn), pp. 214–19.

45 See Petrie, Duncan (2000), *Screening Scotland* (London: British Film Institute Publishing), p. 139.

46 Anderson, Scoular (1990), *A Journey Down the Clyde* (Glasgow: Richard Drew).

47 Morgan, Edwin, 'Strawberries', in *Collected Poems* (Manchester: Carcanet, 1996), pp. 184–5.

CHAPTER 6

Entertainment and Popular Culture
Paul Maloney

Dumbarton's early popular culture reflected its role as a medieval trading centre. From its creation as a burgh in 1222, as part of a royal policy of encouraging commercial growth through new population centres, Dumbarton's burgesses were granted the right to control trade across the Lennox, from Garscube in the east, to Loch Fyne in the west. With the establishment of foreign trading links, the right to levy tolls on Clyde traffic, and a community of tradesmen and merchants, Dumbarton soon possessed the accoutrements of a medieval burgh, including, by 1516, a clock, tolbooth (combined municipal building and prison), and tron, or weighbeam, to regulate weights and measures. All were situated close by the heart of the town, the intersection of High Street and Cross Vennel (later College Street), also the location of the market cross and, in all probability, the market place itself.[1]

In the early years of this period, recreation for the nobility involved sporting pursuits. In his later years, in the 1320s, Robert the Bruce built a manor across the Leven at Cardross, opposite Dumbarton. There he maintained a household which included huntsmen, falconers, dog-keepers, gardeners and rangers, as well as a lion, and a jester, 'Peter the Fool', whose passage to Tarbet is recorded in his household accounts as costing 1s 6d.[2]

For the wider populace, on the other hand, entertainment mostly focused on fairs held on public holidays, which were both important livestock markets and opportunities for drinking, music and revelry. In 1226, Dumbarton was granted the right to hold an annual fair of eight days duration on the Feast of the Nativity of St John the Baptist (24 June). Otherwise, apart from the diversions of the tavern, music and song, communal entertainments revolved around 'ludi' – loosely 'games', or 'play' – quasi-dramatic folk festivities that originally celebrated the old pagan rituals of the spring and winter. Depending on local custom in different parts of the country, these took on a variety of different forms and elements, from processions, pageant, tableau and role-play, to dance, song, mime and storytelling, and probably constituted the roots of Scottish drama.[3] In time, the allegorical reference to regeneration of the land that marked the origins of these fertility rites was overlaid with the Christian symbolism of Christ's resurrection and passion, as the festivities moved from their original emphasis on May to Easter, and from New Year to Christmas. While these more religiously inspired events went under different names, some being termed Clerk or Candlemas plays, while others celebrated the festival of Corpus Christi, the most popular Scottish 'May' folk tradition was the 'Robin Hood' play or game, which, as evidenced by payments to 'certane menstrallis of the toun, and thair Robert Hude', was enacted at Dumbarton in 1547.[4] In 1555, following strong ecclesiastical pressure, Robin Hood games were banned by Act of Parliament, but the tradition proved persistent, as 'the plays [. . .] were exceedingly popular in Scotland, and attempts to suppress them created no small degree of animosity and disturbance'.[5]

With choral music the province of religion, musical education in the fifteenth century was provided by a 'sang school', or song school, kept by Dumbarton's parish church, which trained boys to sing in its choir.[6]

While the Robin Hood games diverted burghers and common people, the courtly spectacles and 'Charivari' enjoyed by the nobility in masques, wedding and baptismal triumphs, and at the elaborate allegorical pageantry of royal entries to towns, shared a common feature in the central role of 'guising', or disguise, the assuming of another identity. In this, as John McGavin has written, these activities, 'so separated from each other by power, class, education, and money, were satisfying the same desire to display oneself metamorphosed and beyond normal social bounds while still within the permissions of custom'.[7] The Reformation, however, brought an almost complete suppression of drama in Scotland. An Act of 1574–5 prohibited plays on the Sabbath, and required all texts, religious and secular, to be submitted to kirk sessions, while religious disapproval acted to dissuade burghs from supporting older customs. As a result, folk drama was in decline by the early seventeenth century, while Scottish drama as a whole did not revive until the mid-eighteenth century.

But, if drama was largely suppressed, and folk customs and pastimes declined in the face of religious disapproval, popular leisure retained a place in seventeenth-century life. In 1639, Dumbarton received parliamentary ratification for its three fairs, held at Patrickmas (17 March), Midsummer (24 June) and Lammas (1 August).[8] And for all the Kirk Session's attempts to enforce strict moral supervision of the community, condemning those found guilty of such offences as fornication, 'charming', slander or Sabbath profanation to stand in repentance by the kirk door, or to banishment from the town, the burgh records, with their references to dicing, fights at dances and booths, drunken misbehaviour and 'tumult', suggest the town also enjoyed its share of raucous ungodly behaviour.[9]

On a more mundane level, such colour and spectacle as was available on a daily basis was bound up with the enactments and rituals of town life, in particular the function of the burgh officers in their ceremonial duties. In 1634, the burgh engaged a drummer 'to stryk the drum evening and morning daily, viz at sex hors at evin, and four hors in the morning, And at all uthir occasionis', one of a series of records of payments to musicians in the town's employ. (In April 1601, it had granted 'to baith the menstrallis ane hundred merks betuix thame at Witsonday and Mertimes' [Martinmas], the recipients of the payment being the drummer and the 'pypaire bye' [piper].)[10] The 'uthir occasionis' included important national events, notably the proclamation of Charles II as King of Great Britain, France and Ireland in May 1660, signified by the singing of psalms at the cross and 'beating of drums through this burgh', while the rejoicings at the king's Restoration in July required Dumbarton demonstrate its loyalty by 'bonfires on throw all this burghe, and drums beating, and cannon shoting from the castel'.[11] Burgh largesse similarly went towards hospitality for important guests. In 1664, entertaining the earls of Argyll and Glencairn, lords Cochrane and Neill Campbell and the Provost of Glasgow cost a total of £18 6s 10d.

The burgh also sponsored horse racing. In 1636 a silver bell was put back into the common kist, 'seeing the horss raisis is ceissit this lang tyme'.[12] They evidently revived, as, in July 1664, the burgh, having promoted a race at the Midsummer fair in past years, and, tiring of the cost of providing a saddle as the prize, 'considering that no benefit has acruit to the burgh tharby', resolved that in future any magistrate sanctioning the race, unless he obtained the council's consent, should be personally responsible for the expenses.[13] However, economic benefit was the motive for the establishment of a race some ninety years later. Then, in 1756, the magistrates and council announced their view that

> it would be of great advantage to the inhabitants of Dumbarton, and would tend to bring the new fair in May to some repute, if proper encouragement were given for a horse race at that fair; therefore they do agree that the town should lay out £5 sterling in the purchase of a piece of plate to be run for on the sands of the burgh on the 1st day of May.[14]

The late eighteenth century saw Dumbarton gain the beginnings of an infrastructure of clubs and societies. The Lang Craigs Club, founded in the 1770s, Salmon Club (1796) and Glenhoulachan, or Midge Club (1824) were all associations based on drinking and carousing, with the former adding cock-fighting, a favourite local gaming pastime, to its activities.[15] In contrast to the increasingly rich texture of burgh life, amusements in rural society barely existed, the routines of work being all-consuming. Such chances as there were for social entertainments came at markets, fairs and feeing days, weddings and funerals, when opportunities to take up the fiddle or pipes were readily grasped. In a rare reference to leisure, the Statistical Account of 1790 noted that the people of Old Kilpatrick 'meet together occasionally and make merry. Their chief amusement is dancing, and upon these occasions there is a pleasing cheerfulness and innocence upon them.'[16]

However, the guising tradition that was central to medieval revels like the Robin Hood games retained a foothold in public consciousness through Galoshins, the Scottish folk play idiom that surfaced in the mid-nineteenth century. Performances were recorded, usually at Hallowe'en, in a number of locations in Dunbartonshire, including Helensburgh, Gartocharn, Alexandria, Balloch and Old Kilpatrick.[17] Terminology varied between areas, with participants known as 'Gloshins' in Dumbarton, and 'Galoshans' in Gartocharn, while the efforts of Vale guisers ('Goloshans') were recalled as constituting

a pretty crude performance, the artistes being backward and cowed, doubtless due to their alleged efforts not being too welcome in houses where they had previously visited. Had the Goloshans selected a season other than round about the close of the year, they might have evoked more enthusiasm. The truth is that the Vale housewives tried to have their homes spotlessly clean – especially at that period – and they simply were not going to allow a wheen laudies wi' glaury feet to come in and make a mess of their kitchens.[18]

The play was performed by groups of performers, latterly children, going from house to house. The texts of two versions collected by James Arnott in the early 1940s, from Helensburgh and Old Kilpatrick [see appendix], demonstrate a considerable overlap, including the combat between 'Slasher' and a second character, the ministrations of a quack Doctor (who boasts a cure for 'the itch, the pitch, the palsy and the gout'), the death of Slasher, and, in the case of the longer Helensburgh version, the intervention of the figures of St George and the Black Prince.[19] Both versions feature a character – Keekum Funny (Old Kilpatrick) or Johnny Funny (Helensburgh) – who collects money from the audience at the end. While the Helensburgh troupe dressed in character, with wooden swords and paper hats, and the doctor in top hat and frock coat, the Old Kilpatrick players were remembered in blacked faces and old clothes. Although the texts are fascinating amalgams, the sources are diffuse and deceptive. Brian Hayward suggests that they are oral transmissions of playtexts originally gleaned from chapbooks, and moreover that the West of Scotland Galoshins tradition, of which the Vale's forms part, probably only dates from the mid-nineteenth century, and seems likely to have been the product of influences connected with industrialisation.[20]

Growth in population and industrial expansion in the nineteenth century brought a range of social problems that found expression in popular culture. The fairs, traditionally agricultural events for sales of live-stock, were also occasions for drinking, dancing and licensed misbehaviour. At the Moss of Balloch Fair in the 1820s, one of three annual holidays taken locally (the others being the Bonhill Sacramental Fast Day and New Year's Day), almost all the inhabitants of the Vale turned out for the festivities, 'lads with their lasses, husbands with their wives and children, old and young, masters and servants, all in Sunday garb'. Alongside the horse-dealing, the shows, with their 'nymph dancers', and vendors like the candy-men and women, lucky poke, rowly-powly, cheap Johns and apple men, attractions included boat rides and meat and drink at the inn. Meanwhile, at a nearby building called the Kiln, 'drink was sold in great quantities' and a fiddler gave penny reels, 'drinking and dancing being kept up till a late hour'. Excessive drinking played a major part in the event, the ground being 'studded over with tents for the sale of beer and whisky' and, as the day wore on and fights broke out, 'fists, sticks and other weapons were freely resorted to'. One man, a quarryman, was remembered as being stabbed so badly by a Glasgow tailor with his shears 'that his bowels protruded, and doctors expected nothing less than a fatal result', although he survived.[21]

By the mid-century such ritualised fairground violence was providing a flashpoint for deeper social tensions. In 1855, confrontations between Irish navvies and local shipwrights, which culminated in a full-scale riot in the centre of Dumbarton in October, had begun in June with fighting at the Carman Hill Cattle Fair at Renton.[22] In 1864, the same fair was the scene of further violence, this time aimed at the authorities. Then county police officers, faced with a crowd of 100 shipwrights who had been drinking heavily, arrested one of their number for striking a horse with a stick, only to be pursued by the crowd. The nine officers, who included the chief con-stable, were forced to flee with their prisoner across open ground, and several were injured, for which five men were subsequently convicted.[23] In this context, the fair incidents were reflective of wider problems associated with violence and policing. In 1856, a further incident in Dumbarton saw an angry mob storm the police station to release three prisoners.[24] In the same year in Duntocher, home to a large community of Irish labourers working on nearby projects, a police superintendent, leading a patrol to combat increasing violence in the area, was himself badly beaten up.[25]

Concern over lawlessness and, particularly, the moral effects of drink on the working classes led to an increasing appreciation of the need for constructive leisure, by which working men could be given opportunities for education and self-improvement and, as importantly, distracted from the temptations of alcohol. As a result a wide range of church and religious groups, temperance bodies and, later, co-operative and working mens' organisations became involved in the promotion of sports, music and social activities. By the 1890s, these included a huge range of concerts, soirees, *conversaziones*, whist drives, *kinderspiels* (dramatic pieces performed by children; see Plate 8), musical competitions, illustrated talks and limelight lectures, as well as sporting and organised outdoor pursuits.

This process had begun early in the century with the founding of the temperance movement in Scotland in 1829 by Greenock-born John Dunlop. By 1833, the soirees held by the Duntocher Temperance Society offered refreshments of bread, coffee and tea, accompanied by vocal and instrumental music, and related societies had been established in Dumbarton, Renton, Alexandria, Bonhill, Row (now Rhu) and Milton.[26] Further temperance organisations followed, including the Teetotal movement (in Scotland from 1832), Rechabites (1838), Good Templars (1869) and Band of Hope (1871), all of which established themselves in Dumbarton and the Vale, offering an increasing range of social and musical activities. Church and evangelical groups, whose membership overlapped considerably with that of the temperance organisations, also provided a network of societies and social activities. While these proselytising organisations used the attraction of brass band music or limelight bible scenes to draw audiences, philanthropists and local employers sought to promote moral education for the betterment of working men. Mechanics' Institutes, which offered facilities for reading and self-improvement, were established in Alexandria, as the Vale of Leven Mechanics' Institution, in 1834, in Dumbarton in 1844, and in Renton in 1882. By the 1850s, the Mechanics' Institutes' extensive programme of lectures, usually delivered by clergymen, combined dry-sounding topics designed to promote self-improvement ('Thinking, not Learning, the true Educator', 'The Duties of the Working Classes') with more lively talks on 'Scottish Song', 'English, Irish and Scottish Music contrasted', and 'A Night with Burns and the Jacobites,' all given with musical illustrations.[27]

However, the worthiness of the reforming agenda sometimes missed the point with regard to the tastes of the wider public. The *Dumbarton Herald*, established in 1851 and a strong advocate of rational recreation, warned against too rarified a view of what constituted entertainment. It argued in pragmatic terms that it was simply no good for religious reformers to dismiss amusements like singing and dancing out of hand; that the severe, instructional approach of the Mechanics Institutes had been tried, with the result that 'as might have been expected, the more intelligent and aspiring have availed themselves of the opportunities afforded, while the mass have continued in their ignorance [. . .] and drunkenness and its concomitants have taken the place of unwisely discountenanced rational amusements'.[28] The point was that people had to be taken as they were:

> The cheering song, and healthful, and morally elevating domestic dance, have been frowned upon by many as ungodly and soul-ruining; and the pent-up stream of human happiness has sought, in not a few instances, free passage in the abodes of vice. No doubt, much that is now sought after as amusement, even of a harmless kind, may be thought weak and unprofitable when viewed through the more enlightened and philosophical minds of future years. In the meantime, however, we are obliged to take the race as it really is as a whole, and by wise, because suitable methods, endeavour to elevate its tastes.[29]

The example evoked in comparison was that of Glasgow's Saturday Evening Concerts, then in their second season, which offered musical pro-grammes that combined soloists in classical and sacred repertoire with music hall comedians and Scots ballads and songs. The formula proved enormously popular, not least because the impetus for the events' estab-lishment came from demands from representatives of the working classes themselves for proper entertainment. As one director put it in a speech from the platform, '[. . .] with respect to the great masses, I do not wonder, con-sidering the way in which the day is spent, that they do not find it very attractive to go out at night and hear lectures on the steam engine'.[30] If Dumbarton's resources could not match those of Glasgow, the *Dumbarton Herald* suggested, the town nevertheless had an abundance of local musical talent, and could surely support an instrumental band.

The Glasgow concerts had a long-standing influence. By 1864, the Vale of Leven Public Hall at Alexandria was presenting concerts in association with the directors of the Glasgow series, who supplied performers from as far afield as Crystal Palace, London, Birmingham and Exeter, supported by the Dumbartonshire Rifle Volunteer Band.[31] The term Saturday evening concert was, with variations, appropriated by a number of different series,[32] as voluntary bodies and associations increasingly featured concerts and musical galas in their activities. The Dumbarton Mechanics' Institute itself offered four concerts per year by the late 1860s.[33]

The demand for leisure activities of all kinds resulted in the building of a series of new venues. The new Public Hall in Alexandria opened in 1862, and Dumbarton's Burgh Hall in 1865. St James' Parish Church Hall, Clydebank, was built in 1891 at a cost of £1,200, with a central hall with seating for 400, plus four other rooms, for use for session meetings, a reading room for young men, and classrooms for the Sabbath school. Part of the hall's stated purpose was to provide facilities for entertainment for local people: 'On Saturday evenings during the winter it is planned to provide a course of illustrated lectures, concerts, instrumental and vocal recitals, etc. for the purpose of meeting a felt want in the district.'[34]

Musical life, firmly rooted in the participatory principle, was rich and diverse. Sacred music received a considerable stimulus from the Moody and Sankey missions to Scotland in 1874 and 1882, when the American revivalists visited Alexandria and Dumbarton respectively, their use of catchy hymns sung to harmonium accompaniment proving highly popular with middle-class opinion. While the use of instrumental music in services remained contentious (with Dumbarton Free Presbytery narrowly rejecting a move to propose its adoption to the General Assembly in 1882), church choirs abounded, and singing was for many the transcendent feature of churchgoing for all denominations. One attender recalled that, on a summer morning at Bonhill Church, 'to hear the congregation lift its voice to the tune "Kilmarnock," was to feel that you had banished mundane affairs and were truly in the house of God'.[35]

Choral organisations proliferated. By 1882, the Vale of Leven Choral Society had ninety-six members, with an average attendance at rehearsals of seventy-seven, while the Dumbarton Choral Union, founded in 1883, had 141 members by 1895, and was giving two concerts annually, of oratorios and sacred music with guest soloists.[36] Other Vale choral organisations included the Teetotal Choir, The Vale of Leven Tonic Sol-fa Association, founded in 1861, The Vale of Leven Choral Union, started in the 1840s, and the Harmonic Society. Clydebank's musical life also included a rich choral tradition. The Clydebank Select Choir, founded in 1887, was followed a decade later by both the Clydebank and District Choral Union, and the Clydebank and District Harmonic Society. The Clydebank Male Voice Choir, originally derived from the Rovers Rambling Club, made its first appearance in 1901.[37]

Brass bands were also extremely popular. Long-established groups such as the Bonhill Instrumental Band (formed in 1817) and the Jamestown and Vale of Leven Instrumental Prize Band (which as a flute band dated from 1872) were both subjects of great local pride, and, in the case of the prize-winning Clydebank Brass (later Burgh) Band and the neighbouring Duntocher Brass Band (founded as the Spinner's Band in 1829), the source of keen local rivalry.[38]

Figure 14 Clydebank Prize Brass Band, which in 1906 became Clydebank Burgh Band.

Sporting and healthy outdoor activities were similarly an important part of constructive leisure, although the dubious gaming and field-sports associations of some older events might have been frowned on by reformers. Dumbarton's annual regattas, which began in 1830, two years after Loch Lomond's, were smart social events at which races were rowed on the Broad Meadow at high tide. The boat races for gentlemen and boatmen held in the afternoon were preceded in the morning by 'foot' races, and horse racing for prize money run around a circuit marked by coloured flags, a bugle sounding the signal to clear the course. The excitement of the scenes was later remembered by those who had watched them as boys from the top of the College Bow, the historic arch then situated on the site of the present railway station, which marked the finishing line.[39] Other events at the regattas in the 1830s, when the proceedings were sometimes termed 'amusements', included fairground-style competitions such as 'climbing a pole for 5s and a blue bonnet', sack races, and walking along a soaped bowsprit to retrieve a bunch of flowers (for a prize of 15s).[40] After an interruption, the regattas resumed from 1853 on the Leven, and the Broad Meadow was subsequently drained for the building of the railway. As late as the early 1860s, however, they retained the air of a rural sporting contest, with patrons advertised as 'The Gentlemen of the Town and Neighbourhood', and events including a 'Duck Hunt for swimmers' ('Duck must be caught within fifteen minutes').[41]

Dumbarton subsequently became famous for its rowing, Dumbarton Rowing Club being formed in 1830, a challenge race between Dumbarton and

DUMBARTON
RACES AND REGATTA,
22nd August 1834.

Order and Arrangement of the Amusements.

I. HORSE RACES.

1st, Race in Heats, for Purse of £15.

HORSES ENTERED.

DESCRIPTION.	NAME.	OWNER.	RIDER'S COLOURS.
1 Bay Mare,	Little-thought-of,	Mr Jennings,	Blue, with Black Cap.
2 Bay Horse,	Auchinleck,	Mr Pearson,	Blue, with Red Cap.
3 Bay Mare,	Velvet,	Mr Cunningham,	Blue and White, Green Cap.

2nd, Another Race in Heats for a Purse of £5.

1 Bay Horse,	Auchinleck,	Mr Pearson,	Blue, with Red Cap.
2 Brown Mare,	Maggie,	J. Milner,	Black Body and Lilac Sleeves.
3 Bay Mare,	Velvet,	Mr Cunningham,	Blue and White, Green Cap.
4 Brown Mare,	Juggler,	Mr Smith,	Yel. and Green Sleeves, Blk Cap

3rd, A Heat by the Horses beat in the former Races for a Purse of £3.

4th, A **CART HORSE RACE.**—first prize 20s. second 15s. third 5s.

II. Climbing a Pole for 5s. and Blue Bonnet.

III. A SACK RACE,---first prize 10s. 2nd 5s.

IV. Walking on and taking a Bunch of Flowers from the End of a Soaped Bowsprit for a Prize of 15s.

V. ROWING MATCHES.

GIGS AND BOATS ENTERED.

1st, Four-oared Gigs for Ladies' Silver Cup, value £15.

NAMES.	OWNERS.	PORTS.	DESCRIPTIONS.	FLAGS.
1 Whistling Swan,	James Colquhoun, Esq. Luss,		White, with black bead,	White, with red ball.
2	W. Colquhoun, Esq.			
3 Water Witch,	W. Lewis, Esq.	Glasgow,	Red,	
4 Highland Mary,	Joseph Turnbull, Esq.	Bonhill,	Cream colour,	Red, with yellow stripe
5 Naiad,	James Robertson,	Paisley,	Red,	Red, with white ball.

2nd, Four-oared Jolly Boats—first prize £4, second £2.

1 Tom Pipes,	R. Arthur, Esq.	Bonhill,	Green, with white bottom,	
2 Hawk,	A. Graham,	Redhouse,	Black, with yellow bead,	White, with red ball.
3 Mary,	A. J. Bonar,	Dumbarton,	Black,	White.
4 Lowland Lass,	W. Cumming,	Bonhill,	Black, with white bottom,	Red, with white star.
5 Maid of the Mill,	James M'Gregor,	Bonhill,	Green,	Blue, with a white cross

3rd, Four-oared Gigs—first prize £4, second £2.

1 Whistling Swan	James Colquhoun, Esq. Luss,		White, with black bead,	White, with red ball.
2 Water Witch,	W. Lewis, Esq.	Glasgow,	Red,	Red, with yellow stripe
3 Highland Mary,	J. Turnbull, Esq.	Bonhill,	Cream colour,	
4 Naiad,	James Robertson,	Paisley,	Red,	Red, with white ball.
5 The Rose,	James M'Farlane,	Dumbarton, Red, with yel. moulding,		Red.
6 Dart,	W. M'Arthur,	Dumbarton, Green, with red stripe,		Yellow.

4th, Two-oared Boats, for Purse of £2.

1 Margaret,	D. Bell,	Dumbarton, Black with white border,		Red, with white ball.
2 Mary,	J. Gilchrist,	Leven,	Black with yellow bead,	Red.
3 Hawk,	A. Graham,	Redhouse,	Black with yellow bead,	White, with red ball.
4 Mary,	A. J. Bonar,	Dumbarton, Black,		White.
5 Lowland Lass,	W. Cumming,	Bonhill,	Black, with white bottom Red, with white star	
6 Thistle,	H. M'Lean,	Dumbarton, Black, with yellow stripe,		White, with blue ball.

☞ It is probable that the Cart Horse Race will be the first started.

DUMBARTON PRINTING OFFICE.

Figure 15 Dumbarton Races and Regatta, 22 August 1834. Order and Arrangement of the Amusements. Contests included a cart-horse race, a sack race, and 'walking on and taking a bunch of flowers from the end of a soaped bow-sprit'.

Cardross ferrymen being staged in 1831, and a team from the town beating the best professionals from England and Wales in the 1850s. There was also a powerful Vale of Leven crew in the 1850s and a revived regatta club was formed in 1853 racing on the Leven between the castle and Dalreoch.[42] An amateur club was established in 1873 and went on to produce both professional and amateur championship-winning crews, with a 'Young Dumbarton' crew dominating professional rowing for a decade from the mid-1890s.[43]

Football, which made its first appearance when a Vale side played Queen's Park in an exhibition game at Alexandria, was first played at Dumbarton on the Broad Meadow in 1872, before the team decamped to Boghead in 1879. As Bob Crampsey discusses in more detail in his chapter, Dumbarton was a founder of the Scottish Football Association. In 1883, it won the Scottish Cup, beating the Renton and Vale of Leven clubs, and in 1890 tied with Glasgow Rangers for the inaugural season of the Scottish League, which it won the following year.[44]

Older sporting clubs included Dumbarton's Curling Club, founded in 1815, and its Bowling Club (1832). Alexandria's Bowling Club was formed in 1870. Hardgate Quoiting Club was formed around 1840, its green adjoining the back door of the Clover Bar, the link with a nearby hostelry being a common feature of bowling and quoiting. Cricket was played in the Vale from 1852, and cycling and rambling became increasingly popular towards the end of the century, as churches in particular became pro-active in their involvement with social activities.

A key reason for the expansion of leisure was the increasing opportunities afforded by public transport. In 1800, the journey from Dumbarton to Glasgow had taken 'three hours by a heavy coach, which ran only twice a-week, and about five hours by a lumbering wagon'.[45] The arrival of the Balloch to Bowling railway to Dumbarton in 1850, and its extension to Helensburgh and Glasgow in 1858 changed the life of the town. With the introduction of Clyde steamers, and access to rail travel, day excursions became extremely popular, and works outings, often sponsored by employers and trade associations, an important ritual of working life. Such events reflected the status of the participants and came in a variety of forms. So, in the early 1890s, fifty merchants' messenger boys from Clydebank travelled in brakes to Row (Rhu) on the Gareloch for lunch, tea and afternoon sports, including sack and three-legged races, and a 'butchers v. grocers' football match; painters from J. & G. Thomson's Clydebank shipyard took a steamer trip to Rothesay; on a more formal basis, the foremen from the same company went by special train to Edinburgh for sightseeing and dinner at a hotel; a party of 700 Oddfellows from the Vale of Leven enjoyed a day excursion to Lanark and the Falls of Clyde; and Clydebank Union Church Choir took its annual picnic at Luss.[46]

Tourism, another product of improved transport, also began to have an economic impact. The first steamer on Loch Lomond, the *Marion*, began advertised excursion sailings in 1818 and, in the late 1830s, the hotel at Balloch underwent extensive refurbishment to cater for the increasing numbers of visitors, who later included the Empress Eugenie.[47] For working people too, leisure time was increasingly available. Half-day holidays for shop workers, and the introduction of annual Fair holidays, during which factories and works closed for a week or ten-day period, brought increasingly affordable opportunities to travel or enjoy holiday breaks. In July 1882, the start of the Dumbarton Fair holiday saw residents leave the town for seaside or inland destinations, as well as for railway or steamer trips 'Doon the watter' to Clyde coast resorts, trains to the terminal at Craigendoran being reportedly crowded. For the affluent, advertisements for destinations further afield included 'a number of excursions to Ireland, England and a few to the Continent'.

With improved communications, town life became more cosmopolitan. The introduction in 1861 of the *Lennox Herald*, the weekend version of the *Dumbarton Herald*, and the availability of affordable popular literature, in the place of poorly printed chapbooks, fed consumer demand for leisure. By the 1890s, the *Herald* carried advertisements from Glasgow dealers for musical instruments such as pianos, melodeons, American organs and harmoniums, previews of plays and concerts, and advertisements for such lurid attractions as 'The Southend Murder' ('portrait model of James Canham Read') at Macleod's Waxworks in the Trongate.

Organisations designed to promote fraternity and self-help among working men were another source of social activities. These included masonic lodges, friendly societies, and orders such as the Oddfellows, Hibernians, Foresters and Shepherds. The Loyal Order of Ancient Shepherds, established in eight locations in Dunbartonshire by the early 1880s, had a sizeable membership distributed between three Vale lodges, the 'Star of Leven' (236 members), 'Rose of the Vale' (198) and 'Flower of Jamestown' (178). At their 1882 united annual Festival in Alexandria, 700 Shepherds, after a service of tea and a long musical programme comprising male and female soloists in songs, quartets and trios, and a choir singing 'Lord, what is man?', were addressed by guest speakers. John Denny affirmed that being a Shepherd 'was a connection to which all young men should aspire', and saluted 'the beneficial effects of working men thus banding themselves together, as making provision for themselves, their wives and their families in times of trouble'. The basis of such fraternity was

Figure 16 The Loyal Order of Ancient Shepherds parade through Dumbarton, June 1905.

mutual financial support: the largest of the three lodges, 'Star of Leven', had an annual income of £403 6s 6d, from which expenditure included £154 19s paid out for sickness, and £46 10s towards funeral claims.[48] Other working-class organisations included the Irish Foresters and Irish National League, and a host of other institutions that included Dumbarton Working Men's Club, the Buchanan Institute, Bowling (opened in 1884), and the Victoria Institute, Renton, established in 1887.

The network of church-derived soirees and socials, Sabbath schools, educational activities and sporting clubs established from the 1850s remained largely unchanged until the First World War. To modern sensibilities, the continuities involved throw up striking examples of social inertia: in 1911 entertainers were still visiting Dumbarton Combination Poorhouse to entertain the inmates as they had done in 1882.[49]

As the nineteenth century progressed, the range and sophistication of activities increased. Church and temperance groups put particular emphasis on their youth wings, which made music and entertainment a key part of their activities. In the 1890s, the Lily of the Valley Juvenile Rechabites held anniversary soirees at the village school in Alexandria, while the Junior Singing Class of Jamestown Church gave a musical service, entitled 'For the Master's Sake', at Jamestown Hall. They also became adept at staging public spectacles and events. In Dumbarton, the Band of Hope Union's semi-jubilee in 1896 was marked by a dramatic 'Grand illuminated procession' through the town, accompanied by flaming torches and limelight views, to a meeting at the Burgh Hall presided over by Lord Overtoun, and attended by the town Bands of Hope, Boys' Brigade, Sons of Temperance, Rechabites, Good Templars and Salvation Army Band of Love. At Clydebank, the day-long celebrations involved speeches, a programme of musical entertainment, and a procession featuring temperance bands and close on a thousand children.[50] The Co-operative movement also used such occasions to demonstrate its breadth through choreographed events. The 1906 semi-jubilee of the Clydebank Co-op featured 6,000–7,000 children, together with pipe and brass bands.[51]

By the 1890s, organised social activities, indeed to a large extent the social fabric of life, were dominated by this network of church and temperance groups. But while these organisations were key sponsors of leisure, their social influence was heavily underscored by the support of prominent local employers and landowners, many of whom were driven by strong religious convictions to play leading roles in improving the moral character of society. Peter Denny, Lord Overtoun, Ewing Gilmour and John Christie, all notable figures with strong evangelical or temperance affiliations, provided financial support and patronage for a wide range of societies and social initiatives designed to improve the quality of life for working people.

However, for all the efforts of moral reformers to improve the character of society, several factors combined to frustrate their success. The first was that, to the dismay of temperance campaigners, the prosperity that was bringing material benefits to workers also served to fuel drunken behaviour and lawlessness. A by-product of Dumbarton's 1882 Fair holiday was a marked increase in cases before the police court, a result of men with money to spend gravitating to the town's bars, giving the High Street on the Saturday evening 'a very disgraceful appearance', and helping account for references to Dumbarton as 'an "El Dorado" for publicans'.[52] Moreover, drink-related violence was a persistent social problem. In June, a fight broke out in the High Street between members of a Protestant fife and drum band and passing Catholic Ribbonmen. Weeks later, a Dennystown correspondent to the local newspaper suggested anyone seeing the scene in the square by Dalreoch station after pub closing time on a Saturday night

> would think the powers of the lower regions had broken loose. The row, the shouts of 'murder,' of 'police,' and the screams of the women are something dreadful. Last Saturday night I am sure there could not be less than four free fights going on at once, and a crowd of about seventy or eighty surging backwards and forwards around them. Respectable people are afraid of venturing out after ten o'clock.[53]

The problem was widespread, and social status offered no guarantee of protection. J. M. Martin of Auchendennen, a JP who was prominent among spectators at the Loch Lomond Regatta in August, had, the previous month, stopped his carriage while passing through Renton to rally bystanders to the aid of a policeman being beaten up, and himself received a cut under the eye.[54] Both the county police force, forty-three strong in 1882, with one constable to every 1,431 citizens, and Dumbarton's ten-strong burgh force, with one officer to 1,378, were reported as needing increasing to reflect growth in the population.[55]

The second point, a broader cultural one, was that the fervour of temperance and evangelical rhetoric could not obscure the fact that certain constituencies continued to ignore their precepts. This was not just in respect of working men's culture centred on pubs, betting and football, but also extended to other classes of society. The conviviality of some of the older Dumbarton clubs was based on heavy imbibing, as evidenced by accounts of their raucous proceedings, as indeed was much of the cultural subtext surrounding Burns appreciation, notwithstanding the speed with which temperance groups formed their own Burns societies. If, by the 1870s, both the libidinous Glenhoulachan or Midge club, and the Hoasting Club, whose members met daily at a local howff for a midday tipple, were long defunct, those of the Salmon Club still enjoyed what was euphemistically termed 'Lochlomond water'.[56] Moreover, before the moral rectitude of the Peter Dennys and Lord Overtouns, a previous generation of industrialists and public figures had enjoyed sports and gaming and indulged in decidedly hedonistic lifestyles. Jacob Dixon, Dumbarton's provost from 1822 to 1830 and, as the proprietor of the glassworks, the town's major employer, was memorably described as 'a lover of pleasure' who 'drained its sparkling, seductive cup to the very dregs'. A well-known supporter of horse racing and sporting pursuits, he had once wagered a thousand guineas on a cock-fight.[57] Although consumption of alcohol had declined from its high point in the 1830s,[58] the older more relaxed culture did not disappear. Horse racing for prize money remained a feature of Dumbarton regattas until the 1840s, whisky tents being remembered 'pitched at Pointfauld principally', while 'there is yet to be seen in that quarter the grave-like mounds which mark the place where many a good gill of *aqua vita* got honourable burial'.[59] For all that temperance was a hugely influential force, particularly among early working-class socialists, pubs retained their place, with the Elephant Inn in particular a focal point of Dumbarton life. A supper for Leven shipyard officials held there in 1882, chaired by a foreman caulker and with guests including William Denny and Walter Brock, toasted 'success to William Denny and Brothers', and 'Educational interests'. After supper, the company enjoyed 'a lengthy and varied programme of toast and song, with instrumental music', singing solos and duets, and providing accompaniment on violin, concertina and piano,[60] a warmly convivial scene redolent of fifty years earlier.

If, notwithstanding these points, temperance and religious organisations remained the most visible sponsors of social activities, other influences reflected the economic relationships of the world of work, as both employers and organisations representing the interests of working people became involved in providing leisure. While employers initially did so through individual patronage, co-operative societies, working-class self-help groups and workers' trade associations also sought to provide leisure facilities and promote social and cultural events.

The development of these interests reflected growing differences in the social and economic growth of the area. While Dumbarton had developed from a country burgh into an industrial town, with commensurate changes and additions to its pre-existing cultural institutions, Clydebank's situation was different, in that it was entirely a product of industrial expansion. The township owed its existence to J. & G. Thomson's relocation of its shipyard there from Govan to Barns o' Clyde in 1871. Not surprisingly, the shipyard dominated the town – which took its name from the yard – and early tenements built by the company for their workers were known as 'Tamson's Toon'. Although churches and social institutions were quickly established, the fact that the workforce were established in the area in advance of many amenities, and before the provision of road access from Glasgow, encouraged them to make arrangements of their own. The 'Tarry Kirk', the wooden hall built on yard land in 1873, was used by the shipworkers for dances, concerts and soirees, and by various religious denominations for Sunday services. It was also the venue for the 1881 meeting that led to the formation of the Clydebank Co-operative society, inspired by the example of that of neighbouring Dalmuir, founded the previous year. The Clydebank society was to prove a major influence on the cultural life of the town, through its annual gala day and the wide range of social activities conducted at the Co-operative Hall in Hume Street, opened in 1908.[61]

Alongside this seemingly dominant sponsorship of recreation by improving interests, or by organisations reflecting either workers' interests or those of employers, there also existed a tier of popular commercial entertainments, which reflected continuities with older strands of popular culture, and continued to bring the whiff of the showground into the regulated world of late nineteenth-century social discourse. Mainly discussed in Chapter 8, these included travelling or fit-up theatres, fairground 'shows', music hall, and barnstorming performances of popular dramas presented at local halls by touring professional companies. Cinema itself was to emerge from this populist fairground context.

The period from the 1890s to 1914 was one of contradictions. Religious, temperance and voluntary associations continued to exert a major influence on organised social activities, indeed on the infrastructure of much of cultural life, and this influence was heavily underpinned by philanthropic support from major employers and landowners. This patrician character was evident in donations towards public buildings and civic amenities, and in personal patronage of societies and trusts. In 1885, John MacMillan and Peter Denny, two of Dumbarton's shipbuilders, gifted the Levengrove estate to the town for use as a park, while, in 1906, Lord Overtoun donated £5,000 towards purchase of 18¼ acres of land for a park in Dalmuir, opened by Lady Overtoun. Also in 1906, Robert McAlpine paid for a bandstand at Radnor Park, Clydebank, and the following year conducted the opening ceremony of the Radnor Park Bowling Club, built with profits from the McAlpine Public House Trust.[62] The Ewing Gilmour Institutes for Men and Women were opened in Alexandria in 1884 and 1891 respectively, new public libraries opened in Dumbarton in 1910 and Clydebank in 1913, both with the support of Andrew Carnegie, and the Brock Memorial Baths in Dumbarton dated from 1914. Industrial consolidation from the late 1890s, however, resulting in the merger and amalgamation of some older concerns, was to lead to the decline of these employers' paternalist influence. This was particularly the case in the Vale, where the four main bleaching and textile companies, established since the 1850s, had by the early 1900s been consolidated into two larger concerns, both run from Glasgow.[63]

In the early twentieth century, the influence of temperance and religious groups on social activities was, in any case, increasingly challenged by employers and working people's organisations, who came to recognise their importance as a tool of social influence. As a result, employers' sponsorship of recreation took on a more corporate face, while the advent of high levels of unemployment and increasingly bitter industrial relations were to lead working-class organisations like the Co-operative movement, trade unions and socialist parties to make increasing use of social activities, both as amenities in times of hardship and as a way of sustaining morale among their memberships. At the same time, the growth in population, introduction of new technologies and increasing demand for entertainment all contributed to a new consumer market for leisure. A newly emergent, assertive working-class culture, based around the pub, music hall, cinema, dance halls, mass spectator sports like football and the bookies, owed more to older 'rough' strains of popular culture than to the improving world of rational recreation, much to the alarm of reformers.

In Clydebank, concerns had been voiced from the early 1890s about the lack of amenities in the burgh where, despite being only 7 miles from Glasgow, life was felt to be 'stripped of the city's attractions, its public parks, its museums, its art galleries, its public libraries'.[64] Commentators reported with dismay on the moral dangers posed by bookies' attendance at meal times outside Thomson's shipyard and the Singer works, and on the presence of illegal huts erected on open ground where, with the 'misguided' indulgence of magistrates, betting on games of chance involving a wheel of fortune took place. One of the reforming campaigners' goals was 'a resort for young men in which they might meet for amusement [. . .] a suitable place for a reading and recreation room with rational and innocent attractions for the youth of the burgh'.[65] Their ideal was no doubt Dumbarton's Young Men's Christian Association, opened in January 1897, which contained a gymnasium, library, baths, lecture facilities and a reading room. In his opening speech, Lord Overtoun exhorted its membership to embrace self-discipline and 'let them not allow sinful pleasure to dim the lustre of their lives'.[66]

However, the democratising effect of the mass popular culture of the early twentieth century was to lead away from moral supervision and, if anything, back towards older patterns of 'rough culture', and of entertainment based on enjoyment, physical exuberance and gratification. The early

1900s brought ice-cream parlours, billiard rooms, roller-skating rinks, aerated drinks and fish and chips, all new forms with seeming delinquent overtones. Clydebank Town Council passed bylaws to limit the hours of billiards and bagatelle rooms, suspected of being used for after-hours drinking, as did Dumbarton.[67] However, despite restrictive licensing, which saw Clydebank pubs close at 9pm as late as 1938 (an extension to 9.30pm the same year only being agreed after considerable debate), the longer-term goals of the temperance movement, the critical force behind most social reform, were to remain unfulfilled.[68] Although one ward in the 1920 plebiscite on the veto of alcohol, Radnor Park, voted to suspend licences, this proved an isolated success. Thereafter, the number of licensed premises in Clydebank remained markedly static throughout the inter-war period, with twenty-nine public houses in 1938 as there had been in 1919.[69] Perhaps as a result, membership of Clydebank's temperance groups seems to have declined over the inter-war period, with a loss of the dynamism that had characterised its Victorian and Edwardian heydays.[70]

The fairs, traditional pretexts for drinking and dissipation, were still in existence. If the Carman Hill event had dwindled by the 1890s, others had been lent a new lease of life by rail travel. In 1910, the historic Cardross Whelk Fair attracted an estimated 6,000 trippers, as 'spring-holiday swells from the city and Vale of Leven appeared almost with the break of day', the station being 'stormed'. While the traditional eating of whelks had declined, the 'shows' did good business, and dancing and games took place on the foreshore until well into the evening, the visitors' behaviour causing the police few problems, in contrast to former times.[71] At Dumbarton Fair, the opening night of the 'shows' on the Broad Meadow in 1910 also attracted an estimated crowd of around 6,000. The following year it was reported that 'the visitor is at first almost blinded by the glare of electric light and the multitudinous paraffin blazes, which cast a light against the sky visible for miles around'. Apart from traditional stalls – aunt Sally's, molly dollies, hoop-la, coconut stalls, cup-shies, shooting saloons and football stances – sideshows included Kemp's ('with its ornately decorated front [. . .] the most attractive on the ground'), and McIndoe's Scottish Show, as well as variety artists, a potted sketch company, 'Little Lady Dot' and 'Major Mite', a tiny Cornishman, Mander's Menagerie, 'a tent of trained animals', and Chapman's American Show. Other attractions included 'a wonderful freak, in the shape of a fossilised two-headed giant, 8 ft 7 inches in length, alleged to have been discovered in Santiago'.[72] Dumbarton Fair continued to offer the queasy attractions of 'freaks' up until the late 1950s.

The authorities did act to regulate such events. In 1891, Dumbarton Council had moved to combine the various shows' appearances into a single

Figure 17 Top: Shows at Dumbarton Common, 1910.
Bottom: The Shows at Dumbarton, 1958.

Figure 18 Concert at Murroch Glen, Dumbarton, June 1908. The young performers are swinging Indian clubs to music provided by the musicians grouped around the piano to the right of the stage. To the left, members of a brass band can be seen sitting on the hillside, their tubas lying on the grass.

ten-day period on the Meadow Park, under the pretext of improving organisation and public safety. The move evidently rendered the event more amenable: by 1910 the showmen were recipients of a church tea party, addressed by the provost, who assured them of the town – and council's – appreciation.[73] Evangelical reformers also sought to use fairs for their message. At Meadow Park in 1895, a stall offering religious literature sold 386 Testaments, 104 Bibles, 5 Douay Testaments, 120 *Pilgrim's Progress*'s, as well as a large number of texts, and distributed 6,000 tracts. The authorities gave the ground for the stand free and Lord Overtoun paid part of the extra expense.[74]

The age was still one of outdoor meetings. A right of way demonstration against plans by Dr Douglas White, a nephew of Lord Overtoun, to close a local road drew a crowd of 10,000 protesters, the biggest in memory, to Dumbarton Common in 1911. Open-air concerts began at Murroch Glen in 1904, initially to raise funds for Dumbarton's Town Band, when the opening programme included the 350-strong chorus of the United Voices of Dumbarton, but proved so popular that they continued until 1913.

Cinema, the key development in the new mass leisure market, first emerged through older amusements such as fairs and music hall. The first generation of promoters included showmen like Joseph Wingate, who was screening films in a tent on Dumbarton Common from 1907, prior to opening the town's first cinema in 1910. But, while films quickly established themselves as the new mass entertainment – by 1920 Dumbarton and the Vale had six cinema venues and Clydebank four – until the 1920s they were accompanied by a pianist or orchestra, and seen in a programme that often included variety acts. And, for all the modernity of coming mass media like film and radio, live performance – everything from amateur dramatics, choral music and band concerts in the parks, to variety, visits by melo-drama companies, circuses and the 'shows' – remained a staple of life well into the 1930s.

If aspects of this expanding commercial leisure market seemed to repre-sent a reconnection with the pleasure principle of older currents of popular amusements, they were complemented by the social activities promoted by working-class organisations. At the forefront of these was the Co-operative movement, which also became involved in screening films at an early stage. The Clydebank Society showed films at its Hume Street hall from 1914 to 1916, while the Vale of Leven Society obtained a licence to show films at the Co-operative Hall in Bank Street.[75] The Co-operative movement was to play an increasingly prominent role in working peoples' lives, particularly in Clydebank and the Vale of Leven. Through their Education Committees, both societies supported a wide range of social and cultural events, from prizes for school children to magic lantern shows, dances and soirees, with Clydebank opening the first branch of the Scottish Co-operative Women's Guild in 1893. New Co-operative Halls at Hume Street, Clydebank (opened in 1908), and at Bank Street, Alexandria (opened in 1904, and holding 800), were let for social functions, such as weekly dancing on behalf of the Jamestown and Vale of Leven Brass Band funds, but were also available for use by workers' organisations. The organisations were by this time long established as supportive of trade union activities. In 1895, the Clydebank Society let the hall in the drapery department at its Alexander Street premises to the engineers to discuss strike action and, during disputes, the Vale Society similarly allowed groups like the Bleachers and Dyers' Union and National Federation of Women Workers to use the Bank Street halls for a nominal charge.

The Co-operative movement was also noted for its sponsorship of music-making, particularly brass bands and choirs. The Vale of Leven Junior Choir were Scottish Co-operative Junior Choir champions in 1904 and 1907, while, in Clydebank, new facilities at Alexander Street, opened in 1920, included a gymnasium and rehearsal space for six choirs, including their Junior Choir, which won the championship at the Scottish Co-operative Music Festival.[76] With its halls as amenities, the Co-operative movement was to be a major provider of leisure throughout the Depression. In the second half of 1926, the year of the General Strike, the Clydebank Society's motor-hiring service provided 805 motor hires, and its charabancs conveyed 5,095 passengers on trips to various parts of Scotland.[77]

While the Co-op movement provided a social network for working people, some employers offered a competing, similarly all-encompassing social vision. William Beardmore & Co.'s vast Naval Construction Works at Dalmuir, established in 1905, made extensive provision for housing for its workforce, building fifty-nine tenement buildings by 1907. By 1918, its Welfare Department had introduced extensive schemes for the education and training of apprentices, as well as the Beardmore Naval Cadets, who enjoyed a summer camp in Perthshire, and works clubs for football, weight-lifting, boxing, badminton, gymnastics, running and photography. There were also societies for wireless and aviation engineering, a ladies' hockey team, and an operatic society, which gave annual productions of Gilbert & Sullivan operettas at Clydebank Town Hall, where their performances were attended by Sir William and his works managers.[78] The Singer Company, following the confrontations with its workforce that led to the 1911 strike, also became increasingly active in providing recreational activities for the staff at its huge Kilbowie works. It introduced, alongside pension schemes, classes in music, dance, elocution, sewing and arts and crafts, as well as bands, literary societies and a wide range of sports clubs.[79] In Dumbarton, Denny also provided sporting and recreational clubs, the Denny Institute, founded in 1892, being followed by the Denny Social Club in West Bridgend in 1917. By the 1920s, employers' inroads into leisure were deeply entrenched. While the actor-manager John Clyde had brought *Jeanie Deans* to Dumbarton in 1911, by 1922 it was the preserve of the Singer Amateur Dramatic Players in the Singer Hall.

While popular entertainment in the inter-war years was dominated by cinema and dancing, the social politics of the period were in turn overshadowed by economic depression, and its devastating effect on the working communities of West Dunbartonshire. Organised recreation was much as it had been for the previous decades, with church influence predominant and an Edwardian sense of order prevailing over the myriad cultural and musical societies. But rising levels of unemployment from soon after the First World War and their impact on the lives of the working classes led both municipal authorities and working-class organisations to act to preserve unemployed people's access to leisure facilities. In Clydebank, where unemployment in 1932 reached 12,545, or 50.4 per cent of registered voters, the Town Council moved to increase its facilities and provide concessions for the jobless. In 1923, a model yachting pond was opened, partly

Singer Sports Gala—The " Queen," Miss Mary Diamond, and her retinue, passing the Grand Stand.

Figure 19 Top: Singer Gala, 1916, with the Holy City visible in the background. Bottom: Mary Diamond, the 1936 Singer Queen.

to generate employment, and a municipal golf course, opened in 1928, proved popular with the unemployed, with the admissions on 6d concessionary tickets rising from 0.3 per cent of total usage in 1930, to 9.5 per cent and 14 per cent in 1931 and 1932 respectively. By 1932, the highpoint of unemployment for the decade, 28.9 per cent of the 5,017 average monthly admissions to the council's Hall Street baths were unemployed. In 1932, additional baths were opened at Bruce Street, where facilities included a swimming pool, Turkish baths, Russian baths, sunray, foam baths and laundry. By 1933, average monthly attendance at the combined baths was 13,594. Public library usage also increased markedly, with 17.2 per cent of the population registered as library users in 1928, while annual issues rose from 124,237 in 1919 to 228,095 in 1926, before reaching their peak for the 1930s at 487,184 in 1932.[80] Other organisations emerged to offer practical aid. The Mutual Service Association was formed in Clydebank in 1932 to help the unemployed through educational classes in hobbies and skills needed for retraining. By 1934, it had 600 members, and was offering classes in a range of different skills, trades and crafts. While such bodies sought to provide practical support, working-class political organisations were also starting to use social activities for more overt political purposes, both for fundraising and as a means of improving morale.

During the disputes of the 1920s and 1930s, music and entertainment, as part of the fabric of life in working communities, came to feature in the context of industrial confrontations. Bands were used for political protests, while theatres and cinemas, normally places of escapism, were regarded as public resources, and, like Co-operative and public halls, employed for meetings during disputes. In Glasgow, theatres were regularly used for political meetings on Sunday evenings, the ILP using the Metropole and the Clarion Scouts the Pavilion. Similarly, in 1911 during the strike at the Singer factory, a mass procession of 8,000 workers from Kilbowie Road to John Brown's had been headed by the Duntocher Brass Band, and the following Sunday a demonstration and rally on Glasgow Green was followed by a mass meeting at the Gaiety Theatre, Clydebank.[81] Cinemas were also used by mainstream parties, the Palace in Dumbarton being hired for a political meeting and an election concert in the same week during the county and burgh elections of 1929.[82]

Militant tactics reached a new level in the politically radicalised Vale of Leven, where, in 1922, with unemployment at 58 per cent of registered workers, a coalition of socialist parties that included the ILP, Communists and Labour, gained control of Bonhill Parish Council, repeating the feat with the District Council in 1935. In this charged atmosphere, the local Vale Unemployed Workers' Movement (UWM) flute band not only played at demonstrations and pickets, but was used to intimidate local political opponents, in one instance following the clerk to the Parish Council to and from work.[83] An Alexandria cinema manager was similarly pressurised into giving the use of his venue for meetings by UWM members picketing outside it. The proliferation of left-wing organisations in the 'Little Moscow' of the Vale in the 1920s and 1930s included the Friends of the Soviet Union, the Young Communist League, Co-operative Men's and Women's Guilds, and the Workers' Charter Committee. These provided a wide range of events between them, including concerts, variety, dances, social evenings, reading groups and sports, with the Communists organising a Burns night at which Hugh MacDiarmid proposed the Immortal Memory.[84]

The cultural activities organised by left-wing organisations, which usually formed part of wider programmes of community involvement or political campaigns, often displayed an emphasis on sociability quite distinct from that of the hedonistic 'rough' consumer culture of commercial entertainments, one that linked them to the political idealism of the period. This was particularly evident in socialist involvement in popular drama. The Clydebank Players, a branch of the ILP, performed Joe Corrie's *The Dreamer* at the 1928 Dunbartonshire Drama Festival, the county section of the Scottish Community Drama Festival.[85] The Glasgow Clarion Players visited the Hume Street Co-operative Hall, while in 1938 the Glasgow Workers' Theatre Group gave performances at Clydebank of Jack Lindsay's *On Guard for Spain* and Clifford Odets' *Waiting for Lefty*, for the Spanish Aid Committee and Clydebank Peace Council respectively. In the post-war period, Glasgow Unity Theatre visited Dumbarton and Clydebank with *The Gorbals Story*.[86]

The influence of these socialist theatre groups was felt in the strong community basis of subsequent theatre in the area. In 1938, the Scottish People's Theatre, formed in 1936, established itself in a hall in Bankend Road, Dumbarton, equipped with a 20ft by 16ft stage, and seating for 250. The first season featured five plays, a puppet show and a revue, given by various amateur societies, while the opening production, Merton Hodge's comedy *The Wind and the Rain*, was performed by a company led and directed by Molly Urquhart. The SPT was praised as a model community theatre, and, after the Bankend Road building was destroyed by bombing in 1941, was reborn as Dumbarton People's Theatre, which continues to the present day.[87] In 1943, Clydebank also established a community theatre, when a public meeting chaired by the provost set up what was to become the Clydebank Repertory Company. A collaborative venture between ten amateur societies, its wartime rehearsals were held in a vacant shop and productions given monthly in the Lesser Town Hall.[88] After the war, it continued as an amateur company at its theatre in Agamemnon Street until the 1980s.

Despite the enormous economic hardships of the Depression, on an institutional level cultural life was rich and assured. Dumbarton celebrated its seventh centenary in 1922. In 1936, the brochure for the Jubilee celebrations to mark Clydebank's fiftieth anniversary, surveying the prize-winning feats of the Clydebank Burgh Band, and Male Voice Choir, and the Union Church and Radnor Park church choirs, suggested that the town could 'justly be regarded as the musical centre of the West of Scotland'.[89] Notwithstanding this cultural capital, Clydebank derived its confidence and prestige from its industrial achievements, and the launch of the *Queen Elizabeth*, the world's largest vessel, on 30 September 1938, was a source of enormous civic pride. The culmination of a week's festivities, the ceremony, conducted by the Queen (the King having been detained by deteriorating events in Europe), was watched by 50,000 people in the shipyard, including 10,000 workers, while thousands more looked on from vantage points at the Singer factory, the Boulevard, canal bank, and the railway embankment, and 'some adventurous people even climbed the roofs of tenements and stood by chimney heads'.[90]

However, Sabbatarianism, or Sunday observance, remained a point of contention. In 1938, Dumbarton Presbytery voted to protest against the proposed Sunday opening of the forthcoming Empire Exhibition at Bellahouston, albeit on the humanitarian grounds that

large numbers of transport workers all over the country would lose their day of rest, in order to convey their fellow men and women to and from the ground that day.[91]

The same year, Clydebank Council's Parks committee voted to open the golf course on Sunday afternoons, by a vote of eight to five. A previous plebiscite organised by the Town Council over whether or not to allow Sunday games, in which 69 per cent of citizens participated, found in favour of the proposal by a small majority, the vote being 9,003 for and 8,925 against. The Amalgamated Wards committee subsequently applied for Sunday opening of putting greens and children's playgrounds. The very narrow margins of approval suggest the strong residual effects of religious conservatism.[92]

With the coming of war, the comparative uneventfulness of the early months of the conflict brought a sense of unreality. By early 1941, government reports of morale on Clydeside were alarmed by this apparent detachment from events, noting that 'only 3% of overheard conversations in Glasgow related directly to the war in any way, as compared with c. 10%

during the same period in southern studies'.[93] At a Dumbarton football ground, spectators were overheard complaining at having to carry gas-masks. There was also 'considerable grumbling about fire-watching, especially noted in the Dumbarton area, people saying that "it's a waste of time", "unnecessary", etc.' Concluding that Glasgow was as remote from the war as London had been on the eve of the invasion of Holland, the assessors regretted the shortage of Ministry of Information 'war talks' designed to raise levels of preparedness for what might lie ahead, particularly in Dumbarton and the Vale of Leven.[94]

One result of wartime adrenalin and full employment was that the entertainment scene was buzzing. In the late 1930s, the Co-operative Hall in Hume Street, Clydebank, had offered dancing to the Philino Dance Band, with Jim Fanning and a lady crooner, with prizes for the Monte Carlo Waltz and 'The Lambeth Walk'.[95] By 1941, people from Clydebank and the Vale could choose from similar local dances, or travel up to one of the super dance halls in Glasgow, where 'the most crowded spot', the Locarno, was 'a seething cauldron of humanity'.[96] Alternatively, there was the huge Playhouse, where bands played in shifts from alternate ends of the floor. Oscar Rabin's featured two female vocalists in red dresses who sat with them to 'clap hands, shake shoulders etc.' during the Jitterbug and finished its set with a 'hot' number entitled 'Six lessons from Madam la Conga'. Not every aspect was so glamorous: on his way out the Mass-Observation reporter noted that 'In [the] gents cloakroom there are patches of sawdust covering vomit, and a sailor has passed out on a sofa'. In the lavatory, several men were taking swigs from bottles.[97]

Both cinema-going and dancing featured prominently in memories of the Clydebank Blitz, with many accounts of the night of 13 March 1941 involving people returning to the town after visiting theatres or dance halls in Glasgow, or being caught in local cinemas at the raid's onset. Walking home after a night at the Queen's Theatre by Glasgow Cross, Alex Hardie and his family were forced to shelter in closes as shrapnel clattered off roofs and pavements, and the impact of one nearby explosion blew Alex into the street.[98] The audience watching a Shirley Temple film at the Regal interrupted by the raid kept their spirits up with community singing:

People began to get up on to the platform and sing and we all joined in [. . .] But suddenly an incendiary bomb came through the roof and landed on the stage. The wardens ran on with pumps and water hoses and everyone in the hall was moved to the back underneath the balcony. That put paid to the singers who were a bit worn out by this time.[99]

Elsewhere, at the Hume Street Co-operative Hall, a concert by the UCBS party was underway when the sirens went off, and the 300 people attending had to spend the night sheltering in the cellar.[100]

While the raids and their aftermath had a devastating effect on the community, the stoicism of Clydebank people's response in the months of evacuation that followed became a defining feature of the town's identity. In practical terms, the effects of the destruction were as damaging to entertainment as they were to every other aspect of town life. Halls, schools, cinemas and dance halls were destroyed, as were the vast majority of public buildings. The loss of the Singer Hall and its contents resulted in the demise of the Singer Pipe Band, while the Duntocher Silver Band and Clydebank Burgh Band lost their halls and equipment.[101]

The post-war period saw the gradual decline and eventual closure of the large industrial manufacturing concerns on which the prosperity of Clydebank, Dumbarton and the Vale had been built. The loss was all the more severe for the fact that, in some cases, the scale of their social activities, and their impact on the social fabric of life in the communities that served them, had never been greater.

Ostensibly, the aftermath to war saw life resume as before. In 1950, Clydebank Council introduced popular 'illuminations' at Dalmuir Park, which, with competitions and concerts, became an annual feature until the 1960s. Singer continued its extensive pre-war infrastructure of sponsored clubs and societies (see Plate 9), with the new Singer Hall hosting annual festivals of drama and vocal music, a flower show, and Caledonian Ball. The Singer Gala and Sports Day, first held in 1916 and now a Clydebank institution, continued at the Singer recreation ground. There its programme of football, track events and Highland dancing culminated in the pageant and crowning of the Singer Queen, a ceremony that seemed to cement civic and corporate bonds in a modern urban version of older folk-based rituals. At the 1950 Gala, Frances Black, 32 Dept., was crowned Queen by the glamorous star of the 'Road' movies, Dorothy Lamour; the following year the ceremony was undertaken by Max Wall, 'King of Comedy', courtesy of Moss Empires.

However, the fabric of life and leisure was changing. The first television set on licensed premises in Dumbarton was installed at the Black Bull Inn, West Bridgend, in 1952. In 1956, rock and roll hit Clydebank, when the arrest of youths after a local screening of *Rock around the Clock* made the national newspapers.[102] But otherwise cinemas were everywhere closing or facing conversion to bingo or dance halls, and the legalisation of betting shops in 1961 ended the illicit and lucrative business of back-street bookies. Although Singer achieved record employment of over 16,000 in 1960, only three years later, on 15 March 1963, the unthinkable happened when the provost ceremonially stopped the Singer clock, the Orwellian symbol of the company's Kilbowie presence since its installation in 1886, prior to demolition, as the factory was redeveloped in an attempt to modernise. In the same year, Denny's shipyard and engineering works in Dumbarton went into liquidation. In September 1967, national and international attention focused on Clydebank and John Brown's for the naming by HM the Queen of her namesake, Cunard's new flagship the QE2, in a scene that echoed the christening of the previous *Queen Elizabeth* in 1938. As before, the town stopped work to witness the event. But, in the same year, the company joined with others to form Upper Clyde Shipbuilders and, in December 1972, the name disappeared when the yard was taken over by Marathon Manufacturing to build oilrig modules. Singer finally closed in 1980.

The loss of these major employers was a devastating blow, not only in terms of their direct economic impact, but also for the role that monumental concerns like Singer's and Denny's had for the communities that they had supported. The desperate attempts to save John Brown's in the summer of 1971 represented concerted community action on behalf of an industry, shipbuilding, whose preservation seemed essential to the very culture and purpose of the town.

While the interactive, communal experiences of cinema-going, dancing and socialising in pubs were increasingly undermined by television, responsibility for providing facilities for leisure and recreation increasingly fell to central or local government. Previously supported by religious groups and temperance campaigners, and then by employers and working-class voluntary and political groups, from the 1960s onwards, this area was increasingly recognised as the province of government planning. Central and local government initiatives designed to aid regeneration also included plans for the provision of leisure and cultural development. The place of leisure was now something that was recognised as integral to plans for the development of new societies. As Roddy Gallacher observed, 'Community now has become defined not by the local working class, but by professional planners acting within a framework of the restructuring of the economic base'.[103]

The most ambitious of these initiatives was the Quality of Life Experiment that took place in west Dunbartonshire between February 1974 and August 1976. This was one of four national Experiments jointly funded by central government in collaboration with local authorities, the Arts Council of Great Britain (including the Scottish Arts Council) and local voluntary groups. Its aim was to see what, in urban areas, a programme of local community-generated activities in culture, recreation and sports could achieve, if given a concerted push.[104] Over its two-year period, the

Figure 20 Dumbarton Arts Bus with Derek Carpenter's Puppets at Bellsmyre, August 1975. Photo by David Mitchell.

Dumbarton Experiment received funding of £260,000, while three specially constituted Neighbourhood Groups, covering Dumbarton, the Vale of Leven and Helensburgh, administered a total of 163 projects. With a brief to expand the range of recreational activities by optimising use of existing resources, rather than through new building, major projects included the Dumbarton Arts Bus, which visited local communities with its cinema, arts workshop and disco; a two-week Dumbarton Arts Festival; a community theatre project with 7:84 Theatre Company; poetry and writers' workshops; and an innovative community television project in Bonhill. Other initiatives included children's play projects, subsidised transport for voluntary groups, funding for a youth centre in Rosneath, and support for a number of community festivals, including the Vale of Leven Gala, Helensburgh Week and Bellsmyre Festival, as well as for a wide range of sporting activities and clubs.[105]

Of their nature, the Experiment's results were complex. Of the area's population of 78,000, it was estimated that in round terms 80,000 (!) people were directly involved over the two-year period, while the total of 'person/sessions' (the number of people involved multiplied by the number of times they took part in activities) was 225,000. Despite this, the difficulty of quantifying quality of life and how it might have been improved led to the final Report's probably overcautious assessment that, given the scale of events and participation, there were reasonable grounds to indicate that 'enrichment' had taken place. Wider conclusions were varied, but reaffirmed the view of observers like Roddy Gallacher – and the intuition of the Experiment's original brief – that action was most effectively generated from grass-roots activists. The report found that surprisingly low levels of funding were necessary to stimulate the creativity of existing voluntary groups, and that the most effective role for authorities, apart for providing financial support, was to supply back-up expertise in areas like marketing and publicity. In effect, it affirmed the counter-view to the Big Brother notion that culture should – or could – be strategically imposed, asserting instead that it should rather be enabled by enlightened support.

Following the end of the Experiment, a new organisation, the Dumbarton District Arts Working Group, emerged to support the continuation of some of its more viable projects, while, in 1980, the arts in Clydebank produced their own co-ordinating organisation, Clydebank Arts and Leisure Enterprises, known as CANDLE, which was established as 'a vehicle to stimulate the growth of arts activities within the Clydebank area'.[106] Co-ordinating with a wide range of local organisations, including Clydebank Pottery Group, Clydebank Lyric Choir, Clydebank Male Voice Choir, Clydebank Musical Society, Clydebank Orchestra, Clydebank Local History Society and Clydebank Photographic Group, CANDLE initiated an Arts Project in the area in 1984. It subsequently employed a full-time Arts Worker and, in 1989, changed its emphasis to embrace education in the arts with particular reference to young people and groups with special needs. CANDLE also developed the theatre in the St Andrew's School, attracting performances by TAG, Scottish Ballet, and, in the mid-1980s, developed a relationship with Glasgow's then-annual Mayfest, whereby productions from the festival, including those by Borderline and Wildcat, also visited Clydebank.

The physical environment of both Dumbarton and Clydebank altered considerably from the 1960s onwards. The random growth of the past was replaced by planned town centre developments, partly necessitated by wartime damage and the need to replace older buildings that were unsafe and insanitary. Although new buildings always attract criticism (in the 1930s George Blake had already denounced the 'architectural chaos' of Dumbarton's pre-war High Street as 'a tragic melange of mingled and competing styles'), there was a price to be paid for redevelopment in loss of character as some of Dumbarton's oldest pubs – the College Bar and Kirk's Bar (later the Railway Tavern) in College Street, and the County Bar in Church Street – were demolished in the reshaping of the central area.[107] Opened in 1969, Dumbarton's new Town Centre included the Concord community centre for youth, and the Denny Civic Theatre, a 340-seat venue funded by a bequest from the Denny family. In Clydebank, high unemployment and the prospect of further social deprivation following the loss of major employers led the Scottish Development Agency (SDA) to designate the town its first Enterprise Zone in 1980. In 1985, the Singer site became the Clydebank Business Park, where new businesses included Radio Clyde. The Clyde Regional Shopping Centre, which opened in 1985, was followed by an adjacent 10-screen UCI multiplex cinema, with seating for over 2,500, and the Playdrome, initially known as Clydebank Tourist Village. This opened in January 1994, containing two swimming pools, including one six-lane, 25m pool with wave machine and flumes, together with indoor sporting facilities. Most recently, new commercial developments have included the Drumkinnon Tower and Lomond Shores complex at Balloch.

Formal provision continues to be developed. The current local arts infrastructure includes West Dunbartonshire Arts Council, which works to promote the arts in the area, while established events include Lomond Folk Festival and Dumbarton's Feis, a community arts festival celebrating music, language and dance. Levengrove and Dalmuir also have annual galas, which include firework displays. Other facilities controlled by the Council's departments include, for visual arts, the Backdoor Gallery at Dalmuir Library, and a network of nine Community Learning and Development Centres. Meanwhile, the area's physical environment is again undergoing major changes. In Dumbarton and the Vale, the Town Centre Initiative is engaged in current projects to improve the town centre through new lighting and shop frontages, and in the clearing and redevelopment of the former whisky distillery site. At Clydebank the large-scale redevelopment of the riverfront area is being undertaken by Clydebank Rebuilt, in a scheme that will accommodate the relocation of Clydebank College and the Playdrome.

These developments and the public provision they represent will obviously have a profound effect on their respective communities. As this chapter has shown, such provision, whether by private benefactors, local authorities or community groups of one kind or another, has marked the provision of entertainment and cultural activity throughout the centuries in West Dunbartonshire. The development of popular culture itself, however, although heavily conditioned by environment, is now recognised as a largely autonomous cultural development. As has been shown, at times, this culture has been at odds with 'official' culture, even violently so. Reliant, as it is, on interaction with the wider range of social factors and circumstances, its vitality is constantly changing. Yet it remains, it seems, beyond shaping by any authority except its own impetus and creativity.

NOTES

1 Dennison, E. Patricia and Coleman, Russel (1999), *Historic Dumbarton: the Scottish Burgh Survey* ([Edinburgh]: Historic Scotland/Tuckwell Press), pp. 8, 15.

2 Irving, Joseph (1857), *The History of Dumbartonshire from the Earliest Period to the Present Time* (Dumbarton), pp. 94–5.

3 Findlay, Bill (1998), 'Beginnings to 1700', in Bill Findlay (ed.), *A History of Scottish Theatre* (Edinburgh: Polygon), pp. 1–79.

4 *Accounts of the Lord High Treasurer*, vol. IX, AD 1546–1551 (Edinburgh, 1911), p. 73.

5 Jackson, John (1793), *The History of the Scottish Stage* (Edinburgh), pp. 408, 415.

6 Dennison, E. Patricia and Coleman, Russel (1999), *Historic Dumbarton: the Scottish Burgh Survey* ([Edinburgh]: Historic Scotland/Tuckwell Press), pp. 16–17.

7 McGavin, John J. (2004), 'Faith, pastime, performance and drama in Scotland to 1603', in Jane Milling and Peter Thomson (eds), *Cambridge History of British Theatre: vol. 1: Origins to 1660* (Cambridge: Cambridge University Press), pp. 70–86 (p. 74).

8 Marwick, J. D. (ed.) (1909), *The River Clyde and the Clyde Burghs* (Edinburgh: SBRS), p. 89; Dennison, E. Patricia and Coleman, Russel (1999), *Historic Dumbarton: the Scottish Burgh Survey* ([Edinburgh]: Historic Scotland/ Tuckwell Press) p. 25.

9 Dumbarton Burgh Records, 21 May 1627 [brawl at dance], 23 August 1627 [disorderly sailor], 1 February 1634 [booths], 8 August 1628 [tumult – drunken brawl], 23 June 1634 [wine and dice]. See Irving, Joseph, *History of Dumbartonshire*, (second edition, 1860) Appendix pp. 475, 480, 491, 505–6.

10 Dumbarton Burgh Records, 24 October 1634, p. 46; Irving, Joseph, *History of Dumbartonshire* (1860), Appendix, Dumbarton Burgh Affairs, p. 171.

11 Dumbarton Burgh Records, pp. 78–9, 18 May, 3 July 1660.

12 Dumbarton Burgh Records, 11 January 1636, quoted in Irving, Joseph, *History of Dumbartonshire* (second edition, 1860), Appendix, p. 511.

13 Dumbarton Burgh Records, 9 July 1664, quoted in Irving, Joseph, *History of Dumbartonshire* (second edition, 1860), Appendix, p. 546.

14 19 March 1753, Irving, Joseph, *History of Dumbartonshire* (1860), pp. 249–50.

15 Macleod, Donald (1877), *Castle and Town of Dumbarton* (Dumbarton), pp. 247, 245–66. Joseph Irving wrote of this time: 'Among members of these clubs deep drinking was carried on to an extent which we fortunately know little about in the present day. The toper of sixty years since rarely thought of rising up the same day he sat down', Irving, *History of Dumbartonshire* (1860), p. 259.

16 Steven, Maisie (1995), *Parish Life in Eighteenth-Century Scotland: A review of the Old Statistical Account* (Aberdeen: Scottish Cultural Press), p. 35.

17 Hayward, Brian (1992), *Galoshins: The Scottish Folk Play* (Edinburgh: Edinburgh University Press).

18 Ferguson, James and Temple, J. G. [1927?], *The Old Vale and its Memories* (London: privately printed), p. 83.

19 Contained in Gazetteer to Hayward, Brian (1992), *Galoshins* (Edinburgh: Edinburgh University Press), pp. 203–5, 256–7.

20 Hayward, Brian (1992), *Galoshins* (Edinburgh), pp. 22–9.

21 'Balloch and Around: Recollections of place and people seventy years ago', *Lennox Herald*, 17 December 1892.

22 *Dumbarton Herald*, 25 October 1855, p. 2; MacLeod, Donald (1877), *Castle and Town of Dumbarton* (Dumbarton: Bennett Bros), p. 167.

23 *Dumbarton Herald*, 9 June, 22 September 1864.

24 *Dumbarton Herald*, 11, 18 September 1856, p. 2.

25 *Dumbarton Herald*, 7 August 1856, p. 2.

26 *Dumbarton Argus: or Lennox Magazine*, No. 21, 30 July 1833.

27 *Dumbarton Herald*, 25 October 1855, p. 3.

28 *Dumbarton Herald*, 11 September 1856, p. 2.

29 *Dumbarton Herald*, 11 September 1856, p. 2.

30 *Glasgow Herald*, reprinted *Dumbarton Herald*, 4 September 1856.

31 *Dumbarton Herald*, 22 September 1864, p. 5.

32 Duntocher & District Temperance Crusaders, 'Saturday Evening Concerts' at New Street Hall, Duntocher, with pianist and a Councillor in the chair; and the League of the Cross Saturday Evening Concerts, at McWhirter's Hall, Clydebank; *Clydebank & Renfrew Press*, 19 October 1895, p. 2, and 27 October 1894, p. 2, and under 'Clydebank' in same issue.

33 MacLeod, Donald (1877), *Castle and Town of Dumbarton* (Dumbarton: Bennett Bros), pp. 158–9.

34 *Clydebank & Renfrew Press*, 12 September 1891, p. 2; see also *C&RP*, 24 October 1891, p. 2.

35 Ferguson, James and Temple, J. G. [1927?], *The Old Vale and its Memories* (London: privately printed), p. 72.

36 'Vale of Leven Choral Society', *Lennox Herald*, 6 May 1882, p. 3; 'Dumbarton Choral Union', *Lennox Herald*, 30 March 1895. The account of the Dumbarton AGM reveals that membership over the previous seven years had remained 'very steady', ranging from 119 in 1887–8, to a high of 174 in 1891–2.

37 For Clydebank musical and sporting organizations, see Malcolm, Pat (1988) ' "Leisure and Recreation", Social trends: 1886–1914', pp. 51–8, in Hood, John (compiler), *The History of Clydebank* (Carnforth: Parthenon).

38 Ferguson, James and Temple, J. G. [1927?], *The Old Vale and its Memories* (London: privately printed), pp. 13, 72–4.

39 MacLeod, Donald (1877), *Castle and Town of Dumbarton* (Dumbarton: Bennett Bros), pp. 148–9.

40 'Dumbarton Races and Regatta, 22 August 1834' (programme), Dumbarton Archives, GDD13/3/2.

41 Dumbarton Regatta Club Minutes Book, 1853–64, GDD13/1/1; bills for 1862 and 1863 Regattas.

42 MacPhail, I. M. M. (1987), *Lennox Lore* (Dumbarton: Dumbarton District Libraries), pp. 56–7; Hood, John (1999), *Old Dumbarton* (Catrine: Stenlake Publishing) p. 34.

43 MacPhail, I. M. M. (1972), *Dumbarton Through the Centuries* (Dumbarton: Dumbarton Town Council), p. 75.

44 MacPhail, I. M. M. (1972), *Dumbarton Through the Centuries* (Dumbarton: Dumbarton Town Council), p. 76.

45 Irving, Joseph (1860), *History of Dumbartonshire* (Dumbarton), p. 261.

46 *Clydebank Press*, 22 August 1891, p. 2; 29 August, p. 2 and p. 4; 23 July 1892, p. 2; 13 August, p. 2.

47 Durie, Alastair J. (2003), *Scotland for the Holidays: A History of Tourism in Scotland, 1780–1939* (East Linton: Tuckwell), pp. 48, 55.

48 *Lennox Herald*, 11 March 1882, p. 2.

49 *Lennox Herald*, 22 April 1882, p. 4; 28 January 1911, p. 4.

50 *Lennox Herald*, 31 October 1896; *Clydebank & Renfrew Press*, 5 November 1897, p. 3.

51 Lawson, William E. (1948), *A History of Clydebank Co-operative Society Ltd* (Glasgow: the Society), p. 45.

52 *Dumbarton Herald*, 19 July 1882, p. 4. For 'El Dorado', see *DH*, 14 June 1882, p. 4.

53 *Dumbarton Herald*, 28 June 1882, p. 3.

54 *Lennox Herald*, 1 July 1882, p. 3.

55 *Dumbarton Herald*, 9 August 1882, p. 4.

56 MacLeod, Donald (1877), *Castle and Town of Dumbarton* (Dumbarton: Bennett Bros), pp. 246–66.

57 MacLeod, Donald (c. 1891), *The God's Acres of Dumbarton* (Dumbarton), pp. 221–2.

58 In West (Old) Kilpatrick, the number of public houses fell from thirty-one in 1841 to twenty-three in 1891, although over the period the population increased from 7,020 to 17,715: Bruce, John (1893), *History of the Parish of West or Old Kilpatrick* (Glasgow: John Smith), p. 147.

59 MacLeod, Donald (1877), *Castle and Town of Dumbarton* (Dumbarton: Bennett Bros), pp. 148–9.

60 *Dumbarton Herald*, 4 February 1882, p. 2.

61 Lawson, William E. (1948), *A History of Clydebank Co-operative Society Ltd* (Glasgow: the Society), pp. 1–3, 67.

62 See Hood, John (compiler) (1988), *The History of Clydebank* (Carnforth: Parthenon), p. 57.

63 Gallacher, Roddy (1982), 'The Vale of Leven 1914–1975: Changes in Working Class Organisation and Action', in Tony Dickson (ed.), *Capital and Class in Scotland* (Edinburgh: John Donald), pp. 186–211 (pp. 186–9).

64 *Clydebank & Renfrew Press*, 15 August 1891, p. 2.

65 'Horse Racing and Betting', *Clydebank & Renfrew Press*, 29 August 1891, p. 3; 'Clydebank Evening resort', 15 August 1891.

66 *Lennox Herald*, 2 January 1897, pp. 2–3.

67 See Brown, Callum G. (1996), 'Popular Culture and the Continuing Struggle for Rational Recreation', in T. M. Devine and Richard Finlay (eds), *Scotland in the Twentieth Century* (Edinburgh: Edinburgh University Press), pp. 210–29 (pp. 218–19). Clydebank's town clerk, John Hepburn, stated that the by-law was intended to target 'persons either taking in liquor into the premises licensed (particularly before the close of public houses at 10 o'clock) or getting it brought in and consuming it there. To allow this would be to encourage drinking on the premise or even playing for drink [. . .] adjournments from public houses to billiard rooms at that hour with a supply of liquor is so common that the council desire to do all in their power to prevent it [. . .] in the interest of good order in billiard rooms'. Letter, 19 January 1905. SRO [now NAS], DD5/1247 Billiard and Bagatelle Rooms.

68 Brown, Callum G. (1996), 'Popular Culture and the Continuing Struggle for Rational Recreation', in T. M. Devine and Richard Finlay (eds), *Scotland in the Twentieth Century* (Edinburgh: Edinburgh University Press), p. 213; *Clydebank & Renfrew Press*, 29 April 1938.

69 Figures from Reports of the Chief Constable of Dumbartonshire, 1919–38, quoted on p. 294.

70 Watson, William Carrick (1984), 'Clydebank in the Inter-war Years: A Study in Economic and Social Change' (unpublished Glasgow University PhD thesis), pp. 300–1.

71 *Lennox Herald*, 2 April 1910, p. 1.

72 *Lennox Herald*, 26 August 1911, p. 2.

73 *Lennox Herald*, 27 August 1910, p. 2.

74 *Lennox Herald*, 31 August 1895, p. 4.

75 Taylor, Mike, Walton, Julia and Liddell, Colin (1991), *A Night At The Pictures* (Dumbarton District Libraries), p. 20.

76 Stirling, Thomas B. (1915), *History of the Vale of Leven Co-operative Society Limited 1862–1912* (Alexandria: Vale of Leven Co-operative Society), pp. 98–101, 129; Lawson, William E. (1948), *A History of Clydebank Co-operative Society Ltd* (Glasgow: the Society), pp. 66–7.

77 Lawson, William E. (1948), *A History of Clydebank Co-operative Society Ltd* (Glasgow: the Society), pp. 69, 75.

78 Johnston, Ian (1993), *Beardmore Built: The Rise and Fall of a Clydeside Shipyard* (Clydebank District Libraries & Museums Department), pp. 102–5.

79 Ballantine, Ishbel et al. (eds) / Glasgow Labour History Workshop (1989), *The Singer Strike, Clydebank 1911* (Clydebank District Libraries), pp. 54–6.

80 Watson, William Carrick (1984), 'Clydebank in the Inter-war Years: A Study in Economic and Social Change' (unpublished Glasgow University PhD thesis), pp. 280–4.

81 Ballantine, Ishbel et al. (eds) / Glasgow Labour History Workshop (1989), *The Singer Strike, Clydebank 1911* (Clydebank District Libraries), pp. 31–3.

82 *Lennox Herald*, 25 May 1929, p. 5.

83 Gallacher, Roddy (1982), 'The Vale of Leven 1914–1975: Changes in Working Class Organisation and Action', in Tony Dickson (ed.), *Capital and Class in Scotland* (Edinburgh: John Donald,) pp. 186–211 (p. 197); also Macintyre, Stuart (1980), *Little Moscows: Communism and Working-class Militancy in Inter-war Britain* (London: Croom Helm), pp. 79–111.

84 Macintyre, Stuart (1980), *Little Moscows: Communism and Working-class Militancy in Inter-war Britain* (London: Croom Helm), p. 103.

85 *Lennox Herald*, 16 February 1929, p. 1.

86 Mackenney, Linda (2000), *The Activities of Popular Dramatists and Drama Groups in Scotland, 1900–1952* (Lampeter: Edwin Mellor Press), pp. 265, 269, 281–2.

87 *Glasgow Herald*, 7 September 1938, p. 6: Murdoch, Helen (1981), *Travelling Hopefully: The Story of Molly Urquhart* (Edinburgh: Paul Harris Publishing), pp. 52–5.

88 *Clydebank Press*, 'Local Repertory Theatre', 5 November 1943; 'Clydebank "Little" Theatre', 25 November 1943.

89 *Clydebank Town Council, Souvenir Jubilee Brochure, 1886–1936* (1936), p. 55.

90 *Clydebank Press*, 30 September 1938.

91 *Clydebank Press*, 6 May 1938.

92 *Glasgow Herald*, 15 June 1937, p. 17; *Clydebank Press*, 24 June 1938, p. 5.

93 Mass-Observation Archive, 600 'Glasgow Morale' (preliminary report), 7/3/41, pp. 8–9. Reproduced with permission of Curtis Brown Group Ltd, London on behalf of the Trustees of the Mass-Observation Archive. Copyright © Trustees of the Mass-Observation Archive.

94 Mass-Observation Archive, 600 'Glasgow Morale' (preliminary report), 7/3/41, pp. 1, 8–11.

95 *Clydebank Press*, 15 April 1938.

96 Mass-Observation Archive, 600 'Glasgow Morale' (preliminary report), 7/3/41, p. 13, no. 35.

97 Mass-Observation Archive. 66/9/G: Glasgow: Entertainment 1941; Handwritten Obs. of visits to Playhouse Dance Hall 24.2.41 & 3.3.41.

98 From Alex Hardie, in Clydebank Life Story Group (1999), *Untold Stories: Remembering Clydebank in War Time* (Clydebank Life Story Group), p. 151.

99 From Helen McNeill, in Clydebank Life Story Group (1999), *Untold Stories: Remembering Clydebank in War Time* (Clydebank Life Story Group), p. 55.

100 Lawson, William E. (1948), *A History of Clydebank Co-operative Society Ltd* (Glasgow: the Society), pp. 91–2.

101 Hood, John (compiler) (1988), *The History of Clydebank* (Carnforth: Parthenon), p. 108.

102 I am indebted to Mike Taylor for the Black Bull information; *Glasgow Herald*, 25 September 1956, p. 7.

103 Gallacher, Roddy (1982), 'The Vale of Leven 1914–1975: Changes in Working Class Organisation and Action', in Tony Dickson (ed.), *Capital and Class in Scotland* (Edinburgh: John Donald,) pp. 186–211 (p. 207).

104 *Leisure and the Quality of Life. A Report on Four Local Experiments*, vols 1 & 2 (London: HMSO, 1977/1978).

105 Local organisations participating in the Quality of Life Experiment were, from Dumbarton: the Dumbarton Society, Dumbarton Arts Club, Dumbarton People's Theatre, Dunbartonshire Operatic Society, Dumbarton & District Pipe Band, Dumbarton Cine Club, Concord Hi-Fi Club, Dumbarton Kayak Club, Dumbarton Sea Angling Club, Dumbarton Amateur Athletic Club, Strathclyde Ladies Athletic Club, Dumbarton Rugby Football Club, Kirktonhill Tennis Club, Dumbarton Bowling Association, Dumbarton Golf Club, Dumbarton Sub Aqua Club, Strathclyde Dog Training Club, Dumbarton Floral Club, Dumbarton Ladies Bridge Club, Dumbarton Community Association BC, Community Involvement, and Citizens' Advice Bureau. Participating organisations from the Vale of Leven were: the Vale of Leven Players, Dalvait Ensemble, Haldane Junior Choir, Lomond & District Pipe Band, Vale of Leven Amenities Society, Lennox Rovers Table Tennis Club, Ladyton Tenants Association, Burnbrae Tenants Association, O'Hare Tenants Association, Riverside Tenants Association, Nobleston Tenants Association, Redburn Tenants Association, Levenvale Tenants Association, Alexandria Central Area Tenants Association, Tullichewan Tenants Association, Impact Youth Club, Vale of Leven Caged Bird Club, Dunbartonshire Budgerigar Society, Vale of Leven Beekeepers Association, An Comunn Gaidhealach (Vale of Leven branch). Information from *Quality of Life Guide*, pp. 17–20.

106 'Application for Funding for Forthcoming Financial Year, April 1989–March 1990', Introduction, p. 2; Clydebank Arts and Leisure Enterprises, Minutes of Meetings, Ref. 790. LC, Clydebank Library.

107 Blake, George (1934), *The Heart of Scotland* (London: Batsford), pp. 49–50; Taylor, Mike (2005), 'Some Notes on Dumbarton's Old Public Houses for Articles Submitted to the Lennox Herald Newspaper in 2005' (unpublished), Dumbarton Library, by kind permission of Mike Taylor.

APPENDIX: OLD KILPATRICK GALOSHINS TEXT

SLASHER

I am a gallant soldier
And Slasher is my name,
My sword and buckle by my side,
I'm sure to win the game.

The game, sir, the game, sir,
Lies not within thy power,
For with my glittering sword and spear
I soon will thee devour.

(*They fight and Slasher is wounded, Keekum Funny calls for a doctor.*)

A doctor, a doctor.

DR BROWN
  Here I am.

Are you a doctor?

DOCTOR
  Yes, you can plainly see
  By my art and activity.

What diseases can you cure?

DOCTOR
  Itch, the pitts [?pilts], the palsy and the gout.
  If you had nineteen devils in your skull,
  I'd cast twenty of them out.
  I cured Sir Harry of the rag nail fifty-five yards long.
  Surely I can cure this man,
  Here, Jack, take a little from my bottle,
  And let it run down thy throttle,
  Thou art not slain,
  Rise up and fight again.

  I have in my pockets
  Crutches for lame ducks,
  Spectacles for blind bumble bees,
  Pack saddles and panniers for grasshoppers,
  Plaster for broken-back mice.

(*They fight again, and Slasher is killed, Keekum Funny goes round with a sea-shell gathering money.*)

[Information: Their faces were blacked and they wore old clothes.]

Source: James Arnott Collection.

From Brian Hayward, *Galoshins: The Scottish Folk Play* (Edinburgh: Edinburgh University Press, 1992). Text format is as presented in source.

CHAPTER 7

Sport and 'King Football': Professionalism and 'Industrialisation'

Bob Crampsey

'Sport' can be divided into two sectors – firstly the amateur games, played essentially for fun, and, secondly, those paid sports that produced some of Scotland's 'Greats' and whose protagonists can be further categorised into 'Officers and Men'. West Dunbartonshire has always had a robust sporting heritage with a broad range of sports and pastimes enthusiastically followed or supported. Bowls (Renton Bowling Club was formed in 1866, the oldest club in the Vale), cricket (Vale of Leven had a cricket club by 1877), rowing, which Paul Maloney discusses in some detail, all had their appointed seasons. Tennis, quoits and fishing had their devotees and the cycling craze looked as if it would last the pace. To avoid overemphasising football, important as that is to the area, this chapter will consider first other, less prominent, but nonetheless important, sports, although all would give way, in the phraseology of time, to 'King Football'. In doing so, the chapter will not only reflect developments in sport from the late nineteenth century on (for, of course, Paul Maloney has dealt with sport in earlier periods), but, in doing so, will set them in the larger context of themes addressed elsewhere in this book.

One of these themes emerges from Paul Maloney's chapter on popular entertainments. This is the tension between the forces seeking social control and those pursuing the principles of pleasure, abandonment and celebration of the human spirit in the, albeit temporary, overthrow of rational order or establishment rules. In some sense, this can be seen as the long-term competition in human life between the Dionysian and the Apollonian. Certainly, sport, as a key element of the expression of human endeavour, can be seen to express such a dynamic. What is more, in the early years of the modern period in West Dunbartonshire, since the middle of the nineteenth century, one of the expressions of this creative human dynamic lay in the development of more systematisation of sports. In this development, the tension between the need for free enjoyment and control, between human aspiration and the perceived need to manage that aspiration, found several points of tension and even conflict that will be discussed in detail. These include the development of professionalism in football – and even the very establishment of a league system – at the end of the nineteenth century. Such a point of tension can also be seen in the middle of the twentieth century when forces of community feeling focused around the controversial establishment of Clydebank Football Club within the Scottish Football League out of an association with East Stirlingshire.

Another theme touched on in other chapters concerns the implications of the processes of industrialisation in West Dunbartonshire. Richard Finlay's chapter, of course, deals with this topic's political and economic implications in illuminating detail, while Alan Riach addresses the arts of industrialised West Dunbartonshire. An underlying theme of this chapter, although one not overemphasised, is that the rise of organised sport and the ways in which it developed were both a result of, and affected by, the changes in patterns of employment and industrial activity in the area.

A third theme of this chapter is that sport has offered a means of personal fulfilment and even of escape from industrialised poverty for talented individuals. These include both such renowned figures as Alec Jackson, Ian McColl and Jackie Stewart and other distinguished, but less famous, sports people whose participation in sport in West Dunbartonshire transformed their lives, if only for a time. Whichever category they belong to, these individuals embody something of the power and impact of sport to express values of individual and team enterprise and human ambition and aspiration. Such figures come to be representative icons of the potential of their home area to produce greatness.

QUOITS, CYCLING, GOLF AND THE PLACE OF FOOTBALL

It was an old saying that where there were miners there would be quoits and, starting from Hardgate near Duntocher, the sport had its strength in the mining villages going east and curving north to Milngavie. Certainly, it was essentially a sport of the mining villages, but there were also quoiting clubs in the douce areas of Glasgow such as Pollokshields. It was the simplest of games in its rules – man throws a ring at a target. Americans threw horseshoes in much the same manner, but in Britain it was the quoit. There was a Dunbartonshire league in the early twentieth century: a game at Renton in which Helensburgh were victors by one shot took place, for example, on 5 July 1913.[1] It has been said that the game was played in parts of the Midlands, Lancashire and Scotland up until the 1930s, but the game lasted much longer than that. In the 1950s and 1960s, there were several international fixtures against Wales with printed programmes to attest the fact.

It was an ideal game for people who had no money. There was no elaborate wicket to maintain, no specialist clothing was required, nor clubs nor racquets such as were essential for golf and tennis. At both ends of the pitch, there were circles of stiff clay, in the middle of which was embedded a steel pin, with an inch or so showing above ground. The main objective was to 'ring the hob', as the steel or iron pin was called. A rare feature of the game was that the duration of the match was entirely in the hands of the players, whether at singles, doubles, foursomes or team matches.

The first reaction of the ruling powers when new games emerged was to forbid them. In the seventeenth century, quoits hovered on the brink of respectability, but fell back at court as being something too rough for scholars and noblemen. On occasions, boisterousness overcame the need for disciplined playing: in England, in earlier times, for example, the Tudors, with memories of the Wars of the Roses, were opposed to the notion of creating occasions that would allow the peasantry to assemble in large numbers. Yet, there was a real discipline and skill required for throwing the heavy rings, although, unlike tennis (and here we are talking of real tennis, not the lawn variety), it never became fashionable. The game increasingly became the property of the new industrial areas as all that was needed was a small stretch of wasteland and a lean-to to act as a pavilion.

As the number of sports, pastimes and recreations open to the working man increased, so the foundations of international cycling were laid. Cycling races including 'De'il Tak the Hin'most' were popular, as was the magazine *The League of American Wheelmen*. Cycling made the headlines when bloomers made their appearance for women, and although there was some opposition to this new form of dress there was less than that which might have been anticipated.

The cyclists were hardy chiels. As the nineteenth century closed, there were cycling parties setting off from Clydebank and Dumbarton with their destination the moorland villages of Stewarton and Fenwick. As noted in *The Scottish Sport* of 1 January 1895, for example, it was the custom for such a party to bring in the New Year in that desolate landscape. In time, the numbers dwindled to a handful of faithful few until the absolute nadir was reached in the 1930s with a single solitary pedaller moving remorselessly over the hostile terrain.

It has been well said that golf courses in Scotland followed the railway tracks and certainly such was the experience along the banks of the Clyde.

The exception to such foundations were the links where golf had been played since the sixteenth century, but these were almost all rooted in the East and attached to one of the Fife or Lothians towns. In the West of Scotland, Old Prestwick stood out like a lonely beacon for many years. In an effort to stimulate passenger railway traffic, the Secretary of the Glasgow & South Western Railway Company wrote to the secretaries of Gailes and Barassie golf clubs inviting them to nominate locations for stations. There was thus a veritable explosion of golf courses in the West of Scotland, with Dumbarton in 1887, Cardross in 1895 and Clydebank and District (Hardgate) in 1905.

Two of these courses produced players who distinguished themselves in very different ways. James Adey had some claim to be the best-known ever member of Cardross. His membership lasted an incredible sixty-one years, from 1944 until his death in 2005. He was born in the old Clubhouse and he came within feet of dying in it as he dragged his mother from the blazing wreckage of that clubhouse during a German raid on Clydebank. About the end of the war in 1945, it became apparent that the Dumbarton Club also had a young member of uncommon ability in one Charlie Green, born on 2 August 1932 and still going strong at the time of writing. For the next forty years, course records fell before him and he was equally able in match play. By the end of the 1960s, he was an automatic pick for Walker Cup matches. In 1962, he finished as leading amateur in the Open Championship at St Andrews. His course records included Windyhills: 66, Glasgow Gailes: 62, Brodick: 60, Turin: 69, Ralston: 66, Cardross: 68 and Killermont: 64. He was certainly capable of playing professional golf at a very high level, had his inclinations taken him that way. In the 1971 Walker Cup at St Andrews, he lost to Lanny Wadkins by one hole, but he defeated A. K. Miller in the afternoon by a similar margin.

The position of golf now in West Dunbartonshire – as in the country as a whole – is currently in a state of flux. In a very few years now the consequences of low birth rate over twenty years will begin to make themselves apparent. The attempt also to keep young girls as members after they first join has proved unsuccessful, and comparatively few under-15 girls go on to achieve full membership. There is some evidence that the tide may be running against the golf club as organised along traditional lines. Judging from the number and content of advertisements in golf magazines there would seem to be quite a strong lobby in favour of the 'Pay and Play' means of organising the game. West Dunbartonshire, of course, lies on the borders of Loch Lomond golf club, which has achieved a certain amount of public attention as one of the few clubs to be able to inform its members that they are playing rather too much on the native sward.

One example from recent history may, however, highlight where the major focus of sporting interest in the West of Scotland has lain. On an August afternoon at the end of the Second World War, Rangers FC were holding their own athletics meeting. The Rangers manager, Bill Struth, had himself been a professional athlete of renown and the Ibrox meeting was an important one. Alan Paterson, a young Scottish high jumper, was attempting to set a new Empire Record in the face of a low, but definite, booing from the crowd. It emerged that the cause of the booing was that the crowd believed this athletic endeavour was preventing Partick Thistle and Third Lanark playing their five-a-side football tie. Clearly, the football was the preferred option. Although Clydesdale Harriers, founded in 1885, had a Dunbartonshire section, supporting, for example, a road race between Balloch and Clydebank in the early 1920s and regularly having members running in the Singer Sports in Clydebank, there was then, and remains now, no large and consistent public for athletics. This is despite the fact that there is usually a temporary stirring of interest when an Eric Liddell or Alan Wells comes along. The tale of Alan Paterson illustrates the dominance that football had quickly come to command over other Scottish sports. In any discussion of sport in Scotland, Association Football must therefore loom large and other games fall in behind. There is a certain rough justice in this since it would be football that would bring such villages as Renton and Alexandria to the public attention and a claim, however spurious, of world domination in a particular sport.

A RESPECTABLE PASTIME

It was a long time before the game of Association Football was properly organised in this country. When the Scots invited England to play an international match in Glasgow on 30 November 1872, under rules only recently then formulated, it could only be done by hiring the major cricket ground, Hamilton Crescent, for the day. As this was the senior sports ground in Glasgow, it did not come cheaply and there were those who thought that the fee of £10, with another £10 payable if the gate receipts totalled more than £50, was mild extortion. In the event, 4,000 came to watch, the gate was £104 and it had been established that such matches could be a considerable attraction. It also gave notice that football could perhaps eclipse cycle racing and even make inroads into that most established of pastimes, rugby football. The success of the match hastened the formation of the Scottish Football Association in 1873, making the eventual advent of professionalism inevitable.

For a sport to be commercially viable then, a sizeable number of the workforce had to be free to play or watch every Saturday afternoon and this had come about by 1880 as a result of legislation to reduce working hours. That first step having been taken, there was the paradox that the initial help being given to the new-born clubs was arriving from the direction of the Public Schools. Here, we must correct a popular and deep-rooted, yet erroneous, belief. For many years, until our own days even, this belief was that one could tell the social status of a school by the type of game that it played. This is the most unreliable of guides. No one would impugn the social credentials of such schools as Westminster, Charterhouse, Repton, Malvern or Eton, yet each of them plays Association Football.

Nonetheless, egalitarianism was not a virtue overprized by the Victorians. The origins of football as we now know it were in the two ancient English universities and the schools mentioned above. A title or two could come in handy in distancing an organisation from the common throng. Thus, the earls of Rosebery – the Primroses of Dalmeny – had a long connection with Heart of Midlothian; Motherwell's ground, Fir Park, was a gift to the club from Hamilton of Dalziel; and the Earl of Portland was a patron of Kilmarnock. These gentlemen were names on a letterhead rather than active legislators, however, and the game drew its strength from mine, factory and foundry.

To play a game for money professionally was social death and initially there was a fierce prejudice against the paid player. 'Base mercenary', 'Hired man at arms' and 'Traitorous wretches' were some of the kinder descriptions sections of the Scottish press had for them, these particular epithets being found, for example, in *The Scottish Sport* in one month alone: December 1888. Some sports were more hierarchical than others and it is perhaps worth noting here that, as late as 1950, it was regarded as unthinkable that a professional cricketer should captain an English Test Eleven. References to footballers and football continued, in general, then, to be patronising. When, in 1884, a competition was established for Glasgow warehouse firms, it got a qualified approval from Mr Lewis McIver, Unionist candidate for an Edinburgh constituency, who declared, according to *The Scottish Referee* in January 1889:

It is an educative pastime and it makes hardy youth of clerks and shopmen who, without it, might be weaklings. Better is it for our youth to be in the open air than in the tavern.

In the tavern, some of the players undoubtedly were. In a famous Celtic v Dumbarton match just after the turn of the century, when Celtic conceded eight goals, not all of their players were pillars of sobriety or so it was widely rumoured. (There was a much later suggestion of a similarly tipsy occurrence in 1937 when, en route to see the English Cup final, Celtic stopped off at Motherwell to play a league game and lost 8–0. Celtic did not look at peak fitness then either, but it has to be said that they finished with nine men.) In a similar vein, at Parkhead in an early Scottish Cup-tie against a country team, the Celtic goalkeeper, anticipating that not much would be coming his way, kept his ordinary trousers on. The country was, therefore, at the end of the nineteenth century, in the death throes of amateurism while simultaneously undergoing the childbirth pains of professionalism.

The attitude of employers vacillated. Much depended on the status of the team involved. The managing director of Denny's shipyard in Dumbarton was thought to be very liberal when, in 1891, the local Dumbarton players, having reached the final of the Scottish Cup against Hearts, the eventual winners, worked as usual until breakfast time, when they ate together before catching the train. This favour was extended because the players were amateurs. A similar request from Renton, where professionalism had taken hold, was rebuffed out of hand in 1895 when they faced St Bernards in the final, losing to the Edinburgh team 2–1. When, in 1896, Hearts again reached the final stage, they spent the week before the big match against Hibernian in a big hotel. To while away the time, they went to theatres and the circus and played golf over Gullane. These excursions were partly due to beneficent paternalism, and perhaps the thought that it would be well to remove the players from the energy-sapping attentions of their wives. Preparation was becoming professionalised in the terms of the time, and the last time a West Dunbartonshire team was to appear in a Scottish Cup final was in the following year, 1897, when Rangers beat Dumbarton 5–1.

It was important then, too, that the game should have clerical approval. As a general rule, ministers of the Church of Scotland were supportive and helpful, as were the vast majority of Catholic priests. Not so the Free Church of Scotland, at whose 1893 General Assembly the Revd John McNeill denounced the new pastime as 'a wile of the serpent'. Meanwhile, the working-class Scots displayed such an aptitude for this new game that they speedily became known as the 'Scotch Professors'. It should be borne in mind that, in 1900, a fitter or a turner in Glasgow was receiving 36s 6d (£1.82) for a 54-hour week, while a top-class footballer could receive three times that. It was, therefore, evident that many players would be lured by the South and lost to their local Scottish employment pool.

Indeed, England had an eight-year head start in professional football, starting it – officially at least – in 1885 to Scotland's 1893, and initially

Scottish faces were set rigorously against the example. It was pointed out that Scotland had a much smaller population, a population moreover that was crammed into the Forth-Clyde valley and thus, it was argued, professionalism was not feasible. Queen's Park was the most vociferous opponent of pay-to-play and pointed to the likelihood of the speedy disappearance of the game in country clubs such as Renton, Vale of Leven (based in Alexandria) and Dumbarton under a professional regime with its emphasis on large crowds and urban centres. This prophecy proved all too accurate. Renton reached the Scottish Cup final in 1895 and, yet, have the melancholy record of having by then lost their league place, from which they were first evicted before having struck a blow in their defence. (They did not survive their first season of professional football because of scandals regarding professional/amateur status, though they were later readmitted for a time.) As long as football was not professional, however, the temptation to pay under the counter would be overwhelming. Factory hands and artisans formed the great bulk of the players. It was naïve to think that they could take two or three days from work to play frequent friendly matches in England without being compensated for loss of earnings and indemnified against the possible loss of jobs in an era of underemployment.

Players who took the Saxon wage had a hard time of it: 'What Scots worthy of the name would be so base as to deliver a fellow-countryman into abject relations of total humiliation and subservience?' thundered *The Scottish Sport* in 1885. Of course, the answer was that quite a few Scots would. They were the agents, whose job it was to cajole the best Scottish players into coming south. These agents led a harassed life and, on at least two occasions, at Kilmarnock and Glasgow, they were physically chastised by supporters of Kilmarnock and Glasgow Rangers. This was in the early 1890s when it seemed certain that Scotland would be bled dry of footballing talent.

The evidence of one agent, Mr Morton, neatly reveals the kind of dilemma and moral quagmire that the clubs faced and the part Dumbarton had to play in exposing it. In 1887, Hibernian won the Scottish Cup, defeating Dumbarton in the final. There were rumours of irregularities in the Hibs accounts and the Scottish Football Association called in the books. The Vale of Leven club, allies of Dumbarton, hired a private detective called Morton to do some investigating on the vanquished club's behalf. It appears that it was 'infra dig' for the wronged side to fight its own corner. He discovered, among other things, irregularities with a Hibs player called Groves, an apprentice stonemason. Groves was marked down as earning between seven shillings and sixpence and ten shillings and sixpence per week, yet he was being paid thirty shillings and sixpence for one morning alone. He was later also paid a (weekly) pound payment for just three days of work.

Moreover, although Hibernian had had three secretary-treasurers in the previous five years, all the entries for that period were written in the same hand. It was obviously a whitewash set of books and yet, astonishingly, Hibernian was cleared. Some weeks later, the Hibs secretary, Mr McFadden, was reported to have absconded to Canada with the club's funds and money belonging to the Catholic Diocese of Edinburgh.

With the coming of professionalism, the social niceties of Association Football first dwindled, then disappeared. No longer was there a pleasant social gathering after the match. The gate money was checked, rechecked and checked again before being divided (with the notable exception of Queen's Park and Celtic who took each other's declarations on trust). The more formal football dinners continued, however, where toasts were drunk and sentiments expressed. One such well-known sentiment – acceptable if somewhat solemn – was recorded in *The Scottish Sport*: 'May the pleasures of the evening bear the reflections of the morning.' There was every excuse at the time in the early 1890s for those sentiments' erring on the side of smugness. Almost thirty years would elapse before the dismal forecasts of the Queen's Park men would see their fears of professionalism – that village clubs would disappear in its onslaught – come fully home to roost. Before that, Vale of Leven (1877–78–79), Dumbarton (1883) and Renton (1885, 1888) would win the Scottish Cup. What is more, Dumbarton would lift the League Flag not once, but twice, in the first two seasons of that competition, being champions in 1890–1 and 1891–2, although, in the first season, the title was shared with Rangers. This was not all the local clubs' achievement: Dumbarton were losing Cup finalists in 1881, 1882, 1887 and 1891, Vale of Leven in 1883 (beaten by Dumbarton), 1884, 1885 (beaten by Renton) and 1890, and Renton in 1886 and 1895. After 1895, though, of the three clubs, only Dumbarton would ever appear again in a Scottish Cup final, when in 1897, as already noted, they were beaten 5–1 by Rangers. In the same year, Renton became bankrupt.

The dominance of the three teams in this early period of organised football is only exceeded in its remarkable quality by their subsequent eclipse. The impact of that dominance can be registered in certain key moments, which also hint at the fall to come. During the earliest period of organised Association Football in Scotland, Queen's Park had never been beaten nor, in fact, had they ever been scored against. It was Vale of Leven who finally took a goal from them in 1875 and founded their temporary supremacy. Vale of Leven wrote themselves into football history with their ceremony of the Loving Cup, which was to be held by each of the players for one year in turn. The last survivor of the Vale side was then to keep the cup and pass it on to his family or, alternatively, bequeath it to some institution in the Vale. Other clubs, notably Stoke City and Rangers, would perform similar rites in the mid–late 1930s. Yet, by the time the Scottish Football League was formed in 1890, Vale of Leven's great days were behind them. This was depite the fact, already noted, that between 1877 and 1890 they won the Scottish Cup three times – in consecutive years from 1877 – and then reached the final, if only to be losing finalist, on four more occasions, the last being 1890. Despite this truly superb Cup record, League football did not seem to suit them. In their second season, they failed to win a single First Division game and did not seek re-election in 1892.

Like a comet, too, Renton streaked across Scottish skies in the last quarter of the nineteenth century. As we have seen, they won the Scottish Cup twice in 1885 and 1888 and came second in 1886 and 1895. They should have been content to bask in the praises men bestowed on them, but the anarchy that seemed to lurk within them ended in undoing them. Such was their falling away that they went from First Division to non-league in just over ten years. From 1883, there was no living with Renton. In 1890, they refused to obey League regulations that they themselves had helped to draw up. They inhabited a mad world akin to human trafficking. There seemed to be a bright future in store when, in a meeting of the cup holders of Scotland and England, Renton beat West Bromwich Albion 4–1 in the 1888 'Championship of the World' game at Hampden Park. They hung on to this title for several years by a masterly process of inactivity and a refusal to give the Albion a rematch. Here was no gracious acceptance of victory, rather a belligerent claim to be World Champions. It was a twilit world of professionalism.

Players played for clubs in suspicious conditions and the Scottish Football Association, as we have noted, inspected club books as a matter of routine, though usually clubs got the tip-off that the officials were on the way. On one such visit, an entry was uncovered in the Renton books that stated a large sum of money had been allotted to the purchase of chickens. The club maintained that the side always dined on 'chicken broth, that is, chicken bree' (reputed to be made with port and fresh eggs) and, henceforward, they were always known as the 'Chicken Bree Club'. So farcical had things become that it was commonplace for a club to carry two sets of books – one for inspection and the other for the general running of the club.

By 1888, the move to start a Scottish League was under way, both in order to facilitate ease of fixtures and to avoid a situation in which one or more of the leading clubs could be eliminated from the Cup as early as the beginning of September. This had hitherto left those eliminated clubs the cold kale of friendly matches and, as the English League flourished, such friendlies were becoming more and more difficult to arrange. The process of organisation

Figure 21 Top: Vale of Leven FC players holding the Scottish Cup, which they won in 1877 and retained the next two seasons. The players are: Back row: W. Jamieson; A. Michie; W. C. Wood; A. McIntyre; A. McLintock. Front row: R. Paton; D. C. McGregor; D. Lindsay; J. Ferguson; J. McDougall; J. C. Baird.

Bottom: Officials and players of Renton FC after they won the 1888 Scottish Cup and then beat West Bromwich Albion, the English Cup-winners, in a challenge match. The players are: Back row: R. Kelso (half back); A. Hannah (back); J. Lindsay (goal); A. McCall (captain, back); D. McKechnie (half back). Front row: N. McCallum and H. McCallum (right wing); J. Kelly (centre half back); J. Campbell (centre); J. McCall and J. McNee (left wing).

seemed to exacerbate the problems represented in Renton, perhaps even more than Vale of Leven, the most celebrated example of a club that found the rigours of League Football too demanding. Through their early expulsion in 1890 for playing against Edinburgh Saints in the first few weeks of league football in Scotland, they totally destroyed what little chance the Dunbartonshire village had of adjusting to the new regime. Edinburgh Saints were in personnel and ground exactly the same side as St Bernards, who had been expelled from the Scottish League for professionalism.

Despite their wilfulness, Renton were readmitted, but their attitude toward league obligations tended to be cavalier. They were clearly out of their depth, gathering only four points from a possible thirty-six in the season 1893–4, when they were expelled again in what proved to be their last season, Hamilton Academicals taking their place. By 1898, after their 1897 bankruptcy, Renton, a club which, from its ground at Tontine Park, had only ten short years before persistently styled itself 'champions of the world', had disappeared totally from top-level existence.

In the next century, the configuration of football teams in West Dunbartonshire, therefore, was quite changed. Certainly, Vale of Leven came back to the Second Division in 1905 and, from then until the outbreak of war in 1914, lived out an undistinguished Second Division existence. They were bottom of the division three times in the five years just before the First World War. Relegated from the Second Division in 1924, they went down with the whole Third Division fleet two years later. Their ground lay empty and ruinous for some years until, with macabre timing, Millburn Park, to which Vale of Leven had moved in 1888 from their first ground in North Street, became the home of Vale of Leven Juniors in July 1939. From time to time, Vale had their moments as a junior club, winning the Junior League in 1946–7 and 1969–70, and having a glory year indeed in 1953 when 55,800 turned out at Hampden to see Vale win the final against Annbank. There was some talk of trying the senior waters again, but it remained just that, talk.

Meantime, the first version of Clydebank came into existence to complement the continuing presence of Dumbarton. This club, it should be noted, bears no relation to the one that would later play under the same name in the Scottish Football League. They were admitted to the Second Division for the last season before the First World War – there was a naval rearmament programme and the yards were busy. The timing of their launch in an area of busy shipbuilding, however, reminds us of the importance of the links between local industry and the health of local football teams.

When the Second Division was discontinued in 1915, Clydebank played for two years in the Western League and, in 1917, had what seemed a great stroke of good fortune. Wartime travelling difficulties meant that Aberdeen,

Figure 22 Triumphant Vale of Leven football players coming up Main Street, Alexandria, after winning the Scottish Junior Cup in 1953.

Dundee and Raith Rovers had to withdraw from League Football and Clydebank were invited to fill one of their places. They spent the next five years in the top flight and, although relegated in 1922 and again in 1924, on both occasions they got back at the first time of asking. Their only claim to fame is that they borrowed the young Celtic player Jimmy McGrory to play against Celtic and he served them well by scoring the winner against his own team. Clydebank were, however, especially vulnerable to the industrial downturn of the late 1920s and, after threatening to resign from the League in 1929, eventually did so in May 1931.

For the next thirty years or so, the burgh banner would be carried into battle by the two junior clubs, Clydebank Juniors and Duntocher Hibs. Both of these junior clubs proved themselves worthy when they had to contend with severe ground damage during the air raids of 1941–2. In a marvellous example of dogged determination, they took the decision, on a casting vote, to carry on and did so with such success that Clydebank won the Scottish Junior Cup in 1942. Yet, there were those who still longed for the thrill of senior football in Clydebank and there were some snide remarks that Dumbarton had found little difficulty in fielding a respectable side during the war. They might only play to a few hundred and their ground might be half-gallant, half-comical, but they kept the senior game alive in West Dunbartonshire.

Other teams, however, appeared for varying periods of time in the senior ranks. Dumbarton Harp, for example, belonged to the category of 'one season wonders' – in their case, the first of the three seasons the Third Division lasted: 1924–5. They attempted another season, but had to resign in January 1926. A club of the same name later featured for a few years in junior football. Nonetheless, it is a remarkable fact that, even for a short period, Dumbarton could support two senior football teams. Helensburgh, then a Dunbartonshire seaside town, also had a club to its name throughout the years of the Third Division. In its last incomplete season, in 1926–7, Helensburgh did very well, finishing third and with a ground of considerable promise: Ardencaple Park. It is surprising that no serious attempt was made to acquire Second Division status, which had certainly been accorded to much less promising material. They did not, however, and, after 1927 until well after the Second World War, Dumbarton remained the only senior football team in the area.

Into a scene of economic and financial scarcity after the Second World War came two brothers who were of that handful of men who understood that the question in Scottish football might just be 'Are the clubs in the right places?' What was about to happen was the first British attempt to set up a football franchise on the pattern baseball employs in the USA. The creation of an entirely new club to Scottish football – East Stirlingshire Clydebank – had a remarkable background in every respect.

In June 1957, two West of Scotland businessmen – Jack Steedman (later to be president of the Scottish Football League) and his brother Charles – became directors of East Stirlingshire Football Club when they bought over 50 per cent of the shares of approximately £1000. They had boundless enthusiasm, a great capacity for hard work and considerable knowledge of football. Almost immediately, East Stirlingshire were transformed from a side whose only objective had seemed to be mere survival in the Second Division to a go-ahead organisation that might one day aspire to the promotion whose day came at the end of the season 1962–3. Then, East Stirlingshire became a First Division side for the first time in thirty years by finishing in second place to St Johnstone. Enthusiasm at Shire's ground, Firs Park in Falkirk, was high and crowds of 7,000 were fairly accepted. Competition in the First Division was too intense for the little club, however, and, after a miserable season in which only twelve points were garnered from thirty-four matches, East Stirlingshire returned to the Second Division as soon as possible. Attendances fell off sharply.

This experience convinced the Steedman brothers that the club would have to be relocated. By chance there was an alternative site ready and waiting. Clydebank Juniors were susceptible to the notion of a merger with

East Stirlingshire and there had, of course, been a brief history, already discussed, of League Football in the shipbuilding burgh from 1913 to 1931. In April 1964, the four members present at a board meeting of East Stirlingshire agreed that the club should move through to the West Coast. By a constitutional quirk, the fact that the Steedmans owned more than 50 per cent of the vote did not make their triumph certain. An Extraordinary General Meeting to block the move was cancelled and some of the brothers' shares transferred to people in Clydebank. The ferocity of local Falkirk reaction was astonishing and quite unlooked-for in an area with no great history of consistently supporting the club. Importantly, East Stirlingshire had acquired considerable skill in their day in Scottish football's C Division and it was now that the East Stirlingshire Shareholders' Protection Association, rather than the Supporters' Club, would bear the burden of the fight as shareholders could be said to have a more immediate interest in the outcome. There were public meetings and there were demonstrations, but none of them was in time to prevent the move to Kilbowie Park in Clydebank where the new side, with its cumbrous title of East Stirlingshire Clydebank, made its first appearance on 8 August 1964. To most people it appeared that, in the face of this *fait accompli*, the old club would die. It did not.

A Glasgow solicitor, Robert Turpie, who had been over the course before, now intervened. He had acted as counsel for five small clubs threatened with extinction in 1955 (one of them Dumbarton). An action to overturn the removal of East Stirlingshire to Clydebank was embarked upon before Lord Hunter in the Court of Session. He found in favour of East Stirlingshire, on the grounds that the shares that had been transferred to those people in Clydebank, under Article 13 of the club's Articles of Association, should have been offered, in the first place, to the other directors.

It was a famous victory and East Stirlingshire were back in Falkirk by August 1965, a year after their first appearance at Kilbowie, rapturously received by a level of public interest that was not sustained for very long. Crowds dwindled and East Stirlingshire sank back to an undistinguished place in the Second Division. Clydebank, meanwhile, began life as a separate entity in the Second Division from season 1966–7. This Clydebank were based on the existing junior team, with a record that included winning the Scottish Junior Cup in 1941–2 and being Central League Champions in 1934–5, 1940–1, 1941–2, 1944–5 and 1949–50.

Although only marginally better supported than East Stirlingshire, Clydebank were good enough to play Premier League football on more than one occasion and produced top players like Frank McDougall and Davie Cooper. They had become a noted nursery for players of quality. In the end, however, they had to stand down from the Scottish League in 2002, returning in 2003 to playing at junior level, now at Glenhead Park, the ground of defunct Duntocher Hibs, in a ground-share arrangement with Drumchapel Amateurs.

So who was right – the East Stirlingshire Shareholders Protection Association or the Steedman brothers? Perhaps in a strange way they were both right, for the whole episode illustrated the conflict of business and sentiment that is forever at the heart of football in Scotland. The Steedmans, dedicated football men though they were, wished to apply the common-sense principles of business to the situation. The viewpoint of the ES supporters and shareholders could be summed up thus: 'If you want a league side in Clydebank, fine but start from scratch. The proper and only place for East Stirlingshire Football Club is the town of Falkirk.' Community loyalty and identity faced down professional acumen.

While Dumbarton, founded in 1872 and a founder of both the Scottish Football Association and Scottish Football League, continues to survive, the history of other West Dunbartonshire senior, and indeed junior, football clubs illustrates less security of tenure. This is surely a reflection of the industrial, economic and social contexts in which they have operated. At the start of the period we have discussed, the surge of industry and the changes in working time laws of the 1870s and 1880s allowed local clubs to develop to a very high level of achievement indeed. These, like the rest of senior clubs of the time, were – at least nominally – amateur and their economic management depended on that status, however at times it might be sham. The smaller town clubs like Vale of Leven and Renton, however, no matter how distinguished they were as footballing teams, could not survive the developing professionalisation and, in a sense, industrialisation of football as it sought the larger crowds and income needed to support an openly professional operation after 1893. For these, larger, even if not very large, towns were required. Even Clydebank, for all its industrialised nature for much of the period under discussion, has not been able to sustain a senior football club. Indeed, in the last thirty or forty years, particularly since the introduction of a five-day working week that allows fans to travel to support clubs in other towns on a Saturday morning, the attractions of larger city clubs like Rangers and Celtic have drawn fans away from local teams.

Perhaps the process that has reached this conclusion was already in train, however imperceptibly, at the beginning of the twentieth century. Certainly, in that century, the West Dunbartonshire senior teams were never to achieve the heights, or anything like them, of the late nineteenth century. It seems certain that the early professionalisation of football with its apparently inevitable drawing of financial resources to larger metropolitan centres contributed to that relative failure. The difficulty of local teams, with the sole exception of Dumbarton, in maintaining a place in senior leagues also surely reflects the ups and downs of industry in West Dunbartonshire, with the related uncertainties of financial sustainability. It may be a symptom of this that two of the greatest footballers to be produced by West Dunbartonshire, Alec Jackson (1905–46) and Ian McColl (1927–), achieved their success outside of the area, even though they were nurtured by local clubs.

Alec Jackson was not only the finest football player that West Dunbartonshire ever fielded, but a native: Renton born and bred. He was a prodigiously skilled player and in his approach to the game he had something of the sophisticated and outward approach that could come from a player of a rather later vintage. His formative years were orthodox enough – Renton School, then on to Dumbarton Academy and then back to Renton. After a time with Dumbarton in the Second Division, a modest £1000 took him to Aberdeen. He took time out to play in the American League with Bethlehem Star, the house team of the Carnegie organisation. Five years passed with Huddersfield Town and then he moved to the infinitely more soigné surroundings of Stamford Bridge. He took to Stamford Bridge as to the manner born. He was well paid by the standards of his time and he enjoyed the whole West End ambience. Chelsea had paid Huddersfield £8,500 for his transfer, an enormous sum by the standards of the early 1930s.

Not afraid of the Continent, Jackson spent his last seasons with Nice in 1934–5. By this time, he had acquired a sort of immortality as one of the Wembley Wizards who inflicted a 5–1 defeat on England at Wembley in 1928. Historical accounts have tended to emphasise the lack of physique of the side, but Jackson, at nearly six feet, was the exception. He was short on needless trickery and indeed his running and strength in the tackle were more trademarks of the English winger. His feat in scoring three goals at Wembley has been equalled only once by a Scot and that was in an amateur international when left winger Dougie Orr also scored three goals. This he did on 29 March 1958 in a match at Wembley when, in front of 7,000 spectators, Scotland defeated England by three goals to two. For all the Scots that have trod that turf since then, the feat has never been repeated.

Jackson had a great capacity for the good life. His was the world of fast cars and nightclubs. His outstanding characteristic was his *joie de vivre* and the feeling that he was genuinely enjoying himself. His nicknames – 'The Flying Scotsman' and 'The Laughing Cavalier' – were tediously predictable, but accurate. His intelligence made it certain that there would be frequent spats with the administration and, in fact, on impulse he walked away from League Football and was quit of it in 1932, before he was twenty-seven, having been capped seventeen times for Scotland, five times against England. It had always been likely that he would die in a traffic accident and so, in 1946, it proved. Then he was a welfare officer, a major serving in the Suez Canal Zone, and a three-ton lorry he was driving skidded and over-turned on a slippery road. He died in hospital in Cairo two days later, on 23 November. With Alan Morton, Alec James, Tim Dunn and Hugh Gallacher, Jackson had set the standard against which every Scottish national side should be judged. He embraced the foreign, the strange and the new, calling to mind the phrase of Coriolanus: 'There is a world outside.'

Born a generation later, in Alexandria on 7 June 1927, and with a grand-father who had played for Rangers, Ian McColl is an example of a player who developed away from the clubs of his home area. After a thorough apprenticeship with Queen's Park for three years, he was well placed to make his mark at Ibrox with Rangers at the start of the 1945–6 season. He was in the tradition of the classic wing-half, although one would have had him just a little speedier. He had been at Ibrox for sixteen years by the time he called it a day in 1960. He had the rare distinction of having been appointed as manager while still a player. He won every prize that domestic football had to offer and the managership he had been offered was that of the national side. His trophy room groaned under the weight of medals, including six League medals, two League Cup medals and five Scottish Cup medals – the last of these won in 1960 when he had played virtually no first-rate football for two years. His record as a manager at Wembley against England was fairly satisfactory, but when he quit the national side in 1965 he spent almost three years as manager of Sunderland without overwhelming success.

McColl was lucky in that, starting, as he did, to play at a senior level towards the end of the Second World War, there was time for him to really learn the skills of the game without feeling coerced or harassed into it. For ten years in the 1950s, he formed a powerful figure in defence alongside Brown, Young, Shaw, Woodburn and Cox. At a time when competition for wing-halves was never more cut-throat, McColl saw off the international team challenges of Evans of Celtic, Docherty of Preston North End, Mackay of Hearts, Redpath of Motherwell and many others. In all, he earned four-teen caps. He was notable for his ability to kill a ball hit almost shoulder-high at him. His 'party-piece' was the great skill with which he took the pace off the ball so that the player taking the pass very often did not even need to break step to bring the ball under control.

Though Jackson and McColl were two of West Dunbartonshire's finest sportsmen, however, and, as such, embody something of the spirit of the area, its resilience and skill, no study of sport in the region could be com-plete without mention of one John Stewart. Born in Milton in 1939, his early involvement with cars was in the family business – Dumbuck Garage – in Dumbarton where he worked as an apprentice mechanic. His brother drove

Figure 23 Jackie Stewart at the civic reception held in his honour in Dumbarton in November 1969 to celebrate his winning the Formula One World Championship. He is being presented with the Jackie Stewart Cup, which he passed on for competition among local schools.

for Écurie Écosse and it was not long before Jackie followed Jimmy into the motor-racing arena. It should also be noted here that, by that time, Jackie had attained Olympic standard in clay-pigeon shooting. While Jackson and McColl made their success in team games, Stewart, like the golfer Charlie Green, made his in sports depending on the highest individual skill, however supported by excellent technical teams.

It was as if he had been born to drive, and drive fast. When he was invited to test Ken Tyrrell's F3 Cooper at Goodwood in early 1964, Stewart bettered the target time set by Cooper's number one driver, Bruce McLaren. Not a little piqued, McLaren then went all out and succeeded in recording a better time. Stewart merely stepped back in his car and repeated the dose. He had driven with such speed and accuracy that John Cooper, the team boss, flew to the pits in an effort to sign him up immediately. His record speaks for itself: twenty-seven Formula One wins, three World Championships and even a win as a constructor with Johnny Herbert in 1999. Among his many honours are included his induction into the International Motorsports Hall of Fame in 1990 and his knighthood, bestowed in 2001. Jackie Stewart has done more than any other racer to revolutionise safety standards in motor racing and remains a superb ambassador for the sport at which he so excelled.

When looking at the potential future development of sports in a community such as West Dunbartonshire, one must examine what land has been made available for the practice of sports and, importantly, what factors may threaten that availability. In the past, a contribution made by big firms to the sports environment was the provision of that rarity of rarities, grass pitches. In recent years, however, the fine pitches and pavilions have largely been abandoned. Where are they now, the splendid playing fields that lined the north and south banks of the Clyde? Is the time right for a counterattack for actually playing games? To take stock of the facilities that would have been taken for granted in places such as Singer's and, within a few miles, the India factory at Inchinnan, Barclay Curle on the upper Clyde, G. & J. Weir and, across the water, Anchor and Ferguslie mills is to consider a much-depleted situation. In recent years, many 'sporting arenas' have come under threat from the construction industry. The ever-increasing demand for housing has led to fields, courts and pitches being commandeered, in particular cricket grounds (as they do not operate all year) and tennis courts (as the sport is not played in any numbers). Additionally, both of these are usually sited in a desirable district, which could mean a very good price for the club, as for the housing, with a consequent redistribution of wealth.

West Dunbartonshire's sporting heritage will no doubt continue, but the emphasis is now more clearly on the individual, while many corporate resources and the possibility of achievement at the highest level from a small-town base seem gone for ever. And yet for all its vicissitudes, Clydebank continues as a football team and Dumbarton has a proud record as one of the oldest surviving senior football teams in Scotland. Even with only two titles, it is still the sixth most successful team in terms of League Championships in Scotland after Rangers, Celtic, Aberdeen, Hearts and Hibernian. West Dunbartonshire teams, even after all this time, have won more Scottish Cup victories, with six, than those of any other non-metropolitan area of Scotland, and more even than those of the city of Dundee with their total of two. It has also produced one of the greatest individual sportsmen in the world in Jackie Stewart. Sport certainly shifts its forms and expressions in tune with economic, social, industrial and cultural change. At the same time, it is clear that, in West Dunbartonshire, sport has been a constant reflector of the nature of the changes in society, the economy and industry at large and still offers a focus for local pride and identity. However much other sports in the period discussed did have to give way to 'King Football', there is still a lively sports culture in the area.

For all that they have never had the prominent place accorded to football, such sports mentioned in the introduction to this chapter as bowls, cricket, tennis, fishing and cycling continue, at a social level, to find their enthusiasts and to thrive.

NOTE

1 Dennett, C. (1995), *The Auld Renton*, vol. 1 (Bonhill: C. Dennett), p. 26.

CHAPTER 8

Theatre, Music Hall and Cinema

Paul Maloney

While the importance of folk drama and popular entertainment has been discussed in some depth in chapter 6, this chapter focuses on theatrical forms that became popular in West Dunbartonshire with the increase in leisure in the nineteenth and twentieth centuries: theatre, music hall and cinema. If these forms were usually associated with purpose-built or adapted buildings, such conditions were by no means a prerequisite of professional activity, as this chapter will demonstrate. The fact that neither Dumbarton, founded in 1222, nor burgeoning Clydebank, established as a burgh in only 1886, had permanent theatres until the twentieth century was more indicative of drama's historic suppression in Scotland following the Reformation, than of any local antipathy. The transfer of the court to London in 1603 – and the subsequent ascendancy of an anti-theatre faction in the Church of Scotland – was a situation from which theatre only began to recover in the mid-eighteenth century. This meant that, until that time, professional drama was consigned to a marginal existence in travelling troupes that performed at fairs.

In fact, in addition to the Dunbartonshire performances of Galoshins folk plays discussed in the earlier chapter, visits by itinerant or travelling theatre companies seem to have been regular occurrences in the nineteenth century. In 1846, Dumbarton was visited by the black American tragedian Ira Aldridge, 'The African Roscius', who played there before going on to appear in Glasgow.[1] And in 1864, the showman David Prince Miller and his partner Walter Edwin established a wooden theatre in Dumbarton called the Adelphi. Named after Miller's former theatre on Glasgow Green, it was situated on Risk Street, in a location remembered as being 'on the High Street opposite the Orchard'.[2] Evidently a fairly substantial semi-permanent structure, it opened in early June to a good reception:

> Though scarcely finished, the inside presents a neat and comfortable appearance and stage appointments of a description for beauty and completeness not often to be met with except in first-class theatres, on

the boards of which not a few of its members are not unknown [. . .] The conduct of the audience, which quite filled the pit and made a goodly appearance in the boxes, was throughout of the orderly description, better by far than we have frequently witnessed at concerts in this and neighbouring towns.[3]

A drop curtain featured a view depicting Dumbarton Castle, and the play, a three-act drama entitled *The Dream at Sea*, which included a hornpipe and various songs, was followed by a farce, *Mr and Mrs White*. With three or four changes of programme each week, repertoire ranged from Shakespeare (*Hamlet, Othello, The Comedy of Errors, Richard III*) to comedies, farces, melodramas (*The Corsican Brothers, Black-Eyed Susan, The Ticket of Leave Man*) and *Rob Roy*. However, despite a talented company, and the advertised patronage of such local eminences as P. B. Smollett, MP for the County (who didn't actually attend the performance) and Lieut.-Col. Finday of Boturich (who did), by mid-August fine weather was still keeping audiences thin. The theatre subsequently failed, bankrupting its managers.[4]

If the Adelphi's failure casts doubt on whether Dumbarton was able to support a theatre company, a later manager found a new method of extending his appeal to working audiences. In 1882, a visitor to George Duckenfield's travelling theatre, erected on the Common at Dumbarton, which he found 'crowded from floor to ceiling by a large audience comprising chiefly young "gutter bloods" ', was appalled when, at the end of the performance, the manager in a speech before the curtain made reference to the fact that he allowed sections of his audience credit. As reported, Duckenfield

> In complimenting the Dumbarton rivet boys and the like upon their honesty [. . .] said he had come to a knowledge of it by the following means. He was in the habit of allowing them to come to the place between the pay days without then calling upon them for their admission money, and he had found it quite safe to do so, as they were always sure to pay what they owed him when they received money into their hands.[5]

Outraged, the complainant denounced what he termed this 'most abominable practice' in the *Lennox Herald*, decrying 'the evil effects which must flow from so pernicious a system being practised among young persons', and trusting 'the man's own sense of moral propriety will induce him to end it at once'. However, Duckenfield's reply in the following issue showed no signs of contrition at his use of 'tick'. He rather observed that, if the 'abominable practices' alluded to were simply 'trusting people who have no money to go into my theatre until they can pay me [. . .] then every trade and profession in Dumbarton (except policemen and pawnbrokers) are guilty of "abominable practices"'. Scorning the term 'gutter bloods', he asserted

> The frequenters of my theatre are the working class. To them alone I owe my success, and to them you owe the prosperity of your burgh. I shall therefore leave them to define whether they belong to the 'gutter' or not.[6]

The spat coincided with reformers' increasing awareness of theatre's potential as a moral agent, with advocates like the Revd W. Stephen arguing for its rehabilitation by suggesting that 'the cultivation of the drama would recover for our people [. . .] a class of literature in which there is a sincere and abounding sympathy with all that is great and good and inspiring'.[7] But while the egalitarian tone of Duckenfield's argument seems remarkably modern, the moral taint of the suggestion that he was somehow entrapping young men by offering them credit, and thus flying in the face of all responsible social injunctions to thrift, was probably inescapable. The paper's editorial comment expressed its disappointment at his response and sympathy with the complainant, and subsequent advertisements for the theatre seem to concede a degree of notoriety by omitting Duckenfield's name and referring to it simply as the 'New Theatre'.

A third travelling theatre appeared in 1896 at Clydebank, run by a manager called Greensmith and 'situated on the Commissioners' grounds opposite Hill View Terrace' where the *Clydebank Press* described it as

> [. . .] proving a big success. Nightly, good houses gather to witness the various pieces. The theatre has now been roofed in in a thoroughly water-proof fashion, and is about as right as what is to be had in such modest erections.[8]

Like Dumbarton's Adelphi, the 'Clyde Theatre' was a semi-permanent wooden structure or travelling theatre, erected on open ground, in which, in this case, performances seem to have begun in partly alfresco circumstances, before the auditorium was even properly enclosed. As in Dumbarton, the company offered three or four changes of programme weekly: a typical week, that of 19 December 1896, involved as principal attraction a five-act drama, *The Grip of Iron* ('Immense production'), followed on Wednesday by a performance 'by special request' of *Hamlet, Prince of Denmark*, and on Saturday, a 'New American Drama'. If the repertoire was generally very similar to that offered by David Prince Miller thirty years previously in Dumbarton, comprising Shakespeare, comedies and melo-dramas, a difference was a more marked emphasis on Scottish plays and the National Drama, which was often based on adaptations of Scott's novels. Those presented included *Wee Curly* (billed as [a] 'Great production of the great local "Scottish" drama'), *Reddie's Bonnie Dochter, Gilderoy, Mary Queen of Scots, Rob Roy, or Auld Lang Syne* and *Jeanie Deans, or The Sisters of St Leonards*. There was also an attempt to cater for different audiences by designating the social tone of particular performances: so a 'Grand fashionable Night' featured *Ingomar, the Barbarian*, while the Saturday performance, termed 'The People's Night', featured *Sweeney Todd, The Demon Barber of Fleet Street*. When Greensmith eventually ended his suc-cessful five-month season, it was to remove his establishment to Perth.[9]

If the seasons presented by these travelling theatres were exceptions, the-atrical life in the late nineteenth century was more varied than the lack of facilities might suggest. By the 1890s, public halls received regular visits from touring companies led by well-known actors and impresarios. W. T. Rushbury, 'a great favourite among Clydebank folks', brought a stream of popular dramas, his advertisements making special play of their scenic splendours, which included a 'beautiful new drop-scene – a view of Dunoon from the East Bay' for *Uncle Tom's Cabin* at the Burgh Hall, Clydebank and 'an Act drop – West Bay of Dunoon' for *Tommy Atkins* at Clydebank Public Hall and Dumbarton Burgh Hall.[10] Popular melodramas included *Greed of Gold* at Dumbarton, and *Alone in London* at the Public Hall, Bowling, while the Brescian Family brought fashionable hits like *Trilby* ('Magnificent scenery, elaborate properties, and London company') to Clydebank, and a Grand Opera company with thirty artistes in Balfe's *The Bohemian Girl* to Alexandria (Mon. & Tues.), Dumbarton (Wed. & Thurs.) and Clydebank (Fri. & Sat.).[11] The fashion for religious dramas also offered opportunities to confront Presbyterian disapproval. A two-night visit of Ben Greet's company with *The Sign of the Cross*, which depicted early Christians facing martyrdom at the hands of the Romans, allowed the *Dumbarton Herald* to cite the enlightened views of the Vicar of Doncaster, who suggested critics 'leave off that silly nonsense which said "I must not be seen in a theatre". They had better die in a theatre than in the most mag-nificent cathedral in a state of unpreparedness.'[12]

Scottish material and the National Drama remained popular. The Perthshire tenor Durward Lely, who had created the role of Nanki Poo in Gilbert & Sullivan's *The Mikado*, frequently appeared in evenings of Scottish Song and John Clyde, billed as 'Scotland's Premier Actor', was also a regular visitor, in April 1897 bringing his barnstorming performances as Rob Roy and as Roderick Dhu in *The Lady of the Lake* to the public halls in Alexandria, Renton, Dumbarton and Clydebank. Most of these managers continued their visits for many years, with Clyde still presenting *Jeanie Deans* at Dumbarton in 1911.

Music hall was also an important presence. Although towns like Dumbarton were not large enough to sustain full-time halls, there was a constant flow of performers to local venues. In the 1850s, John Brand, later manager of the Britannia Music Hall in Glasgow, brought parties of music-hall performers to the Odd-Fellows Hall in Dumbarton, and the company from Glasgow's Whitebait concert rooms were remembered for their 'Glasgow Fast Nights' at Alexandria.[13] By the 1890s, the Scotch comedians J. C. MacDonald and W. F. Frame (whose face, the *Clydebank Press* wrote, 'Every little boy in Clydebank knows') and celebrated tenor J. M. Hamilton were all frequent visitors with their concert parties. Meanwhile, the violinist Mackenzie Murdoch ('The Scots Paganini'), the blackface minstrel Will Candlish ('the Black Emperor'), the soprano Jessie MacLachlan, who sang in Gaelic, and Campbeltown contralto Maggie MacAffer all regularly featured in concerts.

Although music hall involved a cosmopolitan mix of influences, the predominance of Scottish songs and sketches at these events argues its place in the broad continuity of Scottish popular music culture. The programme at Will Candlish's 'Grand Concert', given to a packed Clydebank Public Hall in August 1891, which 'continued without the slightest intermission until far on into the night', included an overture of Scotch airs on the piano, followed by the accompanist, Miss Madline, singing 'The Scottish Blue Bells' and 'Lochnagar'; J. M. Heron, 'The Monarch of Scotch Comedians', with his comic song 'The Wedding Spree', 'which brought out roars of laughter from the audience', and his encore, 'Yer Awfu' Sleakit'; Master Hamish McLean dancing the Highland Fling and Shean Trews; and Will Candlish's 'negro song and dance', followed by Miss Madline with 'The Dear Little Shamrock' and 'Within a Mile of Edinburgh Toon'.[14]

While music hall remained the epitome of godless commercial entertainment for the unco guid, its incorporation into popular concerts along the lines of those pioneered in Glasgow meant that, by the 1890s, it was omnipresent in the entertainments offered by temperance, religious and voluntary organisations. There, displayed in the context of a well-supervised event, under the auspices of an approved body, it was deemed perfectly acceptable.

In the mid-1890s, Dumbarton gained a commercial music-hall venue, albeit one that chose to represent itself in ambiguous terms. In 1896, press advertisements for the Theatre Royal, in College Street, Dumbarton, under the management of C. H. Rea, offered 'Popular Saturday Concerts' each Saturday, listing the artists involved. However, a subsequent letter to the *Lennox Herald*, printed on the front page, complained that, when the correspondent went to attend the event

> [. . .] judge of my surprise, on going there, to find that the 'Theatre Royal' was an old wooden erection situated in the Vennel on a piece of back ground, the approach being badly lit and in a sloppy condition. The only entrance to the booth – or 'Theatre Royal' – was by a few wooden steps leading to a door with a ragged curtain before it; while the approach to the front seats was down a dark, narrow passage, about 2½ feet wide, which was in a most unsatisfactory and filthy state. There being no 'latrine' arrangements, the passage has to serve a double purpose. The house was filled with young people of both sexes. Most of the lads and men were smoking, matches being freely lit and thrown at their feet, even among the girls' dresses. The building being of wood, and with a tar roof, if fire were to take place the audience would be caught in a trap, and many lives would certainly be lost.[15]

The writer further suggested that, as there did not seem to be anyone in charge backstage, 'if fire were to break out here, assuredly it would be disastrous, while the woodyard and other buildings would certainly suffer', and that 'The mere fact of a policeman standing on the landing, talking to the man who took the tickets, is no protection.'[16] The letter seems to provide a valuable description of this sort of wooden theatre, if one rather more primitive than those previously described. The following week, however, the newspaper carried a rebuttal of sorts. It stated that the original letter, published in good faith, had proved to be inaccurate in a number of respects, in that the approach to the theatre was lit by five gas lamps, at some expense to the proprietor; that rather than being one door to the auditorium, there were in fact six, and that the roof was not wood and tarred, as stated, but 'of wood covered with iron'. Of the broader implications of the criticism, the *Herald* stated that 'The entertainments have been much raised in tone during the time of the present proprietor and manager, Messrs W. Robertson and C. H. Rea respectively.'[17]

The truth about the building's condition probably lay somewhere between the two accounts. As described, the Theatre Royal was evidently a fairly crude structure, older than those previously encountered, and possibly a shed of some sort adapted from a previous usage (the editorial implies that it had previously been in operation as a theatre). If it seemed unduly basic to the writer, who signed himself 'Veritas', and who had evidently expected a conventional permanent theatre, it may well have been no worse than other such places of entertainment. Even the appropriation of the title Theatre Royal was not unprecedented (a contemporary theatrical memoir reveals that in an earlier period the Theatre Royal Helensburgh had turned out to be the back room of an inn[18]). At any rate, the newspaper evidently felt able to come to the proprietors' defence, although questions over the motivations of the parties remain.[19]

So, the Theatre Royal then was a wooden shed of some sort, situated in a patch of open ground in the centre of the town near to various business premises, which only operated for one night a week, with just piano accompaniment.[20] Intriguingly, the managers did not choose to title it a music hall, and termed its entertainment 'Popular Saturday Concerts', out of deference to the concert formats of its competitors, even though to all intents it offered straightforward music hall, without the concertising musical elements still usually found in such programmes. In fact, the Theatre Royal entertainments soon faced competition from rival series, in the form of 'Saturday Evening Concerts for the working classes', given simultaneously in the Burgh Hall, Dumbarton and the Public Hall, Alexandria, and concerts under the heading 'Pleasant Evenings for the People' at the Drill Hall, Bonhill, admission for which was 2d.

The example of the Dumbarton Theatre Royal as a part-time venue demonstrates not so much the lack of vibrant music-hall entertainment, but rather the extent to which it was already being provided in more refined contexts, in concert series promoted by local church and voluntary groups. Competition between such groups for leading performers was sometimes intense. The renowned fiddler James Scott Skinner, 'The Strathspey King', related in his memoirs how while visiting the Vale to fulfil an engagement, he found himself mobbed in the street, and then visited before the performance by a deputation from the Committee of the Alexandria Co-operative Society, who had heard him play the previous night in Dumbarton and were anxious to engage him for their own Saturday night concerts, a series Scott Skinner termed 'a power in the land'.[21] But if music hall had broadly been assimilated into acceptable entertainments, and theatre was now at least countenanced, given the popularity of amateur theatricals, and vogue for religious drama, then the moral project to improve society was still by no means secure.

As a key popular form, cinema embodied the democratising nature of the new mass culture. Early systems of moving pictures began appearing from the mid-1890s – the Modern Marvel Company brought its Zoegraph, a form of animated photographs, to Alexandria in April 1897. But the first cinema proper to feature at a local venue was probably the Edison Cinematograph shown at the Theatre Royal Dumbarton in October the same year.[22] While film subsequently became associated with modernity and mass culture, in its earliest phases it retained strong links with older popular amusement cultures, in that its introduction to the wider audience came through travelling fairground booths and subsequently music halls. Indeed, the pioneering generation of cinema proprietors were showmen like the Greens, Wingates and Kemps. Moreover, when cinema did gravitate to purpose-built premises, it did so with live musical accompaniment, and often with variety performers interspersing the film items.

Dumbarton's pioneering cinema promoter, Joseph Wingate, had shown films on Dumbarton Common from 1907, and in 1910 opened the town's first cinema, the Picture Palace (or Wingate's Palace), in Church Street, renamed the Regal in 1936. In August 1914, Wingate opened a second venue, the Pavilion, which combined films and live variety entertainment, accompanied by the 'Pavilion Model Orchestra'. In 1915, Harry Lauder appeared there in a fundraising concert for the Red Cross, and the building subsequently underwent changes of management and name to the Pavilion Picture House (1924) and Rialto (1927). Other Dumbarton cinemas included the Picture House in the High Street (1915) and the La Scala (1920). Of cinemas in the Vale, two were converted from existing public halls after licensing applications to the County Council: Renton's Public Hall (later renamed The Picture House and, from 1939, The Roxy) began showing films from 1912, while Alexandria had the Hall cinema (formerly Alexandria Public Hall in Bridge Square), which began screening films in 1911, and the Picture Palace in Bank Street, opened by Wingate in 1914, but known from 1929 as The Strand.[23]

In Clydebank, early film shows were given by James 'Prince' George,[24] a former bill-poster who, by 1908, was screening films at Clydebank Town Hall on Saturday nights.[25] His pianist in these shows was James Singleton, whose son George, later a well-known Glasgow cinema owner, recalled

[. . .] films were short, seven or eight minutes, maybe ten minutes. A projector was set up at one end and a screen tied up at the other, and the people sat in between. There was only one projector, so there was an interval between each reel, and sometimes to fill in the gaps they put on an illustrated singer, with slides illustrating the song. I can remember very well, quite vividly, and you know it must be eighty years ago, sitting on the platform at the Town Hall, Clydebank, my father playing away.[26]

Figure 24 Staff of the Gaiety Theatre, Clydebank, in 1915. The cap-bands read 'Pickards', most clearly visible on the boy sitting at the front.

Early films were a mixed bag. As well as features like Shakespeare's *Othello* and *The Great Fire Brigade Picture*, George and showmen like him also showed films of local events, known as 'topicals', such as the 'Boy's Brigade Semi-Jubilee Review', 'taken on 5th September 1908', to which local people flocked in the hope of seeing themselves or their friends or family on the screen.[27]

The late establishment of permanent theatres in the area, and rapid development of cinema, meant that venues were often utilised for both purposes. Clydebank's first theatre proper, the Gaiety Theatre on the corner of Elgin Street and Glasgow Road, which seated 1,400, was opened by R. C. Buchanan on 31 January 1902, the curtain rising after the overture to reveal the full company and management assembled to sing the national anthem.[28] The opening production was *On the Frontier*, a dramatisation of Fennimore Cooper's *The Last of the Mohicans*, for which Mrs Bella Frame of Whitecrook later recalled, 'All the actors in the show rode down Glasgow Road dressed in cowboy and Indian outfits in a big parade.'[29] In 1908, the theatre was acquired by A. E. Pickard, the Yorkshire-born proprietor of the Panopticon music hall in Glasgow, who pursued a programme of twice-nightly films and variety. In 1917, it was sold and, after renovation, reopened as the Bank cinema. Other Clydebank music halls included the Cinem [*sic*]

Varieties in Graham Street, opened c. 1908, which, from 1915, became the Palace of Varieties, and then a cinema; the 1,300-seat Empire Theatre (1914) in Glasgow Road, also a cinema from 1928, and the 2,000-seat Pavilion in Kilbowie Road (1919).[30] All these venues combined variety and bioscope presentations before gravitating to cinema usage, with pantomime, amateur nights and Go-as-you-please competitions as regular features. Other local cinemas included the New Kinema opposite Singer station, and the Napoleon Star and Dalmuir Picture House in Dalmuir.

The experience of film-going was intimate and local. Cinema may have been a mass medium, but, in this familiar context, it was also an inclusive, interactive popular culture, which also offered variety acts, charity nights, talent contests, Go-as-you-please competitions and pantomimes. Neighbourhood cinemas, known and celebrated for their individual characteristics and idiosyncrasies, were familiar refuges where young couples did their courting and which developed loyal local audiences. Managers like Jack Short, Jimmy Logan's father, who managed the Roxy in Renton, and kept his regulars entertained by playing the piano when the film broke, were familiar, trusted figures.[31] Incoming managers went to great lengths to cultivate their local clientele. At the reopening of the refurbished Gaiety in 1908, A. E. Pickard engaged two local bands to play selections of music, and dedicated the proceeds of a later performance, attended by the provost, magistrates and members of the Town Council, to the Burgh Unemployed Distress Fund. He also took care to advertise on subsequent posters that they were 'printed in Clydebank by trade union labour'.[32]

The epitome of the synergy between cinema, variety and popular theatre was the Empire Theatre, Alexandria. Opened in November 1910, the Vale Empire, as it was known, embraced most strands of 'rough' live performance, from boxing tournaments and brass bands, to films, variety, benefits for sporting teams like the Vale of Leven Football Club (whose supporters were invited to 'Come and see the Football Match thrown on the screen by the Dreadnought Bioscope') and pantomime (see Plate 6). In its 1911 production of *Aladdin*, the dame's pawky topical song, 'It's time something was done', included digs at the local School Board, Sunday gambling and muddy streets, while the principal girl sang 'Who's going to take me for a walk tonight?' Used by amateur theatrical and operatic societies, the Empire also offered touring thrillers, comedies and revues and, as late as 1929, it was presenting Moss's Selected Players in a season of salaciously billed (and mostly ancient!) melodramas that included *Rogues of Paris* (a version of *The Face at the Window*), Boucicault's *The Colleen Bawn*, *Sapho* ('*The Idol of Paris*' [. . .] 'A tale of a young artist's love for a French Courtesan' [. . .] 'For Adults Only') and *Daft Jamie, or Old Edinburgh in the days of Burke and Hare*.[33]

Figure 25 *Guy Mannering* at the Vale Empire, performed by the Vale of Leven Amateur Dramatic Society, c. 1920s.

If cinema was innovatory, it was music hall that best encapsulated the irreverent tone of the new mass culture, in which performers like Retta Halket ('Clydebank's favourite') and comics like Sam Thomson reflected back at the audience the gallus humour of working-class life and work, with its rituals of tenement living, the public house, football, dancing, betting on horses and the dogs, and backcourt singers. Clydebank also produced its share of performers, most famously Lex McLean, who in 1929 appeared at the Vale Empire as pianist with the eight-strong Leven Entertainers concert party.[34]

Both cinema and theatre declined throughout the 1950s and 1960s, when the community-based Dumbarton People's Theatre and Clydebank Repertory Company helped compensate for the dearth of professional activity. The 1970s, however, brought a revival of interest in the socialist drama of the inter-war years. In a rich period for Scottish theatre, radical companies like 7:84 and its music theatre offshoot, Wildcat, tapped into the vibrant popular theatre tradition that linked the influence of music hall to the social radicalism of the workers' theatre groups of the 1920s and 1930s. The revitalisation and rediscovery of this socialist theatre heritage can be seen to result from two highly influential theatre events. Although both

Figure 26 Billy Connolly appearing in *The Great Northern Welly Boot Show*. © The Scotsman Publications Ltd. Licensor www.scran.ac.uk

took place outside West Dunbartonshire, both were closely engaged with it. The first, *The Great Northern Welly Boot Show*, was premièred during the 1972 Clyde Fair International in Glasgow and then presented on the Fringe of the Edinburgh Festival. It was based on the Upper Clyde Shipbuilders work-in. Put together by a scratch company, it combined dramatic scenes, song and direct address to the audience to celebrate the workers' occupation of the Clydebank shipyard, comically relocated to a Welly (Wellington) Boot factory. It celebrated the possibility of direct action and vernacular language and was immensely popular. It also starred Billy Connolly, who had worked in the shipyards, with music by Tom McGrath and included such performers as Bill Paterson, Alex Norton and John Bett. John McGrath saw this show when thinking about setting up a Scottish 7:84 theatre company and, when he did so in 1973, he engaged such *Welly Boot* stalwarts as Paterson, Norton and Bett. Indeed, 7:84 Theatre Company (Scotland) then became involved in a Quality of Life residency. It presented *Capital Follies, or, A tale of Dumbarton and the Vale*, devised by 7:84 and written by Dave McLennan and John Bett, in the area between 9 June and 6 July 1975. 7:84 Theatre Company (Scotland), whose indirect and direct involvement with West Dunbartonshire was so marked, was also responsible for the second highly important theatrical event: the *Clydebuilt* season of 1981–2 in Glasgow's Mitchell Theatre. This presented Scottish popular theatre from the 1920s, 1930s and 1940s with a particular emphasis on the work of Glasgow Unity Theatre, reminding audience and the profession alike of the powerful impact of the drama of that time. This season, alongside later projects like Bill Bryden's *The Ship* (1990), contributed profoundly to the memorialisation of Clydeside's industrial culture, which, although fast disappearing, was captured in this body of work in a gallus, robustly humorous way that affirmed the continued vibrancy of the people and communities it produced.

In 1989, Wildcat Stage Productions took up residency in Clydebank, in the former Singer social club in Boquhanran Street. After a seven-week refit at a cost of £300,000, the hall reopened as the 900-seat Clyde Theatre with a production of Dave Anderson's *The Greedy Giant*.[35] The flexible layout allowed for both theatre in-the-round or end-on staging, and the company planned to use the venue both as a base for touring and a centre for work with the local community. Although it enjoyed critical success, however, including with a revival of John McGrath's *The Cheviot, the Stag and the Black, Black Oil*, the company, by 1992, was facing a reported financial deficit of £100,000. The theatre closed in 1992 and was subsequently demolished.

The Civic Theatre and Clydebank Town Hall remain the leading entertainment venues, the absence of professional theatre companies enabling them to be used for extensive programmes of community activities, including amateur societies, film nights, dances, musicals, choir concerts and a sell-out annual Christmas show. Community drama remains, however, a touchstone locally, and is regularly employed to mark important events. In 1986, *Risingest* was produced to celebrate Clydebank's centenary, while at Clydebank Town Hall on 13–14 March 2001, *The Night of the Big Blitz* was presented to commemorate the sixtieth anniversary of the bombing of Clydebank. This performance combined amateur and professional performers, and included the final stage appearance of the late Jimmy Logan. During the 2005 VE Day commemorations, the Town Hall was transformed into a 1940s cinema, screening Movietone news, cartoons and features from the period.

It is possible, of course, that, in the near future, professional theatre will again come to play a more prominent role in West Dunbartonshire, perhaps under the auspices of the new National Theatre of Scotland. In the interim, however, imaginative community-based theatre projects are increasingly valuable. They provide a means by which the area's vibrant history and rich cultural heritage, both rural and industrial, can be brought alive for younger generations, who grow up in the shadow of a sleeping giant that is the region's industrial legacy.

NOTES

1 *The Era*, 1 and 15 February 1846, p. 6.
2 MacLeod, Donald (1877), *Castle and Town of Dumbarton* (Dumbarton: Bennett Bros), p. 147.
3 *Dumbarton Herald*, 9 June 1864.
4 Miller's statement reveals that the reason for the venture was the previous failure of their theatre in Coatbridge. 'For this reason we were in Dumbarton during the summer where we had not success, and having been advised by friends in Dumbarton to return there in winter, we did so with an expensive company, costing about £40 a week. The first week that season we scarcely took £20 and we closed it', *Airdrie, Coatbridge, Bathgate and Wishaw Advertiser*, 28 January 1865, p. 2. Although the theatre was used by Harry Clifton for a Grand Concert in April 1864, later the same month it was advertised as being for sale. With no buyer forthcoming, in May the theatre's furnishing and materials ('quite fresh') were advertised for sale by lots. For Adelphi, see *Dumbarton Herald* 9 June–25 August 1864; 23 March, 27 April, 18 May 1865. In Miller's autobiography he briefly refers to the venture, stating: 'Proceeded to Scotland, managed to commence a small theatre in Coatbridge with a gentleman, Mr Walter Edwin. We succeeded very well, and tried another town, Dumbarton; this experiment was a failure, and we lost both.' David Prince Miller, *Life of a Showman* (1869), p. 11.
5 'A Theatrical Practice which should be stopped', *Lennox Herald*, 22 April 1882, p. 5.
6 'The "Tick" at Duckenfield's', *Lennox Herald*, 29 April 1882, p. 4.
7 'The Place of the Drama in Popular Education' (paper to the Dumbarton Philosophical and Literary Society, conclusion), *Dumbarton Herald*, 8 March 1882, p. 5.
8 *Clydebank & Renfrew Press*, 17 October 1896, p. 3, and 3 October, p. 3; see also advertisements for Clyde Theatre, Clydebank, *Clydebank & Renfrew Press*, 19 December 1896–30 January 1897.
9 *Clydebank & Renfrew Press*, 12 December 1896, p. 4 and 30 January 1897.
10 For *Uncle Tom's Cabin* see advert, *Clydebank & Renfrew Press*, 18 August 1894, p. 4; for *Tommy Atkins*, see advert, *Lennox Herald*, 24 October 1896, p. 8.

11 For *Greed of Gold* & *Alone in London*, see advert, *Lennox Herald*, 28 August 1897; for *Trilby*, see advert, *Clydebank & Renfrew Press*, 10 October 1896, p. 2; for *Bohemian Girl*, *Lennox Herald*, 12 October 1895, p. 5.

12 *Dumbarton Herald*, 10 March 1897.

13 For *Brand*, see *Dumbarton Herald*, 1 November 1855, p. 2.

14 *Clydebank & Renfrew Press*, 29 August 1891, p. 2.

15 *Lennox Herald*, 7 November 1896, p. 1.

16 *Lennox Herald*, 7 November 1896, p. 1

17 *Lennox Herald*, 14 November 1896, p. 1.

18 Coleman, John (1904), *Fifty Years of an Actor's Life* (London: Hutchinson), pp. 216–29.

19 'Veritas', who apparently proved uncontactable, seems almost excessively public-spirited in his zeal over fire precautions; however, despite the newspaper's insistence that there were three attendants on duty in the stage area, it was also the case that Rea, the manager, was also the pianist ('accompanist') for the performances, and would therefore have been unlikely to have been of much use after curtain up. Perhaps the key to the paper's speedy defence lies in the fact that Rea's partner, Mr Robertson, was a well-known local businessman, a joiner and funeral undertaker, who may well have owned the theatre building itself, and whose business premises at 62 College Street were situated close by. These factors, and the fact of the theatre's advertising with the paper, might have contributed to the *Herald*'s defence of the venue; see W. Robertson advertisement, *Dumbarton Herald*, 2 December 1896.

20 The 1898 Ordnance Survey map of the town centre shows a structure marked 'Theatre' standing in open ground apart from other buildings in the area indicated.

21 Skinner, James Scott, *My Life and Adventures* (orig. published in *The People's Journal*, 1923; City of Aberdeen & Wallace Music, 1994), p. 63.

22 *Lennox Herald*, 17 April 1897; 2 October 1897.

23 Taylor, Mike, Walton, Julia and Liddell, Colin (1992), *A Night at the Pictures* (Dumbarton District Libraries).

24 A fashion among showmen of the time, there was also a Prince Edward, who brought film and variety entertainments to Dumbarton and Alexandria c. 1911; and Prince Bendon was a well-known ventriloquist and later cinema owner.

25 Hood, John (1986), 'No Waits, No Flickers, No Breakdowns', pp. 11–16, *Clydebank Historical Journal*, vol. 6, Spring 1986, p. 14.

26 Quoted in McBain, Janet (1985), *Pictures Past: recollections of Scottish cinemas and cinema-going* (Edinburgh: Moorfoot Publishing), pp. 26–7.

27 Prince George Advertisement, *Clydebank & Renfrew Press*, 18 September 1908, p. 4.

28 *Clydebank & Renfrew Press*, 3 January 1902.

29 *Clydebank Press*, 22 September 1961.

30 Peter, Bruce (1999), *Scotland's Splendid Theatres* (Edinburgh: Edinburgh University Press), pp. 150–2.

31 Logan, Jimmy (1998), *It's A Funny Life* (Edinburgh: B&W), pp. 16–17.

32 *Clydebank & Renfrew Press*, 18 September 1908, p. 8; Scottish Theatre Archive, playbill for Clydebank Theatre, Monday 26 December 1913, STA Xa 4/14.

33 For *Aladdin, Lennox Herald*, 7 January 1911, p. 4.; for Moss's Players, *Lennox Herald*, 27 April 1929, p. 5, and 4 May 1929, p. 5.

34 *Lennox Herald*, 9 February 1929, p. 5.

35 *Lennox Herald*, 10 and 17 November 1989.

CHAPTER 9

Ancient Identities – Changing Routes

Ian Brown

The title of this chapter puns to purpose on this book's title. Not only has this history explored the many developments and changes that have taken place in West Dunbartonshire in well over two millennia, it has also highlighted the ways in which, time after time, the area has reformed and recreated itself. The 'journey' that the area has gone on is reflected in its very nature as a centre of travel and trade, and latterly industry. The importance of waterways, for example, in the development of the area has repeatedly been highlighted, as has the importance of the region as a throughway between cultures. The name of one of its ancient towns, Balloch, is derived, as Simon Taylor has noted, from the Gaelic *bealach*, meaning 'pass or way'. Certainly, the ways of travelling to and through the region have changed as technology has changed. Yet, it remains a constant in all of this change that West Dunbartonshire is a bealach encompassing the often-craggy complexities of the history and culture of Scotland. Understanding the history of West Dunbartonshire is a way of understanding the issues that have formed not only the area, but also Scotland as a whole.

It could, of course, be argued with some force that any similar area of Scotland would represent somehow in microcosm (and the limitations of such an undynamic conception were discussed in the first chapter of this book) the totality of Scotland, its culture and history. Perhaps such a case might be made, and for some areas it would be true. It is likely that in others, however, the range of cross-reference from specific to general and general to specific would be limited, inevitably, by the narrowness of the range of individual geography or particular cultural history or the absence of adequate historical records. What is striking about West Dunbartonshire is the extent to which it combines within itself the elements of, to borrow from Ted Cowan's chapter title, the Highland and Lowland, the Gael and non-Gael. It has become a cliché, however true, to talk of the diversity of Scotland. Yet, in this area, as has been demonstrated clearly by this book, there has been a very wide diversity of experiences, of identities, of ways of being and travelling through life, of economic activity, trade and industry, political and governmental processes and entertainment and sporting activities. Such diversity marks the area as somehow embodying and representing many of the major strands in the development of Scottish history and whatever may be signified by Scottish 'identity'. The complexity of that identity, or rather those identities, is shown even in such a specific matter as the complexity of the linguistic history of the area, encompassing British, Gaelic, Scots and English, with further military and religious input from Norse, Norman French and Latin. The fact that the current local government entity of West Dunbartonshire is, at the time of publication, only ten years old is neither here nor there in this regard. Indeed, the very fact of such a relatively new identity in an area with a long, diverse and important history simply serves to underline the point being made. The area has constantly recreated and redesigned itself and may still be part of yet other local government organisations in the future. Yet, it retains its own core of identities, which mark it as a distinct contributor to the body, cultural and politic, of Scotland. Its *distinctiveness* may be understood in terms both of its having a distinct individuality and representing distinguished achievement.

It is as much the geographic features and the topographic location of the area as anything else that facilitates this distinctiveness. The relationship of humanity and its environments is, of course, a complex and deeply researched issue. Yet, in West Dunbartonshire, the nature of that relationship is on one level simple. The lie of the land makes it the natural western terminus for both the Antonine Wall and the Forth and Clyde Canal. It nestles between hills and loch and is defined by the River Leven and the Clyde as it changes from a river to a firth. The metaphor is, however, deceptively cosy, because its clearly defined nest-like qualities make the area also attractive as a centre for military aggression and defence and a nexus for trade and industry. Dumbarton Rock has, from the earliest times, been a centre of defence, while the travel ways north and south and to east and west from and through the central area of West Dunbartonshire are still marked out in the main roads of the area. In a sense, it is a difficulty in that many more people pass through West Dunbartonshire than stop in it on their journeys, and so do not fully absorb the nature of the area they travel through. Yet, to resist that character of being a transit hub for the nation is as futile for those that live in the area as Liverpool or Southampton denying their history as major terminals for sea-going liners. Whether as home to the capital in the time of the British kingdom or as, later, in 1222, containing a burgh founded at what seemed like the edges of the sort of civilisation based in towns and a centralised system of government, the area's location between, and so at the centre of, cultural and trade links gave it an identity at the heart of political and economic change. And while its later industrial identity has marked the appearance and perceptions of the area, it is surely noteworthy that its qualities as a suitable location for a king's residence must be a reason for the Bruce electing to build his manor house at Cardross. Its location must certainly have had symbolic force for him, lying on a boundary between Highland and Lowland and the Gael and non-Gael, on important lines of communication by water and in the shadow of the ancient symbol of power and military strength represented by Dumbarton Rock. But it must also have had the simple rural attractions that anyone would seek in a country residence with access to good hunting and a high quality of life.

At several points in this book, the fact that West Dunbartonshire is a remnant, as it were, of the ancient region or kingdom of Lennox has been remarked. As Simon Taylor has reminded us, it is only too possible to understate the significance of the area defined by modern West Dunbartonshire within that ancient region of Scotland. The seat of kings was in Dumbarton; the seat of earls was at Balloch. West Dunbartonshire, as it now is, is in effect the heart of Lennox. As Lennox changed, as governmental structures developed and boundaries were drawn and redrawn, so new industrial strengths developed and Clydebank came to be founded as a major international shipbuilding centre, where all three great liners, *Queen Mary*, *Queen Elizabeth* and *QE2*, were built. Other areas of Scotland would dispute the claim, but in a real sense the area became, if not the heart, a key hub in the industrial vitality of nineteenth- and twentieth-century Scotland. In all regions, there are local rivalries: this is inevitable and often healthy. Those in the heart of Lennox, between the ancient burgh of Dumbarton and the modern burgh of Clydebank – however much Dumbarton itself was a famous shipbuilding and industrial centre – are surely charged by the poles of ancient and modern, of historic resonance and innovative urgency.

The earlier history of West Dunbartonshire reveals rivalries, tensions and variations central to the nature of Scotland itself. Simon Taylor's analysis of the historic development of the kingdom of Al Clud into the medieval earldom of Lennox illustrates major political and military changes that, in turn, defined the shape and nature of modern Scotland. His analysis of the place-names of the region marks the ways in which the ancient languages of the kingdom survive today ingrained in everyday usage, however submerged, taken for granted and only partly understood. The forces of centralisation and change in governance of the later Middle Ages and Renaissance are marked clearly by Ted Cowan. Time and again, central figures in the development of Scotland as a nation were deeply involved in the life and affairs of the area. Meanwhile, in and around it was unfolded one of the archetypal struggles of the creation of modern Scotland. This was the process by which the MacGregors found themselves in a conflict that may, at the time, have seemed to be local and economic. From a modern perspective, however, it can now be seen to have been also about the underlying direction of the clan system, the values of centralisation versus family loyalty and what is now often summarised as Celtic against Lowland. Yet, as Professor Cowan so clearly shows, in part the conflict was within the Celtic world itself. And the complexity of identities in Scotland now is bound up with just such conflicts of loyalty and the intermingled nature of modern Scots as historically Anglian, Scots, Gaelic and Nordic, to name only four elements in their make-up. The modern rivalry between Dumbarton and Clydebank already referred to is also the rivalry between a town with a Gaelic name and one with a Scots/English name. Indeed, the very word 'Scots', used for our national sister language to English, is a term for a Gaelic-speaking people. In that irony lies an entire history of cultural interchange and political conflict.

While the advantage that Dumbarton had as a port for Glasgow because, upstream of it, the Clyde was not navigable to substantial ships, was to be lost when Dumbarton retained its own identity and turned down the offer to be what is now Port Glasgow. Yet, the town also retained a variety of other commercial advantages. These led to its becoming, as the technologies of the eighteenth century developed, a major centre for the making of glass, while the landward area of the Vale became central in the Scottish textile industry. In the nineteenth century, the advantage of location on the Clyde gave rise to the establishment of the shipbuilding industry, first at Dumbarton and then in the foundation of Clydebank. By the beginning of the twentieth century, West Dunbartonshire was home to a major industrial complex and, with the advent of Singer, was adoptive home to a modernising production technology. The vibrancy and innovation of the area drew in new citizens from a variety of areas, including the Highlands and islands and Ireland.

The process of identity change and the integration of varieties of history and culture into the area continued. Paul Maloney describes with great liveliness and detail the ways in which, over the centuries, the popular entertainments of the area had developed. By the time of industrialisation, while the folk-based traditions of entertainment continued, the professionalisation of the entertainment industry was under way. Maloney points to the dialectic between entertainment that was officially approved whether by Kirk or law-court – drunkenness for example being a major leisure activity neither much approved of – and a counterbalancing Dionysian strain in the people's pleasures. Even as the more formalised and commercially managed theatre and music hall developed, the manifestation of popular culture continued. The process of industrialisation and urbanisation in nineteenth-century Scotland is often represented in economic terms, understandably enough. It also, however, represented a process of change in popular culture in which traditions that had once been rural were brought into urban contexts, subtly both changing and yet maintaining their historic identity. Maloney's discussion of the Galoshins play is a fascinating example of just such a process. What we see is that the commercial advantages that made the area a centre of the Industrial Revolution also meant that, within it, the way people lived inevitably changed, but, within that inevitability, older ways of life and entertainment and culture survived.

In literature and the other arts, West Dunbartonshire reflects a complex picture. Two substantial authors, each in their different ways highly influential, were born in the area: Tobias Smollett and A. J. Cronin. The area has also both acted as a source of inspiration for writers and attracted them to stay, sometimes for only a short visit and sometimes for longer. Alan Riach reminds us that one of David Lyndsay's small Renaissance masterpieces, *Squire Meldrum*, is set in the area, while he concludes with the reflections of Edwin Morgan on the Kilpatrick Hills. In between these two, a wide range of visitors has found inspiration both in the old county of Dunbartonshire and modern West Dunbartonshire and in the environs of Loch Lomond. While Burns famously received the freedom of Dumbarton, a perhaps surprising number of modern authors, including Cecil Day Lewis and W. H. Auden, lived and worked for a time in the area. Ian Crichton Smith spent an influential three years living in Dumbarton and teaching in Clydebank before returning to the West Highlands. His first collection was published while he lived in the area and he returned to it in his writing often. And, of course, Maurice Lindsay moved to live and write in Milton. In short, as Alan Riach demonstrates in chapter and verse, the literary history of West Dunbartonshire and the surrounding area is full of life and of achievement. Of course, the area has appeared also in a wide variety of paintings, including some of industrial subjects. Yet, it is a factor often forgotten in seeking the cross-over between arts and industry that the highly important 1972 *The Great Northern Welly Boot Show* was based on the workers' occupation of Upper Clyde Shipbuilders in Clydebank. The interaction between different aspects of the society and arts of West Dunbartonshire is intricate and complex. It is full of surprising elements and remarkable for the impact of a number of artists – and of the experience of those living in the area itself – in influencing larger artistic, literary and theatrical developments. Not only are its varied identities expressed in these artworks, but these artworks come to stand as exemplars of some of the most important works in their genres, often not simply in terms of importance in a Scottish context, but in international terms.

In sport, too, West Dunbartonshire has had a powerful impact. It has contributed, in particular, significantly to the development of football in Scotland. Bob Crampsey's chapter is very clear about the astonishing achievement of football clubs like Vale of Leven, Renton and Dumbarton towards the end of the nineteenth century in establishing organised football competition in Scotland. Renton even achieved, if by a device, the title of World Champions – and remains undefeated in that particular version of the title to this day. While, however, these clubs succeeded at the highest level in those amateur days, the advent of professionalism meant that by the turn of the twentieth century their glory had faded. The football of even the early twentieth century came to depend on the economics that meant that teams from small burghs could not sustain consistently high levels of achievement. In future, while there would be sports achievers of the highest rank from the area – Jackie Stewart being perhaps most prominent, but certainly not alone as a prominent sportsman – their achievement would be based on their leaving the area and on individual, rather than concerted team, effort. In this, of course, West Dunbartonshire reflected early the model of sports achievement prevailing in the modern world.

The first paragraph of this chapter closed with an observation that 'Understanding the history of West Dunbartonshire is a way of understanding the issues that have formed not only the area, but also Scotland as a whole.' Repeatedly, this chapter, and indeed the whole of this book, has reminded the reader of just how this is so. It is to be hoped also, however, that this book has offered a vision of the complex range of identities that have gone to shape the individuality of modern West Dunbartonshire as it is now and as it will be. If this book has demonstrated anything, it is that identities change, and yet retain deep roots. It also implies that, if history is anything to go by, further reshaping of its identity will come about. As its arts, industries, sports and popular life change, develop and reconfigure, though, the heart of Lennox will still remain, in a very particular sense, at the heart of Scotland.

Bibliography

BOOKS AND JOURNALS

Accounts of the Lord High Treasurer, vol. IX, AD 1546–1551 (1911) Edinburgh.

Adomnan of Iona, *Life of St Columba*, translated by Richard Sharpe (1995), Harmondsworth: Penguin Books.

Aitken, Archibald M. (2003), *Jamestown and Balloch as I remember them*, Dumbarton: West Dunbartonshire Libraries and Museums.

Anderson, A. O. (ed.) (1990), *Early Sources of Scottish History, A.D. 500 to 1286*, 2 vols (first published, Edinburgh 1922; reprinted with preface, bibliographical supplement and corrections by M. O. Anderson), Stamford: Paul Watkins Press.

Anderson, Alan Orr and Marjorie Ogilvie (eds and trans.) (1991), *Adomnán's Life of Columba* (originally published 1961, revised edition), Oxford: Oxford University Press.

Anderson, Scoular (1990), *A Journey Down the Clyde*, Glasgow: Richard Drew.

Annals of Ulster (to 1131) (edited and translated by Mac Airt, S. and Mac Niocaill, G.) (1983) Dublin: Dublin Institute for Advanced Studies.

Ashe, Geoffrey (1983), *A Guidebook to Arthurian Britain*, Wellingborough, Northamptonshire: The Aquarian Press.

Ballantine, Ishbel et al. (ed.) (1989), Glasgow Labour History Workshop, *The Singer Strike, Clydebank 1911*, Clydebank: Clydebank District Libraries.

Barrow, G. W. S. (1988), *Robert Bruce & The Community of the Realm of Scotland* (3rd rev. edn), Edinburgh: Edinburgh University Press.

Batey, Colleen (1994), 'The sculptured stones in Glasgow Museums', in Ritchie, Anna (ed.), *Govan and its Early Medieval Sculpture*, Stroud: Alan Sutton Publishing, pp. 63–72.

Bieler, Ludwig (ed. and trans.) (1979), *The Patrician Texts in the Book of Armagh* [with a contribution by Fergus Kelly], Dublin: Dublin Institute for Advanced Studies.

Bisland, Ian (1997), *McDougall's of Bonhill*, Alexandria: Ian Bisland.

Bisland, Ian and Lobban, Malcolm (2004), *Behind the Silken Veil: the Story of the British Silk Dyeing Ltd.*, Alexandria: [Bisland and Lobban].

Blake, George (1934), *The Heart of Scotland*, London: Batsford.

Blake, George (1937), *Down to the Sea: The Romance of the Clyde, Its Ships and Shipbuilders*, London: Collins.

Blake, George (1945), *The Constant Star*, London: Collins.

Blake, George (1946), *The Westering Sun*, London: Collins.

Bold, Alan (1989), *Scotland: A Literary Guide*, London: Routledge.

Breeze, Andrew (1999), 'Some Celtic Place-Names of Scotland, including *Dalriada, Kincarden, Abercorn, Coldingham* and *Girvan*', *Scottish Language*, 18, pp. 34–51.

Bromwich, Rachel (1961), *Trioedd Ynys Prydein: The Welsh Triads*, Cardiff: University of Wales Press.

Brown, Alan (c. 2000), *Loch Lomond Passenger Steamers, 1818–1989*, Nuneaton: Allan T. Condie Publications.

Brown, Callum G. (1996), 'Popular Culture and the Continuing Struggle for Rational Recreation', in Devine, T. M. and Finlay, Richard (eds), *Scotland in the Twentieth Century*, Edinburgh: Edinburgh University Press, pp. 210–29.

Brown, Michael (2003), 'Earldom and Kindred: the Lennox and its Earls, 1200–1458', in S. Boardman and A. Ross (eds), *The exercise of power in medieval Scotland c. 1200–1500*, Dublin: Four Courts Press, pp. 201–24.

Bruce, John (1893), *History of the Parish of West or Old Kilpatrick and of the Church and Certain Lands in the Parish of East or New Kilpatrick*, Glasgow: John Smith & Sons (reprinted Clydebank: Clydebank District Libraries, 1995).

Buchan, John, *Mr Standfast* [1919] (1964), London: Pan Books.

Burgess, Moira (1999), *The Glasgow Novel: A Complete Guide – Third Edition*, Glasgow: The Scottish Library Association and Glasgow City Council Cultural and Leisure Services.

Cain, P. J. and Hopkins, A. G. (1993), *British Imperialism: Innovation and Expansion, 1688–1914*, London: Longman.

Cairney, John (2000), *On the Trail of Robert Burns*, Edinburgh: Luath Press.

Calder, Angus (1992), *The Myth of the Blitz*, London: Pimlico.

Calder, Clair and Lindsay, Lynn (2002), *The Islands of Loch Lomond*, Formartine: Northern Books.

Camb. Reg. Registrum Monasterii S. Marie de Cambuskenneth (printed by Grampian Club, 1872).

Campbell, Robert D. (1999), *Loch Lomond and the Trossachs*, Edinburgh: Mainstream.

Campbell, Roy Hutcheson (1980), *The Rise and Fall of Scottish Industry, 1707–1939*, Edinburgh: John Donald.

Candon, Anthony (1988), 'Muirchertach Ua Briain, Politics and Naval Activity in the Irish Sea, 1075 to 1119', in Gearóid Mac Niocaill and Patrick F. Wallace (eds), *Keimelia: Studies in Medieval Archaeology and History in Memory of Tom Delaney*, Galway: Galway University Press, pp. 397–415.

Castle, Colin (1996), *Clydebank 100: Ships from Clydebank and District*, Dumbarton: West Dunbartonshire Libraries and Museums.

Chirrey, James (1994), *The Royal Naval Torpedo Factory, Alexandria*, Dumbarton: [James Chirrey].

Clancy, Thomas Owen (ed.) (1998), *The Triumph Tree: Scotland's Earliest Poetry AD 550–1350*, Edinburgh: Canongate.

Clydebank Life Story Group (1999), *Untold Stories: Remembering Clydebank in War Time*, Clydebank: Clydebank Life Story Group.

Clydebank Town Council (1936), *Clydebank Town Council, Souvenir Jubilee Brochure, 1886–1936*, Clydebank: Clydebank Town Council.

Cowan, Edward J. (1984–6), 'Fishers in Drumlie Waters – Clanship and Campbell Expansion in the Time of Gilleasbuig Gruamach', *Transactions of the Gaelic Society of Inverness*, vol. liv, pp. 269–312.

Cowan, Edward J. (1990), 'Norwegian Sunset – Scottish Dawn: Hakon IV and Alexander III', in Norman H. Reid (ed.), *Scotland in the Reign of Alexander III 1249–1286*, Edinburgh: John Donald, pp. 103–31.

Cowan, Edward J. (1997–8), 'The Discovery of the Gaidhealtachd in Sixteenth century Scotland', *Transactions of the Gaelic Society of Inverness*, vol. lx, pp. 259–84.

Coleman, John (1904), *Fifty Years of an Actor's Life*, London: Hutchinson.

Cronin, A. J. (1931), *Hatter's Castle*, London: Gollancz.

Cronin, A. J. (1945), *The Green Years*, London: Gollancz.

Defoe, Daniel (1979), *A Tour through the Whole Island of Great Britain [1724–6]*, ed. Pat Rogers, Harmondsworth: Penguin Books.

Dennison, E. Patricia and Coleman, Russel (1999), *Historic Dumbarton*, [Edinburgh]: Historic Scotland in association with the Tuckwell Press.

Devine, T. M. (1990), *The Tobacco Lords: a Study of the Tobacco Merchants of Glasgow and their Trading Activities c. 1740–90*, Edinburgh: Edinburgh University Press [originally published, Edinburgh: John Donald, 1975].

Devine, T. M. and Jackson, G. (eds) (1995), *Glasgow vol. 1: Beginnings to 1830*, Manchester: Manchester University Press.

Donnelly, Joe (1990), *Bane*, London: Barrie & Jenkins.

Dennett, C. (1995), *The Auld Renton, volume 1*, Alexandria: C. Dennett.

Dumville, David N. et al. (1993), *Saint Patrick A.D. 493–1993*, Woodbridge: Boydell.

Duncan, A. A. M. (2002), *The Kingship of the Scots 842–1292: Succession and Independence*, Edinburgh: Edinburgh University Press.

Dunn, Douglas (ed.) (1979), *The Poetry of Scotland*, London: Batsford.

Dunn, Douglas (1986), *Selected Poems 1964–1983*, London: Faber & Faber.

Durie, Alastair J. (1979), *The Scottish Linen Industry in the Eighteenth Century*, Edinburgh: John Donald.

Durie, Alastair J. (2003), *Scotland for the Holidays: A History of Tourism in Scotland, 1780–1939*, East Linton: Tuckwell Press.

Ferguson, James and Temple, J. G. (1927), *The Old Vale and its Memories*, privately published.

Findlay, Bill (1998), 'Beginnings to 1700', in Findlay (ed.), *A History of Scottish Theatre*, Edinburgh: Polygon, pp. 1–79.

Forbes, Alexander Penrose (1872), *Kalendars of Scottish Saints*, Edinburgh: Edmonston & Douglas.

Forsyth, Katherine [with an appendix by Koch, John T.] (2000), 'Evidence of a lost Pictish source in the *Historia Regum Anglorum* of Symeon of Durham', in *Kings, Clerics and Chronicles in Scotland, 500–1297*, ed. Simon Taylor, Dublin: Four Courts Press, pp. 19–34.

Fraser, James E. (2005), 'Strangers on the Clyde: Cenél Comgaill, Clyde Rock and the bishops of Kingarth', *Innes Review*, pp. 102–20.

Fraser, William (1874), *The Lennox, vol. 1, Memoirs*, Edinburgh.

Fraser, William (1869), *The Chiefs of Colquhoun and Their Country*, 2 vols, Edinburgh.

Gallacher, Roddy (1982), 'The Vale of Leven 1914–1975: Changes in Working Class Organisation and Action', in Tony Dickson (ed.), *Capital and Class in Scotland*, Edinburgh: John Donald, pp. 186–211.

Galbraith, Iain (1989), *By the Rivers of Water: Portrait of Bonhill Parish*, Stevenage: Spa Books Ltd.

Glas. Reg. Registrum Episcopatus Glasguensis (printed by Bannatyne and Maitland Clubs, 1843).

Gunn, Neil [1939] (1991), *Wild Geese Overhead*, Edinburgh: Chambers.

Halliwell, Leslie (1991), *Halliwell's Film Guide*, Eighth Edition, ed. John Walker, London: HarperCollins.

Harrison, Margaret (1981), *Iona to Canterbury: Pilgrims for Peace*, Dumbarton: [Harrison].

Hayward, Brian (1992), *Galoshins: The Scottish Folk Play*, Edinburgh: Edinburgh University Press.

Hempstead, James L. (1996), *Robert Burns and Dunbartonshire*, Dumbarton: Dumbarton Burns Club.

Hempstead, James L. and Taylor, Michael C. (2004), *History of Dumbarton Burns Club*, Dumbarton: Dumbarton Burns Club.

Henderson, Meg (1997), *The Holy City*, London: Flamingo

Heron, Robert (1799), *Scotland Delineated, or A Geographical Description of Every Shire in Scotland, Including the Northern and Western Isles*, Edinburgh: printed for Bell & Bradfute; G. G. & J. Robinson, London.

Historia Ecclesiastica Bede's Ecclesiastical History of the English People, edited and translated (1969) by Bertram Colgrave and R. A. B. Mynors, Oxford: Oxford University Press.

Hogg, James (1981), *Highland Tours*, ed. William F. Laughlan, Hawick: Byway Books.

Hood, John (1982), *The 1st Old Kilpatrick Boy's Brigade Company 1932–82*, Clydebank: Clydebank District Libraries.

Hood, John (1986), *Clydebank: 100 years Souvenir Edition*, Clydebank: Clydebank District Council/James Paton Ltd.

Hood, John (1986), *Duntocher Trinity Parish Church, 1836–1986*, Clydebank: Clydebank District Libraries.

Hood, John (1986), 'No Waits, No Flickers, No Breakdowns', *Clydebank Historical Journal*, vol. 6, Spring, pp. 11–16.

Hood, John (1987), *Gavinburn Primary School 1887–1987*, Clydebank: Clydebank District Libraries.

Hood, John (1988) (compiler), *The History of Clydebank*, Carnforth: Parthenon.

Hood, John (1999), *Old Dumbarton*, Catrine: Stenlake Publishing.

Hood, John (2004), *Old Bowling, Duntocher, Hardgate, Milton and Old Kilpatrick*, Catrine: Stenlake Publishing.

Hood, John and McIntyre, Wallace (1992), *Clydebank Historical Journal, volume 10*, Clydebank: Clydebank District Libraries and Museums Department.

Hopner, Graham (1996), *Mick McFall: The Mythical Man*, Balloch: Blackhouse Land Publishers.

Irving, John (1928), *Place Names of Dumbartonshire*, Dumbarton: Bennett & Thomson.

Hutchison, I. G. C. (1986), *A Political History of Scotland 1832–1924: Parties, Elections and Issues*, Edinburgh: John Donald.

Irving, Joseph (1857), *The History of Dumbartonshire from the Earliest Period to the Present Time*, Dumbarton.

Irving, Joseph (1860), *History of Dumbartonshire* (2nd edn), Dumbarton.

Irving, Joseph (1879), *The Book of Dumbartonshire*, 2 vols, Edinburgh: W. & A. K. Johnston.

Jackson, John (1793), *The History of the Scottish Stage*, Edinburgh: printed for Peter Hill, and G. G. J. & J. Robinson, London.

Johnman, Lewis and Johnston, Ian (2001), *Down the River*, Glendaruel: Argyll Publishing.

Johnston, Ian (1993), *Beardmore Built: the Rise and Fall of a Clydeside Shipyard*, Clydebank: Clydebank District Libraries and Museums Department.

Johnston, Ian (2000), *Ships for a Nation 1847–1971: John Brown and Company, Clydebank*, Dumbarton: West Dunbartonshire Libraries and Museums.

Kelman, James (1989), *A Disaffection*, London: Secker & Warburg.

Kirkwood, David (1935), *My Life of Revolt* [foreword by Winston S. Churchill], London: George G. Harrap & Co.

Lappin, A. Graham (1999), *Old Alexandria, Bonhill and Renton*, Catrine: Stenlake Publishing.

Lawson, William E. (1948), *A History of Clydebank Co-operative Society Ltd*, Glasgow: the Society.

Lee, Clive (1999), 'The Scottish Economy and the First World War', in Catriona M. M. Macdonald and Elaine McFarland (eds), *Scotland and the Great War*, East Linton: Tuckwell Press, pp. 11–36.

Leisure and the Quality of Life. A Report on Four Local Experiments, vols 1 & 2 (1977/1978), London: HMSO.

Lenn. Cart. Cartularium Comitatus de Levenax ['Cartulary of the Earls of Lennox'] (printed by Maitland Club, 1833).

Levitt, Ian (1988), *Poverty and Welfare in Scotland 1890–1948*, Edinburgh: Edinburgh University Press.

Liddell, Colin M. (1994), *Memories of the Vale, 1940–1950*, Dumbarton: Colin M. Liddell.

Lindsay, Maurice (1979), *The Lowlands of Scotland: Glasgow and the North*, London: Robert Hale.

Lindsay, Maurice (1983), *Thank You for Having Me: A Personal Memoir*, London: Robert Hale.

Lindsay, Maurice (1990), *Collected Poems 1940–1990*, Aberdeen: Aberdeen University Press.

Lindsay, Maurice (2000), *Worlds Apart*, Callander/Edinburgh: diehard publishers.

Logan, Jimmy (1998), *It's A Funny Life*, Edinburgh: B&W.

Lyndsay, Sir David (2000), *Selected Poems*, ed. Janet Hadley Williams, Glasgow: Association for Scottish Literary Studies.

McAllister, Jim (2002), *The Sons of the Rock: the Official History of Dumbarton Football Club*, Dumbarton: Dumbarton and Vale of Leven Reporter.

McAusland, Brian (1988), *Clydeside Harriers: A Centenary History 1885–1985* [Glasgow: Clydeside Harriers].

McBain, Janet (1985), *Pictures Past: recollections of Scottish cinemas and cinema-going*, Edinburgh: Moorfoot Publishing.

McGavin, John J. (2004), 'Faith, pastime, performance and drama in Scotland to 1603', in Jane Milling and Peter Thomson (eds), *Cambridge History of British Theatre: vol. 1: Origins to 1660*, Cambridge: Cambridge University Press, pp. 70–86.

Macintyre, Stuart (1980), *Little Moscows: Communism and Working-class Militancy in Inter-war Britain*, London: Croom Helm.

MacIvor, Iain (1981), *Official Guide to Dumbarton Castle*, Edinburgh: HMSO.

Mackay, James (1993), *Burns: A Biography of Robert Burns*, London: Headline.

McKendrick, Tom (1993), *Rivet Temple*, Clydebank: Clydebank District Council.

Mackenney, Linda (2000), *The Activities of Popular Dramatists and Drama Groups in Scotland, 1900–1952*, Lampeter: Edwin Mellor Press.

MacLeod, Donald (1896), *Ancient Records of Dumbarton*, Dumbarton.

MacLeod, Donald (1877), *Castle and Town of Dumbarton*, Dumbarton: Bennett Bros.

MacLeod, Donald (c. 1891), *The God's Acres of Dumbarton*, Dumbarton.

MacPhail, I. M. M. (1963), *Short History of Dumbartonshire*, Dumbarton: Bennet & Thomson (reprinted, Stevenage: Spa Books, 1984).

MacPhail, I. M. M. (1972), *Dumbarton Through the Centuries*, Dumbarton: Dumbarton Town Council.

MacPhail, I. M. M. (1974), *The Clydebank Blitz*, Dumbarton: West Dunbartonshire Libraries and Museums (2000 reprinting).

MacPhail, I. M. M. (1979), *Dumbarton Castle*, Edinburgh: John Donald.

MacPhail, I. M. M. (1987), *Lennox Lore*, Dumbarton: Dumbarton District Libraries.

Macquarrie, Alan (1993), 'The Kings of Strathclyde, c. 400–1018', in Alexander Grant and Keith J. Stringer (eds), *Medieval Scotland, Crown, Lordship and Community*, Edinburgh: Edinburgh University Press, pp. 1–19.

Macquarrie, Alan (1996), 'Lives of Scottish Saints in the Aberdeen Breviary: some problems of sources for Strathclyde saints', *Records of the Scottish Church History Society*, 26, pp. 31–54 [St Patrick: pp. 44–50].

Malcolm, Pat (1988), '"Leisure and Recreation", Social trends: 1886–1914', in John Hood (compiler), *The History of Clydebank*, Carnforth: Parthenon, pp. 51–8.

Marwick, J. D. (ed.) (1909), *The River Clyde and the Clyde Burghs*, Edinburgh: SBRS.

Maughan, William Charles (1897), *Annals of Garelochside Being An Account Historical and Topographical of the Parishes of Row, Rosneath and Cardross*, Paisley: Alexander Gardner.

Maxwell, Gordon S. (1989), *The Romans in Scotland*, Edinburgh: Mercat Press.

Miller, David Prince (1869), *Life of a Showman*, London.

Mitchell, John (2000), *The Shielings and Droveways of Loch Lomondside*, Stirling: John Mitchell.

Munro, Hugh (1961), *The Clydesiders*, London: Macdonald.

Munro, Hugh (1964), *Tribal Town*, London: Macdonald.

Munro, Neil (1907), *The Clyde: River and Firth*, London: A. & C. Black.

Murdoch, Helen (1981), *Travelling Hopefully: The Story of Molly Urquhart*, Edinburgh: Paul Harris Publishing.

Neill, John (1912), *Records and Reminiscences of Bonhill Parish*, Hoddesdon: Wentworth Book Company Ltd (reprinted 1979).

Neville, Cynthia J. (2005), *Native Lordship in Medieval Scotland: The Earldoms of Strathearn and Lennox, c. 1140–1365*, Dublin: Four Courts Press.

Nicholson, Colin (1992), *Iain Crichton Smith: Critical Essays*, Edinburgh: Edinburgh University Press.

Nicholson, John (1994), *Liners of the Clyde*, Glasgow: Hart, Maclagan & Will.

Nicolaisen, U. F. H. (1976), *Scottish place-names: their study and significance*, London: Batsford (second impression with additional information 1979).

Osborne, Brian D. (1991), *Robert Napier 1791–1876: The Father of Clyde Shipbuilding*, Dumbarton: Dumbarton District Libraries.

Osborne, Brian D. and Armstrong, Ronald (eds) (1999), *Mungo's City: A Glasgow Anthology*, Edinburgh: Birlinn.

Pais. Reg. Registrum Monasterii de Passelet (printed by Maitland Club, 1832; New Club, 1877).

Pearson, Joan (1971), *Loch Lomond Village: the story of Gartocharn and the parish of Kilmaronock, Dunbartonshire*, Gartocharn: Famedram.

Pearson, Joan [1982], *Loch Lomond: The Maid and the loch*, Gartocharn: Famedram.

Peter, Bruce (1999), *Scotland's Splendid Theatres*, Edinburgh: Edinburgh University Press.

Rae, Peter (1718), *The History of the Late Rebellion; Rais'd against His Majesty King George, By the Friends of the Popish Pretender etc*, Dumfries: printed by Robert Rae.

Rankin, Robert A. (1993), *March Stones in the Kilpatrick Hills: a Feuars Dispute of the 1850s*, Clydebank: Clydebank District Libraries and Museums Department.

Reid, Jimmy (1976), *Reflections of a Clyde-Built Man*, London: Souvenir Press.

Report of the Royal Commission on the Housing in Scotland [Cd. 8731] (1917), Edinburgh: HMSO.

Rivet, A. L. F. and Smith, Colin (1979), *The Place-Names of Roman Britain*, London: Batsford.

Rodger, R. (ed.) (1989), *Scottish Housing in the Twentieth Century*, Leicester: Leicester University Press.

RMS Registrum Magni Sigilli Regum Scottorum (*Register of the Great Seal*), ed. J. M. Thomson and J. Balfour Paul, Edinburgh 1882–1914 (reprinted by The Scottish Record Society, 1984), 11 vols, Edinburgh: Scotland's National Archives.

Ross (1777), 'A map of the Shire of Dumbarton', [Charles Ross] National Library of Scotland Map Library, EMS.s.182.

RRS ii Regesta Regum Scottorum vol. ii (*Acts of William I*) ed. G. W. S. Barrow (1971), Edinburgh: Edinburgh University Press.

RRS v Regesta Regum Scottorum vol. v (*Acts of Robert I*) ed. A. A. M. Duncan (1988), Edinburgh: Edinburgh University Press.

RRS vi Regesta Regum Scottorum vol. vi (*Acts of David II*) ed. B. Webster (1982), Edinburgh: Edinburgh University Press.

Scott, Sir Walter, *The Heart of Midlothian* [1818] (1982), ed. Claire Lamont, Oxford: Oxford University Press.

Shiels, Edward (1937), *Gael over Glasgow*, London: Sheed & Ward.

Skinner, James Scott (1994), *My Life and Adventures* [orig. published in *The People's Journal*, 1923], Aberdeen: City of Aberdeen & Wallace Music.

Slaven, Anthony (1975), *The Development of the West of Scotland 1750–1960*, London: Routledge & Kegan Paul.

Smith, Iain Crichton (1986), *Towards the Human: Selected Essays*, Edinburgh: Macdonald.

Smith, Iain Crichton (1986), *A Life*, Manchester: Carcanet.

Smith, Iain Crichton (1992), *Collected Poems*, Manchester: Carcanet.

Smith, Iain Crichton (2001), *Murdo: The Life and Works*, ed. Stewart Conn, Edinburgh: Birlinn.

Steven, Maisie (1995), *Parish Life in Eighteenth-Century Scotland: A review of the Old Statistical Account*, Aberdeen: Scottish Cultural Press.

Stirling, Thomas B. (1915), *History of the Vale of Leven Co-operative Society Limited 1862–1912*, Alexandria: Vale of Leven Co-operative Society.

Stokes, Whitley (ed. and translator) (1887), *Tripartite Life of St Patrick*, 2 vols, Rolls Series.

Struthers, Sheila (1994), *Old Clydebank*, Catrine: Stenlake Publishing.

Taylor, Mike, Walton, Julia and Liddell, Colin (1991), *A Night At The Pictures*, Dumbarton: Dumbarton District Libraries.

Taylor, Mike (2001), *Lennox Herald 150 Years*, Irvine: Scottish and Universal Newspapers.

Taylor, Mike (2005), 'Some Notes on Dumbarton's Old Public Houses for Articles Submitted to the Lennox Herald Newspaper in 2005' (Unpublished: held in Dumbarton Library).

Taylor, Simon (1996), 'Place-names and the Early Church in Eastern Scotland', in B. E. Crawford (ed.), *Scotland in Dark Age Britain*, Aberdeen: Scottish Cultural Press, pp. 93–110.

Todd, James Henthorn (ed. and trans.) (1867), *Cogadh Gaedhel re Gallaibh: The War of the Gaedhil with the Gaill*, London: Longmans, Green, Reader & Dyer.

Walker, Marshall (1996), *Scottish Literature Since 1707*, London and New York: Longman.

Watson, Angus (1995), *The Ochils: Place names, History, Tradition*, Perth: Perth and Kinross District Libraries.

Watson, William Carrick (1984), 'Clydebank in the Inter-war Years: A Study in Economic and Social Change' (Unpublished Glasgow University PhD thesis).

Watson, William J. (1926), *The History of the Celtic Place-Names of Scotland*, Edinburgh and London: Royal Celtic Society by W. Blackwood (reprinted with an Introduction by Simon Taylor, Edinburgh: Birlinn, 2004).

Watts, Victor [with contributions by John Insley] (2002), *A Dictionary of County Durham Place-Names*, Nottingham: English Place-Name Society.

Whyte, Hamish (ed.) (1983), *Noise and Smoky Breath: An Illustrated Anthology of Glasgow Poems 1900–1983*, Glasgow: Third Eye Centre and Glasgow District Libraries Publications Board.

Wilson, David A. L. (1998), *The History of Dumbarton Kilwinning Lodge No. 18*, Dumbarton: Dumbarton Kilwinning Lodge No. 18.

Winter, C. W. R. (1994), *Long Live the Queen Mary*, Whitwell, Isle of Wight: Forget-Me-Not Books and the Manor Design and Publishing Partnership.

Woolf, Alex (2006), 'Dún Nechtain, Fortriu, and the geography of the Picts', *Scottish Historical Review* 85, pp. 182–201.

Wordsworth, Dorothy [1804], *A Tour in Scotland in 1803* (reprinted, Edinburgh: James Thin at the Mercat Press, 1973).

ARCHIVES AND NEWSPAPERS

Airdrie, Coatbridge, Bathgate and Wishaw Advertiser

Clydebank Arts and Leisure Enterprises, Minutes of Meetings, Ref. 790. L.C., Clydebank Library.

Clydebank Press

Clydebank & Renfrew Press

Dumbarton Burgh Records

Dumbarton Argus: or Lennox Magazine, No. 21, 30 July 1833.

Dumbarton Herald

The Era

Glasgow Herald

Lennox Herald

Mass-Observation Archive, 600 'Glasgow Morale' (Preliminary Report), 7/3/41, p. 13, No. 35.

Mass-Observation Archive. 66/9/G: Glasgow: Entertainment 1941; Handwritten Obs. of visits to Playhouse Dance Hall 24.2.41 & 3.3.41.

Notes on the Contributors

Ian Brown is a freelance scholar, cultural and educational consultant, playwright and poet. He is General Editor of *The Edinburgh History of Scottish Literature* (Edinburgh University Press, 2006).

Edward J. Cowan, Professor of Scottish History at Glasgow University, is currently Director of Glasgow's Crichton Campus at Dumfries. His most recent book is *'For Freedom Alone': The Declaration of Arbroath 1320* (2003).

Bob Crampsey is a leading sports journalist and broadcaster and a historian and biographer. His work includes the definitive *The Scottish Football League: The first 100 years* (1991).

Richard Finlay is Professor of Scottish History at the University of Strathclyde. His most recent book was *Modern Scotland, 1914–2000* (2004).

Paul Maloney is completing a PhD in the Department of Theatre, Film & Television Studies at Glasgow University. He is the author of *Scotland and the Music Hall, 1850–1914* (2003).

Alan Riach is Professor of Scottish Literature at Glasgow University as well as a poet. He is the author of *Representing Scotland in Literature, Popular Culture and Iconography* (2005).

Simon Taylor is research fellow, Department of Celtic, Glasgow University, with a special interest in toponymics (the study of place-names), working on the project 'Gaelic in medieval Scotland: the evidence of names'. He is the author of *Place-Names of Fife* Vol. 1 (West Fife) (2006).

Index